KILLING SACRED COWS

OVERCOMING *the* FINANCIAL MYTHS
that are DESTROYING *your* PROSPERITY

GARRETT B. GUNDERSON
WITH STEPHEN PALMER

Published by Greenleaf Book Group LLC
4425 S. Mo Pac Expwy., Suite 600, Austin, TX 78735
www.greenleafbookgroup.com

Distributed by Greenleaf Book Group LLC

For ordering information or special discounts for bulk purchases, please contact Greenleaf Book Group LLC at 4425 S. Mo Pac Expwy., Suite 600, Austin, TX 78735, (512) 891-6100.

Design and composition by Greenleaf Book Group LLC
Cover design by Greenleaf Book Group LLC

Gunderson, Garrett B.
  Killing sacred cows : overcoming the financial myths that are destroying your prosperity / Garrett B. Gunderson with Stephen Palmer. -- 1st ed.

   p. : ill., charts ; cm.

   ISBN: 978-1-929774-51-7

1. Finance, Personal. I. Palmer, Stephen (Stephen Daniel), 1976- II. Title.

HG179 .G863 2008
332.024   2008925604

Printed in the United States of America on acid-free paper

08 09 10 11 12 13   10 9 8 7 6 5 4 3 2 1

First Edition

Contents

Introduction   v

Myth 1: *The Finite Pie*   1

Scarcity thinking brings out the worst in us including fear, pride, jealousy, selfishness, and adversarial competition. Replacing scarcity with abundance helps us to increase our creativity, productivity, health, wealth, and happiness.

Myth 2: *You're in It for the Long Haul*   25

The accumulation theory of wealth creation, which teaches us to save money and compound interest for long periods of time, prevents us from achieving our full potential. A more productive financial theory is utilization, which helps us to maximize our value creation and therefore our wealth in the present moment.

Myth 3: *It's All About the Numbers*   57

Prosperity has less to do with our financial numbers on paper and more to do with our happiness and fulfillment. This shift in mindset helps us to put numbers in their proper perspective.

Myth 4: *Financial Security*   85

True financial security does not come from the government, corporations, benefits, and entitlements; it comes from within us. Taking responsibility for our wealth leads us to transcend false security to find both true security and freedom.

Myth 5: *Money Is Power*   109

Money has no power except the power that people give it. Money is an effect, or a byproduct; value creation is the cause.

Myth 6: *High Risks = High Returns*   139

"High risk equals high return" is a gambling, not a true investing, philosophy. The best and safest investments are those that align with our passions, knowledge, and abilities and that we can control.

Myth 7: *Self-Insurance*   163

"Self-insurance" really means no insurance. The best way to reduce your insurance expenses is to get the best insurance and as much of it as possible.

Myth 8: *Avoid Debt Like the Plague*   187

People fear debt because they don't understand the technical definition. Understanding the technical definitions of debt and liabilities opens up a world of possibility.

Myth 9: *A Penny Saved Is a Penny Earned*   211

Value is a far more important consideration than price when it comes to our purchases and investments.

Defeating the Myths: *The Formula*   231

Acknowledgments   249

The 401(k) Hoax   251

Special Offers   257

Index   265

Advance Praise for *Killing Sacred Cows*

"It's refreshing to hear another voice who understands that 401(k)s, home equity, and other 'traditional' investments are lazy assets and how to transform them into productive, cash-flowing investments. In *Killing Sacred Cows*, Garrett Gunderson breaks through the herd mentality to present the innovative approach to wealth creation employed by the wealthiest individuals. Forget what you think you know—read this book if you want to learn how to become financially successful."

—**LORAL LANGEMEIER**, author of the National Best Seller, *The Millionaire Maker: Act, Think and Make Money the Way the Wealthy Do*

"*Killing Sacred Cows* isn't a light or comforting read . . . it's disconcerting and thought-provoking. Transcend mediocrity and find true prosperity via this exceptional book."

— **CHRISTINE COMAFORD-LYNCH**, *New York Times* bestselling author of *Rules for Renegades: How to Make More Money, Rock Your Career, and Revel in Your Individuality*

"The vast majority of people plan and organize their economic lives with faulty and counterproductive ideas, attitudes, and strategies. Garrett Gunderson throws out all of the bad stuff and then supplies rules and methods that bring substantial and satisfying progress over a lifetime."

—**DAN SULLIVAN**, President and founder of Strategic Coach

"Because of a learning disability, my high school graduating class voted me most likely to fail. What neither my classmates nor I realized at the time was that my 'broken' way of thinking prepared me for success much more than those who thought in conventional ways. Through my disability, I've developed a unique perspective that has allowed me to far exceed the predictions of my high school classmates.

If you want to succeed, ignore the crowd and follow your passion. In *Killing Sacred Cows*, Garrett Gunderson proves his understanding of this by detailing a 'broken' perspective on personal finance that is plain right. If you want results like everyone else, do what everyone else is doing—if you want to succeed financially, break the traditional rules and follow the path of the truly wealthy. Buy and read *Killing Sacred Cows* to discover that path."

—**ROBERT SHEMIN**, *Wall Street Journal*, *USA Today*, and *New York Times* bestselling author of *How Come That Idiot's Rich and I'm Not?*

"Success can be directly determined by your ability to build quality relationships and *Killing Sacred Cows* offers refreshing, realistic ways to get to the heart of prosperity by shifting your focus toward improving your relationships."

—**IVAN MISNER**, *New York Times* bestselling author and founder of BNI

No actual cows were killed or harmed during the creation of this book.

Introduction

Find the sacred cows, slaughter them, sell the meat, make a profit.

—Dan Sullivan

Why do so many of us struggle financially when we live in the most free and prosperous country in the history of the world? Why do we continue to struggle when we are bombarded daily with information on how to become wealthy? I believe that most of us are kept from our potential because we labor under false ideas and perceptions about money, wealth, and prosperity.

The dictionary defines a "sacred cow" as an individual, organization, institution, teaching, or belief often considered exempt from criticism or questioning. In the financial world, sacred cows are the myths and traditions that distort our thinking about money, wealth, success, and prosperity. These myths are widespread and constantly reinforced through advice from friends and relatives, financial institutions, and the financial media. Because these financial sacred cows are so pervasive, they are rarely questioned and even less often defeated. But learning and applying the fundamental truths that counter the myths is the most direct path to the prosperity we're all capable of.

The purpose of this book is to help you kill these sacred cows—to identify and overcome the subtle and destructive myths, lies, and fallacies about money that are perpetuated through social programming and unquestioned traditions. These myths are crippling us—individually and societally. They limit and destroy our potential. They drastically and negatively influence our decisions on a daily basis, and most of us aren't even aware that they exist or how destructive they are.

> What if everything you thought you knew to be true about money and finances was actually completely false? How soon would you want to find out, and what would you do about it?

Throughout the course of this book, we will explore the most common financial fallacies. Upon close scrutiny, you'll see that these myths are at odds with common sense at best, and at worst, destructive of our potential as creative beings.

Much of the material covered herein will undoubtedly be controversial, because it will challenge some of your most cherished beliefs and core assumptions. But it will also be enlightening. It will expand your thinking. It will help you to question things that most people never question. And with that critical analysis will come deeper understanding and more empowering perceptions and beliefs.

 Enslavement by illusion is comfortable; it is the liberation by truth that people fear.   —David Hawkins

Origins of the Myths

The question arises, "If much of what we're taught about money is false, then why are these myths so prevalent, and where do they originate?" I believe that most of the myths about money that we are taught today originated during major economic or cultural developments (such as the Great Depression), are solidified by financial institutions that have a vested interest in maintaining the status quo, and are spread through the misguided advice of well-intentioned family members and friends.

A myth is a fixed way of looking at the world which cannot be destroyed because, looked at through the myth, all evidence supports that myth.
—**Edward de Bono**

We rarely think to question the financial concepts we believe in and follow. Seldom do we consider that these "tried-and-true" strategies might in fact be false. This happens because we are trained in our perceptions of money from a young age. Our parents pass along to us their own ideas about money. Even if their ideas are not explicitly stated, we absorb them through observation of our parents' use of money. If they were careless spenders, we will likely spend our money carelessly. If they were cautious and suspicious of others, we will hold tight to our money in like manner and miss opportunities to grow our wealth. Or we will adopt the polar opposites of their behavior about money and get ourselves into entirely different trouble. Without even knowing the source of our feelings about money, we will behave in ways that perpetuate financial mismanagement through our lifetimes and those of our children.

The members of our families and communities contribute to our miseducation through their own buying habits, through employment and investment advice, and through other motivating behaviors. Most people have good intentions, but their advice relies on the same myths they were taught or information that may be pertinent to their situations but does not relate to our own.

The myths we absorb from our parents and community are supported by society as a whole. Our culture offers "wisdom of the ages" in the form of clichés about money that we rarely question. These clichés are often rooted in historical events that have little to do with our current economy or our personal financial situations. For example, the Great Depression resulted in hoarding and a scarcity mindset that permeated American culture and heavily influenced succeeding generations. And the post–World War II boom led to the belief that financial security came from tying oneself to a corporation. These beliefs are perpetuated by institutions within our society because they support their goals or because the people within the institutions don't know any better either.

Nothing is more difficult than competing with a myth.   —Françoise Giroud

Financial services companies sell their products by promoting perspectives and methods with fancy names such as "The Miracle of Compounding Interest." These marketing messages have been used for so long that we have come to accept them as viable and trustworthy financial strategies. But financial institutions have always practiced and continue to practice the very things that we are either told to avoid or are completely unaware of. The ideas they promote are good for them, but not necessarily good for us.

Conventional retirement planners are usually no more helpful in the quest for true financial freedom. Not only do retirement planners receive their training from financial institutions, but they often work directly for these companies as well. Even if a retirement planner is knowledgeable in correct economic principles, he usually has an underlying incentive to sell suboptimal products.

This does not mean that financial institutions are inherently evil because they pursue their own interests. It does mean, however, that we must be aware that institutions are in business for a reason: to increase their revenues and their bottom line. My goal is not to tell you to completely avoid financial institutions; it is simply to point out that they have their own distinct interests and those interests may not coincide with yours. The better we understand the agendas of financial institutions, the more wisely we can utilize their policies for our benefit.

Educational institutions aren't effective at combating the myths that financial institutions propagate. American schools fail at educating students in correct principles of personal finance. A very different approach to money management is taught to students in personal finance courses as opposed to those in corporate finance courses. Personal finance directs learners to accumulate net worth, pay off debt, invest for the long term, and protect their possessions with term insurance. The corporate finance course teaches velocity of money, cash flow, risk management, and permanent insurance strategies. These principles and methods are far superior to and less risky than the personal finance techniques. In fact, corporate finance strategies are intended to take advantage of the investment dollars tucked away by people using personal finance methods. What isn't taught to the average American is that corporate finance strategies can be employed on a personal level and used to achieve far greater wealth with equal or better security.

To combat the compounded influence of family, community, experts, education, and society—a daunting task—we must realize that popularity and the majority's opinions don't necessarily point to the truth. In other words, fifty million people saying a dumb thing doesn't make it any less dumb. The herd mentality is destructive. Consider this question: If only a minority of people are wealthy, why do we follow what the majority of people do financially? True principles of personal finance exist that can lead to prosperity for anyone in almost any circumstance. But succeeding with these principles requires the courage to step away from the crowd and to choose "the road not taken."

The Destructive Nature of Financial Myths

Buying into myths about money and finances destroys our prosperity and limits our productivity. It prevents us from seeing empowering and enlightening truths. It makes us stumble in ways that we never would have had we known the truth. For example, my friend Garrett White routinely does the following exercise at seminars: He asks a person to walk from the front of the room to the back, get a glass of water, and bring it back to the front. He promises that if they do it correctly, they will receive a prize. Each time, when the volunteers return to the front of the room with a glass of water in hand, he informs them that they did it all wrong—they were supposed to turn around three times, walk a certain way, and go around a few chairs. His exercise shows that we can't succeed at anything unless we know the rules. Myths and false information keep us from learning the natural rules of wealth and prosperity.

When we accept financial myths, we accept untold opportunity costs. Every single thing that we do comes at a cost, the cost being everything we could have done instead of what we actually did. For example, every time we decide to accumulate money in a bank account because it's "safe," it comes at the cost of the returns we could have earned had we found a more productive use for the money. Every time we choose to follow the myth that developing our passion is risky and that finding an unattractive career is safe, it comes at the cost of achieving our full potential and influencing people for good.

When people are confronted with myths, they commonly experience mental dilemmas. In fact, this phenomenon is one way to detect an underlying myth impacting a decision. Dilemmas come about when false beliefs leave us paralyzed, caught in a catch-22 where we see no way to win no matter what we do. For example, many people desire to be highly successful and wealthy but believe (often subconsciously) that achieving success would mean acting against their moral principles. They believe they are forced to choose between their principles and their prosperity.

What can you do in a situation like this? Instead of just taking action and feeling guilty with any choice, those who understand that myths are prevalent in our financial thoughts question the basic assumptions that they are facing and see past the myth. This helps resolve the dilemma and grants new access to power and the ability to take action in a way that promotes a feeling of prosperity and certainty, rather than frustration and confusion. The difficulty is in finding the myth that is crippling your progress among the many subtle beliefs about money and productivity you've absorbed over a lifetime of learning about them.

Why We Can't Let Go

 Education is the slow process of learning our ignorance. —**Will Durant**

It's human nature to relate things that we are unfamiliar with back to the things that we are already familiar with, or with the things that we *think* we know. But what if the things we think we know are false, or at least misguided? How can we make sense of new things when our frame of reference is distorted or not founded in truth? One of the most critical steps we can take toward financial freedom is to accept the possibility that what we thought to be true may be completely false, and that there are infinite truths we have yet to learn.

I believe that the financial sacred cows give us distorted views of money and prosperity that we are rarely able to defeat because these fallacies appear to be self-evident. Because modern life is complicated and we have to make decisions about so many different kinds of issues, we often depend on the opinions of specialists and experts in a field instead of learning about it ourselves. We've become used to accepting assumptions and handed-down advice and often choose not to make the time and effort to question them. We are too busy (or so we think) to learn the world anew, from its very foundations on up. We take the word of experts, or we trust in the advice of those we love and who love us. I certainly started out well indoctrinated into the myths, and it was only through trial and error, a willingness to experiment, and the guidance of wise mentors that I managed to shake free of their grasp and create the life I want to live.

However, when I teach people about financial myths and how to overcome them, there are three statements or sentiments that I routinely hear: "It sounds too good to be true," "Why haven't I heard of this before?" and "You have to be a financial genius and learn the secrets to be really successful or wealthy."

When I hear people say "It sounds too good to be true," my answer is that we only believe this about things with which we have no experience. All great human achievements sounded too good to be true at one time. Can you imagine teaching a nineteenth-century pioneer living in a dirt-floor, one-room cabin about how cell phones and computers work? When we say "It sounds too good to be true," what we really mean is that we don't know how to do it, so we are skeptical. This attitude limits our potential by giving us negative and suspicious lenses through which we view the world.

Granted, a healthy tendency to critical analysis can save us a lot of headaches, and I am not saying that we should be naïve and blindly accept whatever we're told. But it is much more healthy and conducive to happiness and creativity to remain open to learning how and why things work, even if we don't initially understand. Casually discarding everything that sounds "too good to be true" will lead to a life of poverty even if we are surrounded by success and prosperity.

Likewise, when people demand why they haven't heard my strategies before, the implication is that they have a monopoly on all truth and find it hard to accept that there are things that they don't know.

In reality, there are four realms of knowledge relating to all of us: the things we know that we know; the things that we think we know; the things that we know we don't know; and the things that we don't know that we don't know. Obviously, the last realm—the things that we don't know we don't know—is infinitely larger than all of the other realms combined. It's human nature to relate things that we are unfamiliar with back to the things that we are already familiar with, or with the things that we *think* we know.

Those who say it can't be done are usually interrupted by others doing it.

—Joel Barker

On the other hand, believing that financial success is a product of genius or secret strategies is a recipe for irresponsibility and inaction. Those who believe this tend to think that their lack of success is a result of market and societal forces beyond their control. This group fails to realize that universal principles of wealth creation are available to all of us equally. These people don't realize their full potentials because they believe—consciously or subconsciously—that success comes from sources outside of themselves, and that if they aren't lucky enough to have been born into the circles of the wealthy who know the "secrets," then the quest for wealth is a futile search.

Financial success is the product of finding and applying universal principles. It is available to every one of us. It is achievable. It is integral to our progress and development as creative beings with infinite potential. If we can train ourselves to question and attack the myths that are limiting our potentials, we can be infinitely prosperous.

There are risks and costs to a program of action. But they are far less than the long-range risks and costs of comfortable inaction.

—John F. Kennedy

Replacing the Subtle Lies with the Elusive Obvious

This book is primarily concerned with exposing elusively obvious ideas that combat the subtle lies we labor under. Blatant lies are easy to recognize and avoid; the subtle lies can ultimately be more destructive because they are much more difficult to detect and uproot.

Subtle lies seem to make sense and to carry a certain air of credibility. They are often supported by supposed proof and factual evidence that spread and perpetuate them. Many times they appear in the form of half-truths, or truths taken out of context. As these myths gain hold in society, they seem obviously sound—so obviously so that we don't question them. They are sometimes indications of good intentions, but they carry unintended and often unseen negative consequences.

Myths which are believed in tend to become true. —**George Orwell**

Subtle lies also take root in times of chaos and conflict; they can appear as saviors in times of extreme circumstances. They find fertile ground in atmospheres of fear and greed. They appeal to the baser side of human nature. They make destructive paths seem better by focusing on short-term rewards while disguising long-term consequences; by their very nature they encourage shortsightedness. They make us forget the big picture and lure us into focusing on unimportant, trivial matters. In the words of Stephen Covey, they get us into the "thick of thin things."

When we begin to strip the myths bare, we quickly find that declaring them false takes nothing but common sense. We have all had experiences where, after a significant change in our mindset, the new truth that we have discovered seems so obvious that we wonder why we haven't seen it before. So it is with these myths—as soon as we turn our full attention to evaluating their worth, it becomes clear that they are nonsensical at best, and at worst, actively destructive.

Men occasionally stumble over the truth, but most of them pick themselves up and hurry off as if nothing had happened.

—Winston Churchill

The "elusive obvious" is the truth that lies just under the surface of the hype, rhetoric, and propaganda that distracts us from seeing it. For instance, many of us are taught to go to school, get good grades, choose a traditional career, and aim for jobs at a stable corporation with good benefits—even if all of this means that we spend our lives stuck in a situation that doesn't bring real joy. We're taught that it's "risky" to pursue our passions—especially if those giving the advice can't see a way for us to make money by doing so.

But when we carefully analyze such traditional advice, we begin to see how ridiculous it is. When we study the lives of the ultrasuccessful, we find a common thread: all of them pursued their passions instead of ignoring or stifling them for the sake of security. Where would the world be if Walt Disney, Warren Buffett, and Bill Gates had followed this terrible advice?

How can it be risky to wake up each morning and do what we love doing, provided it is moral, principle based, and creates value in the world? Sacrificing the things that bring us the most joy for an imaginary security, and therefore not living up to our potential, is actually the more risky thing to do. This, then, is the elusive obvious behind the advice to sacrifice passion for security.

Do what you love in the service of people who love what you do.

—Steve Farber

Redefining Prosperity

One of the most important subtle lies we must combat—one that lies at the root of so many other myths—is that prosperity is nothing more than the accumulation of material wealth. The elusive obvious is that true prosperity is different for every person and rarely has much to do with how much money she has in the bank or how many cars he has in the garage.

Prosperity and happiness are closely related (as we'll discuss throughout the book). They are both dependent upon two key elements: Soul Purpose and human life value.

Each of us was born for greatness, and every one of us has what I call "Soul Purpose." Soul Purpose is your unique set of talents, abilities, and passions applied productively and effectively, making tremendous impact upon the world and bringing the highest levels of joy and fulfillment for you and everyone you touch. It's the mission that you were born for; it's what you would do every day even if you didn't get paid for it. When you've truly found your Soul Purpose, you create so much value for others that you're almost inevitably paid very well indeed. My friend and colleague Steve D'Annunzio says of Soul Purpose, "Living your Soul Purpose does not mean that you have to own your own business or be famous. It means that you are doing what you are naturally passionate about doing every day, whether working for yourself or as an employee. Many people know their Soul Purpose but refuse to acknowledge it because doing so may require uncomfortable decisions. The real pain and suffering from human existence come from not making these decisions."

The mass of men lead lives of quiet desperation and go to the grave with the song still in them.

—Attributed to **Henry David Thoreau**

Human life value is our own particular combination of knowledge, skills, and abilities—everything that we are when we take away all of our material resources. It is our character and integrity, our ability to think creatively and uniquely, our relationships, our faith—or the lack of each of these things. It is our knowledge and ability to shape materials and information in new ways that are valued and utilized by others and ourselves. Every material thing we enjoy today came from the utilization of individual human life value. The materials in our homes already existed in the earth, but until human life value was applied to natural resources, that matter was nothing but potential value. When human life value is applied to physical matter, it becomes shaped and manipulated into something valuable to us.

If we think of prosperity in terms of achieving and applying our greatest human life value in order to live our Soul Purpose, many of the myths that we labor under instantly come into question. If our new goal is to create value in the world, not simply build our net worth, then how we go about becoming prosperous changes forever.

Try not to become a man of success, but rather try to become a man of value.

—Albert Einstein

The Purpose of *Killing Sacred Cows*

The most important factors in economics that directly affect your wealth and prosperity are the factors that initially go unseen, the forces at play beyond the myths perpetuated by people and institutions that have a vested interest in your belief of the myths. The purpose of this book is to train your mind and help you to cultivate the ability to be able to see through the myths that limit wealth creation. If this is accomplished, you may well experience a productivity breakthrough on an unprecedented scale.

Specifically, here are some of the things you will learn from reading this book:

> How the scarcity paradigm, which is at the root of so much common financial advice, limits our financial success

> How the "accumulation theory" of wealth that most of us subscribe to destroys our potential

> Why "investing" in the stock market for most people is little better than buying lottery tickets—and how you can create real wealth instead

> How most people are in a security dilemma caused by avoiding things they fear, which actually decreases their security—and how to find true security yourself

> Why money doesn't equal power

> Why the most lucrative investments are by nature the lowest risk

> Why the best way to reduce the cost of insurance is to buy the most you possibly can

> How false beliefs about "getting out of debt" may be keeping you from financial freedom

> Why value is infinitely more important than price

After reading this book, the next time your brother-in-law advises you to maximize your 401(k) contribution, you won't blindly accept the fallacy that there will be an automatic "100 percent rate of return" because of the employer match. The next time your parents tell you to get a fifteen-year mortgage and to pay if off as quickly as possible, you'll stop and think about it, analyze it from every angle, and be able to see the unseen falsehoods behind the myth that this practice is safe. If you do contribute to a 401(k) or pay off your mortgage quickly, it will be because it is part of a macroeconomic plan with other moving parts that will actually bring you the best return, not because of a false perception of the employer match and tax deferral. And instead of questioning if you will have enough money to retire, you'll question the concept of retirement itself.

You will, in short, be better prepared to think like a wise economist instead of like a confused consumer. You will find that what you see on the surface is often, if not always, deceptive, and that real truths lie under the surface of what is obvious. Becoming empowered financially will help you unleash your creative genius and reach your full potential. We cannot become financially successful until we learn to recognize myths and then overcome them with truth and principles.

My purpose isn't so much to identify and answer every myth for every reader as it is to just get readers thinking about the rhetoric, propaganda, and traditional "logic" that we're fed through the financial media. If after you are finished reading this book, you are still depending on me or anyone else to give you answers on how to recognize and see through financial myths, I have failed my purpose. Many more myths exist than we'll cover here, and this book is not meant to be an exhaustive study of each one; it's meant to be a catalyst to set you on your own path to true financial freedom.

Immerse yourself in the real facts and begin to break through the barriers that the myths about money have created in the minds of so many people. As you read this book, you will get beneath the surface to the root of money matters. You will see that the invisible chains holding you back are merely illusions that you accept from other people, the media, and financial institutions. Unlock the genius within by educating and investing in yourself.

My challenge to you is to take this book personally. As you read, think about how you can apply these concepts and how they would be useful for you. When you feel compelled to have a conversation about what you are learning, engage in one. If at any time you question what you're reading, think it through and apply the concept in your life. Keep reading, learning, and questioning the assumptions and beliefs you face every day. Live extraordinarily; this may not be easy, but it is more than worth it.

MYTH 1:

{ **The Finite Pie** }

The number of mouths to be fed will have no limit; but the food that is to supply them cannot keep pace with the demand for it; we must come to a stop somewhere . . . In this state of things there will be no remedy . . . famine, distress, havoc and dismay will spread around; hatred, violence, war and bloodshed will be the infallible consequence; and from the pinnacle of happiness, peace, refinement and social advantage we shall be hurled once more into a profounder abyss of misery, want, and barbarism than ever by the sole operation of the principle of population!

—Thomas Malthus (1766–1834)

T he way we think is costing us money—and more than money, our quality of life. Without knowing it, we're missing opportunities, wasting our potential, and letting our dollars and destinies stagnate. But all of this comes from one pernicious root belief: Most of us believe that there is a finite resource "pie" from which we all share and that the more we have, the less others have, and vice versa. We believe that all resources are scarce. It's not unusual that so many of us believe this, though. From birth a mindset of scarcity is ingrained in us. In school we're taught that economics is the science of allocating scarce resources. On television, in magazines, in newspapers, on the Internet, and in virtually every other form of media, we are bombarded with claims that there isn't enough to go around. The theories and strategies of intellectuals like Thomas Malthus articulate such a convincing case for scarcity that it becomes difficult to see the deeper truths beyond what the data seems to suggest on the surface.

In the scarcity mindset, we take it for granted that our society does not have enough resources or productive capacity to fulfill everyone's needs and desires. Consequently, we believe that our material gains come only as a loss to others, and that when others possess more it means less for us. It's easy to see how a culture that accepts the notion of scarcity quickly becomes ultra-competitive and selfish.

But the scarcity mindset is predicated on false beliefs, misinformation, outdated ideas, and fear. While scarcity may be a valid concern at times in the physical world, I will show how human innovation and the principle of exchange render those facts obsolete and add much deeper context to the surface realities, and how we can overcome scarcity and its ill effects in both our minds and our finances.

scarcity:
The belief that resources are limited, and the world is a stage for a zero-sum game of accumulation. In a zero-sum game, anything that another wins is no longer available to all others playing the game.

Scarcity is the belief that resources are limited, and the world is a stage for a zero-sum game of accumulation. In a zero-sum game, anything that another wins is no longer available to all others playing the game. Further, these winnings are not replaced or transformed into anything of equivalent or greater value that remains in the game, available to other players. In scarcity, ownership by another means the loss of opportunity for oneself.

The opposite of scarcity is abundance. The concept of abundance is that there are more than enough resources to fulfill the desires of all the people within a society, a far more inspiring and productive way to look at the world and well supported by the facts, as I'll show you. This is the approach that many successful people and organizations take to their financial decisions, and for obvious reasons. This mindset sets a positive, clear path to achieving your financial potential and your purpose.

The Destructive Nature of Scarcity Thinking

At some point or another in their lives, most people experience scarcity as a reality on a personal scale. But to extrapolate this beyond its true importance and adopt the belief that scarcity represents the nature of our economy, our culture, our environment, or even our universe is destructive and limiting in every aspect of our lives.

When our actions are based on a scarcity mindset, we are acting on fear: fear that we won't get our fair share, that somebody else will reap rewards that we won't, or that we'll have to fight tooth and nail against others to achieve the level of success or prosperity we desire. And this fear causes us to make irrational decisions (especially when it comes to our finances) that limit our potential rather than enhance it.

Nevertheless, the scarcity paradigm dominates our culture today. Consider an example from the media:

> Of all the impulses in humanity's behavioral portfolio, ambition—that need to grab an ever bigger piece of the resource pie before someone else gets it—ought to be one of the most democratically distributed. *Nature is a zero-sum game, after all.* Every buffalo you kill for your family is one less for somebody else's; every acre of land you occupy elbows out somebody else. (Jeffrey Kluger, "Ambition: Why Some People Are Most Likely To Succeed," *Time*, November 14, 2005, vol. 166, no. 20.)

Note the author's assumption that scarcity is the nature of the universe, and how he perceives that human behavior should flow from that assumption. That philosophy justifies hostile, destructively competitive action and the perception that all economic transactions are win-lose, and unapologetically so. After all, if we do not "[elbow] out somebody else," according to Kluger, we are left with nothing ourselves.

Here is another example about Wal-Mart, the company that zero-sum thinkers love to hate:

> Wal-Mart's ascent . . . has already placed it in the exclusive club of companies whose raw power makes them the most feared corporate animals of their time. Wal-Mart has killed or wounded competitor after competitor . . . there's little doubt that Wal-Mart is among history's premier practitioners of Darwinian capitalism, red of tooth and claw. (Matthew Maier,"How to Beat Wal-Mart," CNN Money.com, May 1, 2005.)

Notice the words "feared," "killed," "wounded," "Darwinian," and the references to Wal-Mart as a corporate beast "red of tooth and claw." The underlying assumption here is that Wal-Mart's gains are painful wounds or losses to every other retail store.

It's clear that the scarcity mindset pervades our media and culture, but how does it practically affect us in our daily lives? Reacting out of fear of loss causes us to accept false theories on how to succeed, to neglect the opportunities that would lead us to true prosperity, and to suffer in bad jobs and unfulfilling lifestyles working for nothing but an illusion of security. And perhaps most important, scarcity negatively affects the way we interact with others because it's characterized by an adversarial, win-lose perspective of the world and relationships. When we compete in scarcity, we try to do so at the expense of others—we believe that we can only win if someone else loses. We view others as competition, as roadblocks in the way of our getting what we want. The destruction this attitude wreaks on our prosperity and our contributions to the world is wide-reaching and hard to see at first, but much of this book will be focused on uncovering it and helping to restore a more natural worldview.

In the thrall of scarcity thinking, we make faulty financial decisions. We buy things we don't need because we can never have enough, and we also postpone appropriate purchases, even when we have the money, because we can't let go of our precious dollars. We pull money out of investments when we should be buying more, and we buy investments at their peak when we should be selling. We're naïve when we should be cautious, and skeptical when we should be optimistic. When we encounter challenges, our minds automatically focus on all the reasons why we can't succeed. We feel jealous and envious of others when we perceive that they are more intelligent or beautiful, make more money, have more friends, or have more opportunities than us. We feel superior to those who have less than us. We sue and are sued at the slightest grievances, and for trivial amounts of money, then complain when insurance rates raise. Scarcity even leads some to lie, cheat, and steal to get what is wanted, at the expense of others and our own integrity.

In the commission-based financial services industry, scarcity leads to a focus on making a sale instead of what our clients really want, which hurts both parties. My friend Dean, who is also in the financial services industry, told me about a realization he had as he was working with a client. His client came to him seeking advice on a new job. The client had to make a decision between two pay structures, and was also trying to weigh his children's school and his own work situation, which would be changing, into the equation. As the client bared his deepest concerns and hopes for the future, Dean found that he wasn't really listening or trying to meet the client's needs; rather, his thoughts were focused on how he could sell the client a life insurance product to generate a commission. After he made his presentation and the client shared more information, it became clear that the life insurance policy was completely unnecessary and Dean lost the sale. As he tried to figure out what had gone wrong, it became clear to Dean that he had acted with a scarcity mindset, and hadn't met the client's actual objectives, nor had he created real value for fear of losing a commission. Instead he lost the client altogether—after realizing Dean was only in it for the commission, the man never came back again.

THE MYTHS IN REALITY:
Cash in Coffee Cans

My own great-aunt destroyed her relationships with her siblings because of her struggles with the scarcity mentality. A first-generation immigrant, she came to America from Italy with her brother, sister, and parents when she was young, and all the family scrimped and saved for years to build up a nest egg, which they put in the bank in her name. As she got older, my great-aunt told everyone how poor she was, and she applied to every government program that might offer her assistance. My grandfather was always over at her twenty-five-thousand-dollar house fixing her faulty appliances, and she continued to economize on every possible purchase.

Then she got very sick and was expected to die soon. That's when my grandfather pulled me aside and explained that the siblings' money was all in her name, and probably about to be lost to medical expenses or taxes—and they had accumulated over half a million dollars. As my aunt lay on her deathbed, she asked that we move the money to a safe place.

Against the odds, my aunt recovered and we moved the money to a high-yield investment. Instead of being pleased that we'd found a way to turn their nest egg into usable cash, she was furious and accused my grandfather of stealing from her. He took the money out of the high-yield investment and gave it back. My aunt took some and buried it in her backyard, sealed some more in coffee cans in her cellar, and returned to living a life of poverty—but this time, without my grandfather's help and support. The two siblings still don't speak to each other, despite the seventy-five years of closeness that came before.

When we live in scarcity, greed can blind us to common sense. My friend Cory lost fifty thousand dollars in a scam because he became overwhelmed with the prospect of high returns and thought that if he didn't act immediately, he would lose out. He was approached by a company who asked him to invest in a debt-restructuring and -assistance program and promised him a 10 percent per month return. Without doing any due diligence, he quickly wrote them a check for twenty-five-thousand dollars, and a couple days later gave them another twenty-five thousand because he was so excited about the potential returns. The next month Cory and the other "investors" were told that the company was still working through some issues and would be unable to pay. Each month after that brought another excuse, and several months later, with no returns ever paid, Cory found out that the company was a scam. The founder went to prison. Cory discovered that this person had already been convicted of similar activity and was on probation at the time Cory gave him money. A simple Internet search would have uncovered the fraud, but the lure of high returns prevented him from acting wisely.

Scarcity is about so much more than money and material resources. It's a mindset, a way of viewing and interacting with the world, and it permeates everything we think and do. In large part, it determines who we are and how we act. It robs us of hope, steals our dreams, presents us with supposed evidence for living small and treating others badly, and renders us impotent, despite our infinite potential to create and make the world a better place. In a world of possible freedom, joy, abundance, and service, a scarcity mindset cripples us and aids us in seeing not much more than limitations, suffering, poverty, and selfishness.

The scarcity mindset can also limit the potential of the people around us, our community, our economy, and our society. This is because the scarcity mentality is characterized by adversarial, win-lose relationships. When we compete in scarcity, we try to do so at the expense of others—we believe that we can only win if someone else loses.

Some people might argue that adversarial competition is a critical element of free enterprise, that it's impossible to have a free market economy without it. However, it's clear that a free market economy is more productive when everybody adopts an attitude of cooperative competition and fosters win-win relationships. That sounds a lot better than "for every winner there must be a loser," doesn't it? The myth of scarcity destroys our potential because it pits us *against* each other rather than helping us work *with* each other.

More than simply derailing individual financial success and human potential, scarcity thinking tears apart communities, relationships, and families. Under the scarcity paradigm, money and goods aren't the only finite resources—*everything* is grounds for competition and resentment, from jobs to abstract qualities like beauty and intelligence. Everything someone else possesses represents something that you cannot have.

Even people who consciously reject the idea of scarcity can be *subconsciously* subject to the negative effects of the myth, whether because they copy behaviors their parents and family members have modeled, because scarcity simply feels safer, or for some other unexamined reason. Most of us operate with unconscious paradigms of scarcity that we don't verbalize or try to express. If we did, we might recognize their destructive nature and seek out a better ideology that wouldn't cripple our ability to think and act creatively or productively. This is exactly what the concept of abundance can do for us.

YOU KNOW YOU'RE IN SCARCITY WHEN...

Your friend at work gets a promotion and you find yourself feeling jealous, rather than happy for him.

You see a person driving an expensive car and find yourself feeling resentful or judging her.

You make purchases on credit and live beyond your means; you're dissatisfied with what you have.

You postpone important purchases that would add dramatic value to your life, even when you have the money to make them, because you can't stand to part with your cash.

When your spouse or child asks you to buy something, more often than not your immediate response is that you can't afford it.

You find yourself frequently wishing for a better life, yet you think that it would be futile to strive for something better; there's never enough time or money to do the things you want to do.

You have ideas about how to make your life better, like switching careers or starting your own business, but are afraid to put them into action.

You keep your money in "safe" investments like CDs and money market accounts because you fear losing it.

You pick the riskiest investments, cross your fingers, and hope for high returns, thinking that gambling and luck is your best path to wealth.

Replacing Scarcity with Abundance

Scarcity thinking is holding us back, individually and as a society. Because of this, we must find a way to replace scarcity thinking with a mentality of abundance. Scarcity thinking says, "I can't afford it," or "I just don't have any options," or "I never have enough time to pursue my ideal life." Abundant thinking says, "How can I afford this?" or "I know I have unlimited options; I just have to find a way to realize them," or "How can I *create* more space so I have time to pursue my passions?" Scarcity is limited; abundance is limitless.

We can consciously choose to view life abundantly, to think and act abundantly, and to eliminate our fear of loss. The path to overcoming the myth of scarcity requires us to recognize and accept the abundant nature of our environments and of our potential as creative beings. When we face hardships that seem to reveal that life is harsh and the nature of our existence is combating scarcity, we need to take a broader view and realize that what has happened is that principles of abundance have been violated. If more people live with an abundance mindset, we will all experience less hardship.

QUIZ: What Is Your Mindset?

Rank the following statements on a scale of 1–10, with 10 being "true" and 1 being "false":

1. You are living something close to your ideal life today.
2. You feel confident, assured, and in control of every place you invest your money.
3. All of your financial components are working together and you have the right team in place to see them through.
4. You feel energized and empowered by your finances right now.
5. You do what you want to do on a daily basis, without fear over money.
6. There are no money worries you could remove from your life to improve it.

Add your answers together and divide by 60. What's your grade? A+? C-?

Take, for example, people who have lost money through investments in mutual funds or the stock market. With a scarcity mindset, they will believe they have learned that investing is risky and that profits from investments are scarce. But the true lesson could be that a person or group of people involved with the investment—the investor, the fund manager, the CEO of a business in which the money was invested—made choices that limited or destroyed the potential return of the investment. Investors could also learn lessons from the experience that will propel them to greater success with investments in the future—such as better ways to select fund managers or businesses to invest in. They might examine their investment options more closely in the future to ensure that they are aligned with the principles of abundance, or think of a new way to earn returns from their money. Through abundance, they can view their mistakes as positive lessons that can be applied to minimize risk, and continue to invest, becoming wiser with each investment, each success, and each mistake.

Overcoming the myth of scarcity and replacing it with an abundance mindset is achieved by understanding the following truths, which I'll explore throughout the rest of this chapter.

> People, not material things, have intrinsic value, and people make individual, personal determinations of the value of material things.

> The principle that exchange creates individual and community wealth implies that by continuously exchanging goods and services we can create infinite value from those goods and services. Even if resources are finite, scarce resources plus human ingenuity, individual ideas of value, and continual exchange can create infinite productivity from the available resources.

> The quality of our lives is not determined by the quantity of our stuff.

> Adversarial competition is not conducive to a healthy free market. Enlightened, cooperative competition helps us transcend win-lose relationships and serve one another more effectively and efficiently.

Intrinsic Value and Infinite Value Determinations

One of the key fallacies that helps propagate scarcity thinking is the belief that material things, rather than people, have intrinsic value. Valuing material things in themselves, instead of for their worth to people, inevitably leads to a scarcity mindset, because if material things have intrinsic value, the only way to increase your wealth is to hoard these things. Then, when you lose material things, even in an agreeable trade, you have reduced your wealth. But this is illogical thinking.

How much is your home worth? You probably have a specific dollar amount in mind and would staunchly defend that estimate. But consider this: Would the value of your home change if it were moved to a different city? To a different state? To a different climate? To a different country? Will your home be worth the same amount a year from now? Five years from now? The value of any home depends on many factors and can fluctuate depending on market conditions. But if a home has intrinsic, or inherent, value, how could its market value change?

The first answer to the question, "How much is your home worth?" is always another question: "To whom?" Material things only have value and utility because people value and use them, and people *do* have intrinsic value. People determine what a particular thing is worth to them individually, and each one of us will value any given material resource differently from every other person. This is why the value of any material good or resource can be infinite—because it exists only in our minds and perceptions. A home worth $1 million to you could be completely worthless to me. I might pay $100,000 for a car that you would never consider driving. The intrinsic value lies in the people living in homes and driving cars, not in the homes and cars themselves.

More gold has been mined from the thoughts of men than has ever been taken from the earth.

—Napoleon Hill

None of us value material things equally. This means that resources are infinite according to our individual perceptions of value. There's no productive reason to hoard material things, because since we all have different desires, we can fulfill those desires through efficient, free-market distribution of material resources. When we operate in abundance instead of hoarding

Q: If I have a book and you have $20, and we mutually decide to exchange my book for your $20, what was the book worth to you? What was the book worth to me?

everything for ourselves, resources go into the hands of those who value them the most, and, in most cases, who use them the most effectively.

Our individuality makes for infinite value perceptions and determinations. Why worry that there aren't enough BMWs to go around? Not everyone wants a BMW. Even if it appears that we are going to run out of something, those who value that thing the most will continue to use it, and those who value it the least will create other resources to fulfill the desires previously fulfilled by that resource. This ingenuity will create more markets and more products, and it will ultimately satisfy more wants and needs than ever before.

Consider the example of currency: Even though the amount of currency in circulation is finite, we can use every dollar bill in infinite transactions to create infinite value. One dollar bill can literally become millions—a concept that will be discussed more in chapter 3. I can buy something from you for a dollar, you can take that dollar and buy something from someone else, who can then use it to buy something else, and so on. There are finite dollars, yet infinite value can be exchanged with that finite currency.

Value Exchange Facilitates Wealth

If I have a book and you have $20, and we mutually decide to exchange my book for your $20, what were the book and the $20 worth to you? What were the book and the $20 worth to me? Most people answer that the book was worth $20 to both you and me. This is wrong. *We only give up something in an exchange when we value what we're receiving more than we value what we're giving up.* Hence, there is no way to quantify an exact amount that the book or the $20 was worth to you or me. All we can conclusively say is that to you, the book was worth *more* than $20 and the $20 was worth *less* than the book; to me the book was worth *less* than $20 and the $20 was worth *more* than the book. We both walk away wealthier than before the transaction because we both have something that is worth more to us than what we had before.

We only exchange when others have something that we value more than what we currently have. We never trade like value for like value, because we have no incentive to do so. We trade what we have for what we actually want more. Therefore, hoarding of goods, money, or resources for their own sake—which often comes about as a result of scarcity thinking—limits our personal wealth and precludes personal joy and fulfillment. When we refuse to spend or exchange, we eliminate the joy that comes from activities and possessions that cost money and the increased satisfaction that comes from exchanging something we value for something we value more.

Exchange can only occur in an atmosphere of disagreement. In a free market, the final sale price of any object is always an amount that the seller and the buyer both disagree that the object is worth. This principle is vital to overcoming the myth of scarcity, because one way we create infinite value is through the process of exchange. Just as we can exchange the same dollars an infinite number of times, so we can exchange any and every form of material wealth. The value is not in the things—it is in the minds of people.

Human Ingenuity

Even if we are unable to accept that material resources are essentially infinite, the fact remains that human beings are creative by nature and able to apply their creativity and ingenuity to scarce resources in ways that make those resources abundantly productive. Take, for instance, the case of oil, which is available only in limited quantity. The same ingenuity that gave us the products and resources that have diminished the supply of oil can provide a way to stretch what is left and discover new sources of energy. Oil was used very little until we invented automobiles; then it became one of our biggest sources of energy. The free market is now seeking to replace oil with other, more viable and sustainable sources of energy. How many resources are yet to be discovered, awaiting our creativity to find a use for them?

A: The book was worth more than $20 to you, and the book was worth less than $20 to me.

In *The Ultimate Resource 2*, economist Julian Simon provides empirical data to support the idea that resources can be made abundant by intelligent people working to solve their problems and the problems of their communities. He argues that through economic and political freedom, human ingenuity (which is the "ultimate resource") can manipulate scarce resources to create a prosperous future for the world. For instance, as he explains,

> Agricultural land is not a fixed resource. Rather, the amount of agricultural land has been increasing substantially . . . In the countries that are best supplied with food, such as the United States, the quantity of land under cultivation has been decreasing because it is more economical to raise larger yields on less land than to increase the total amount of farmland. For this reason, among others, the amount of land used for forests, recreation, and wildlife has been increasing rapidly in the United States.

Simon also gives highly optimistic evidence on pollution, natural resources, human fertility, immigration, and the unhealthy effects of population density, among other things.

Fear of innovation and "disruptive" technology has always been a fact of civilization, despite the progress that it actually inspires. For example, even Gutenberg's printing press, which completely revolutionized the world for the better, was initially feared and criticized. Historian Will Durant wrote that when the printing press was introduced, "not all welcomed it. Copyists protested that printing would destroy their means of livelihood; aristocrats opposed it as a mechanical vulgarization, and feared that it would lower the value of their manuscript libraries; statesmen and clergy distrusted it as a possible vehicle of subversive ideas" (*The Reformation*, 159).

In spite of protests that it would destroy livelihoods, with the printing press came countless new jobs and industries including printing and publishing, journalism, ink production, and increased paper production. Furthermore, the indirect benefits of the press contributed to more widespread and democratic education, which in turn led to even more jobs and industries. It may have put a handful of copyists out of work, but the net effect was a dramatic increase in production, jobs, industries, and outlets for human creativity and ingenuity.

In our society, there is a similar outcry against jobs lost to outsourcing and innovation. What many who bewail these trends fail to realize is that *precisely because of innovation* outsourcing can create more and better jobs than those that are lost. Russell Roberts, an economics professor at George Mason University and a research fellow at Stanford University's Hoover Institute, confirms that

> . . . imports don't destroy jobs. They destroy jobs in certain industries. But because trade allows us to buy goods [and services] more cheaply than we otherwise could, resources are freed up to expand existing opportunities and to create new ones. That's why we trade—to leverage the skills of others who can produce things more effectively than we can, freeing us to make things we otherwise wouldn't be able to afford. The United States has run a merchandise trade deficit every year since 1976. It has also added more than 50 million jobs during that time. ("Why We Trade," November 2007, www.foreignpolicy.com)

On the level of our day-to-day lives, the inexhaustible supply of human ingenuity means that we're never truly trapped in a problematic situation, only that we haven't yet found the best solution. It means we can always find a way to make the money we need to make to be happy and prosperous, and that the resources and material goods we already have can probably provide more value to us than we may expect at first. At the heart of abundance is a belief in human ingenuity and human value, and a dedication to applying as much of our own value and ingenuity as we can to improve our societies and reap the rewards.

Regardless of the changing availability of any other service or substance, human ingenuity remains the one most important resource. Ideas are not and will never be scarce—and ideas lead to innovation, which leads to increased efficiency and the ability to use resources in ways that were previously unimaginable, as well as the creation of new and better resources. Human ingenuity is like a piano: although there are a finite number of keys on a piano, there are infinite ways to combine the notes they play to create music. While many scientists observe the seemingly finite nature of material resources, they fail to realize the infinite abundance that arises when human creativity is applied to scarce resources.

Quality of Life vs. Quantity of Stuff

When we understand that people, not things, are the real assets, we naturally stop placing so much value on material goods. We diminish the tendency to base our sense of self-worth on how much stuff we have. We find more happiness in relationships than we do in homes, cars, and boats. We realize that prosperity is more a state of mind than it is columns of numbers on paper.

What you leave behind is not what is engraved in stone monuments, but what is woven into the lives of others.

—**Pericles**

Our quality of life is closely tied to our level of financial freedom. I define financial freedom as the choice that money will no longer be the primary factor in our decision-making processes. This doesn't mean that it's not *a* factor—it's just not the main factor. This is the point at which we scrub phrases like, "I can't afford it" from our vocabulary. This is where we commit to no longer let our money rule us, but rather, to govern our money. According to this definition, every person reading this book can become financially free immediately. What it takes is commitment—not interest, but a committed choice.

When we become mentally free, this internal freedom is reflected in our external, physical world. Our material wealth becomes a mere reflection of our abundance perspective.

What I'm talking about is a three-part formula: our beliefs determine our behavior, and our behavior determines our results. Another way to state this is "Be-Do-Have." Most people put these in the exact opposite order, as in "Have-Do-Be." People think that if they could just *have* more, then they would *do* the right things, and then they would *be* who they want to be. But abundance works in the opposite order: If we want to *have* more, then we should start by *being* better people; in order to be better, we start *doing* better things, which leads to having more of what we want. When we become who we were born to be—or, in other words, start living our Soul Purpose—every resource imaginable becomes available to fulfill our mission.

If we want to prosper, we must learn that happiness does not come from material things. We must become aware that happiness comes from inside

If I **had** what I needed,
I could **do** what I want to,
and then I would **be** happy
and productive.

ourselves; nothing external can dictate our lasting happiness. Taking responsibility for and shaping our beliefs and habits is the first step toward happiness and prosperity. The irony is that the healthier our beliefs are, the more material and spiritual prosperity we will experience.

All external changes in the forms of life, not having a change of consciousness at their base, do not improve the condition of the people, but generally make it worse . . . A better life can only come when the consciousness of men is altered for the better; and therefore all the efforts of those who wish to improve life should be directed to changing their own and other people's consciousness.

—**Leo Tolstoy**

Competition + Cooperation

Scarcity results in a competitive approach to economics and personal finances. If resources are limited, if there's only so much wealth to go around, and another's gain results in my loss, then I must compete with that person for all available resources. Adversarial competition results in hoarding and mismanagement of resources. If another's gain represents my loss, then I must strive to be the winner in every transaction. I must view every other person as a threat to my prosperity.

This type of thinking limits our financial potential because we frequently miss or reject the opportunities that could result from cooperation and sharing with others. The opposite of competition is, of course, cooperation and interdependence. When individuals bring unique skills and talents to a combined project, the total value of that project increases at a greater rate than the individual value each of those people contributed. Through the synergy created by sharing and exchanging our full human potential, everyone benefits and becomes far wealthier than if they were to hoard their talents and energy to themselves. (This energy, talent, and potential is what I call *human life value*, and I'll explain more about it throughout the book.) This is the type of thinking Dr. Ivan Misner has used to create Business Networking International (bni.com), the largest business networking organization in the world. BNI creates an abundant-minded atmosphere where individuals understand that cooperation and exchange are prerequisites for success.

When we are in scarcity mode, we are faced with many dilemmas, one of them being that if resources are scarce and material things have static, intrinsic value, then every transaction is a win for one person and a loss for another. By definition, according to the scarcity paradigm, no person can ever engage in a win-win transaction. If resources are so scarce, the dilemma becomes, "If I want to be happy, I must do it at the expense of the happiness of other people, and if I want to be moral, I must sacrifice my own happiness to do so."

The abundance paradigm helps us to see the possibility of and the value in win-win exchanges and transactions. People who are operating in abundance know that by serving the wants and needs of others, and thus creating happiness in the lives of others, they actually bring more happiness to themselves. The goal is to serve others, not to exploit or dominate them. They are able to serve wholeheartedly and completely because they know that by so doing, they aren't in any way diminishing their own happiness; in fact, they are generating *more* happiness and success in their own lives.

In an abundance paradigm, we fulfill our needs and wants by helping others fulfill their own; transactions are always win-win. In abundance, all of our thoughts, words, emotions, and actions are motivated by contributing to our personal success and the success of others. In abundance, no one is jealous or envious of another's money; there is infinite wealth to be created and put to use.

People who are committed to free enterprise, entrepreneurs who deeply understand abundance, don't operate a business in order to put another institution out of business and give their customers no alternative. They bring products and services to the market in order to serve others. They understand that it is in their best interest to serve others. They believe in efficient and effective service. They know that there are limitless opportunities to serve and to create wealth. They know that through abundance *everyone* can win and that each of us can have our individual desires satisfied without harming other people. Free enterprise is about excellence and unique offerings, not about destroying competition (although there are certainly many misguided individuals out there who have given free markets a bad name). The more people who understand this and become true creators of free enterprise, the easier it becomes for free-market businesses to succeed through cooperation.

I learned the value of cooperation early on in my career. I moved from a small town in Utah to Salt Lake City to expand my financial services practice, but I was worried about how I was going to build a career and make it work because I didn't know anyone there. Fortunately, Dee Randall, an insurance agent, had heard about the many financial courses I had been taking, and asked me if I would come and present to his agency. I did, and after the event three agents asked me to help them with clients. This led to a lot of joint work with other agents (the year after I graduated from college I made $133,000), and an idea.

My idea was to start a regular training course for agents. I immediately had several people tell me that it was a big mistake, that I was training my competition. But I knew it was right so I persisted. I started teaching about a hundred agents on a regular basis in what I called the "Mission-Driven Forum." Although I was brand new to the area, my business exploded, and I started receiving more referrals than I could handle. I went from making $133,000 one year to $450,000 the next, all because I did what many people thought didn't make sense: I cooperated with my competition, and the result was more business for all of us.

The free market inherently tends toward abundance, not scarcity. This is due to the principles of exchange, cooperation, and innovation, among others.

Abundance creates opportunities; it doesn't destroy them. If a business fails in a free market it is because customers are being served more efficiently and effectively elsewhere, not because the business somehow "lost." This actually becomes an opportunity for a business to learn how to serve others better, which is exactly how successful people and businesses handle temporary failure. Successful entrepreneurs view temporary setbacks as steppingstones to success, allowing for increased knowledge and thus greater ability to succeed; in other words, temporary failures are part of the market research process.

YOU KNOW YOU'RE IN ABUNDANCE WHEN . . .

Your primary focus in life is to lift, serve, and bless the lives of others.

You feel happy when others succeed—even those who may be viewed as your competition—and you never feel threatened by others.

You feel satisfied, complete, joyful, and calm.

The purchases you make align with your core values.

Your investments are wise; you're not naïve, nor are you overly skeptical. You perform wise, patient research and make an educated decision.

Rather than saying "I can't afford it," you ask, "*How* can I afford it?"

You consistently overcome fear, through faith and courage, to pursue your dreams and a career that aligns with your passion and purpose.

You're able to work with others to achieve things that you couldn't do alone.

You take full responsibility for your life and your work and use your internal strength to overcome all challenges and transcend external circumstances.

Throughout my career, I've had the benefit of witnessing firsthand the hold that scarcity can have on people's lives, and then the empowering change that occurs when they make the transition to thinking abundantly. One couple that I've had the privilege of working with, Ben and Heather Corrales, told me of their struggles with scarcity. They always felt paranoid about finances and were always focused on worrying about the lack of money in their lives. They thought that no opportunities would come their way, and that opportunities were a product of luck, rather than factors that they had control over. Even when they found opportunities, they analyzed them through the eyes of scarcity, and so they developed a "too good to be true" mentality and were afraid to act.

When they started educating and investing in themselves, I watched a significant transition occur. They experienced the paradigm shift, embraced abundance, and began viewing the world through entirely new eyes. Where all they saw was lack before, now they were seeing multiple opportunities. More important, they realized that they had the ability to control the productivity of their opportunities through their own education. They started reading and studying more. They found and began utilizing resources that were previously unavailable to them. Now when they choose to engage in an opportunity, they do it not because of how much money it will make, but because it aligns with their purposes and unique abilities. The time spent worrying when they were in scarcity is now time that they spend increasing their knowledge and productivity; they've learned to reduce their fear through education and the abundance mindset. In just a short time, they felt liberated. Money no longer dictates their lives or provides the primary motivation for their actions, and yet they make more money in safer ways.

Though it is perhaps easiest to see the financial and relationship benefits of an abundance mindset, the power of this way of thinking extends to all aspects of life. I also have the privilege of working with some spectacular individuals who have overcome challenges by embracing the freedom of abundance. One associate in particular, Anthony Andelin, discovered abundance after an agonizing car accident when he was twenty-one. On the way to a movie with friends, the car he was in was broadsided, leaving Anthony with a broken sternum, a broken pelvis, two broken ribs, and a separated shoulder. In the hospital, he was told that he might not walk again.

Anthony says that he quickly fell into scarcity, overwhelmed with thoughts and feelings about all the things he would miss out on in life, all the things he wouldn't be able to do. Then, at 3 A.M., as he lay wallowing in his perceived limitations, a thought entered his mind that completely changed his focus and outlook. He realized that his ability to walk again was dependent upon him, not on any doctor or other external factor. In the quiet hours of the night, Anthony made a decision that changed the course of his life. He decided that he would walk again, that he was responsible, and that he would live a productive life despite anything that happened to him.

Now, in spite of all evidence to the contrary, and after a formidable rehabilitation process, Anthony is able to do everything as before, with no limitations. He attests that it all came down to that one decision between scarcity and abundance, victimhood and heroism, that determined the outcome. Scarcity thinking told him to stop trying, to wallow in the pain, misery, and deprivation. But he knew that he was born for something greater. He understood his power as a creator, and he used that understanding to create his ideal life. Now he finds fulfillment in teaching others the same empowering truths: that abundance is the true nature of the universe and of human beings, and that we can be and do what we choose to be and do.

* * *

We were born to be creators and to make our lives extraordinary with the gifts we're given. By becoming consciously aware of our own nature, we can begin to let go of scarcity and fear and begin to accept and express abundance. As we begin to think abundantly, the changes in our thoughts and behavior are manifested externally. As James Allen wrote, "Men do not attract that which they *want*, but that which they *are*."

MYTH 2:

{ **You're in It for the Long Haul** }

Remember, if you are able to save just $100 a month and you faithfully transfer it to your nest egg, in forty years (compounded at the average S&P 500 rate of 10.2 percent) that little extra saving will be worth close to $700,000!

—Richard Paul Evans

Myth:

Put all your money in a 401(k) and forget about it. Retirement is going to cost you everything you can possibly save and maybe a little more.

401(k)

Reality:

Don't let your money stagnate beyond your control— Put it to productive use immediately so it can benefit you now and in the future.

I n our society, there is a strongly held belief that wealth is determined by how much money we have accumulated in the bank, in investments, and in retirement accounts, regardless of any other factor. This is one of the most ridiculous myths that I confront on a regular basis. It's ridiculous because it's so easy to demonstrate its fundamental flaws, and yet the myth dominates our thinking and our conversations on personal finance—we accept it unquestioningly.

According to the mainstream financial media, the road to wealth is to save and accumulate money, with a pie-in-the-sky dream of living off the interest of all of the money we've saved and invested. We're taught to reduce our expenses at all costs, put money away in 401(k)s and IRAs, never touch our principal, and find our risk tolerance and develop an appropriate asset allocation model.

Risk tolerance is "the degree of uncertainty that an investor can handle in regard to a negative change in the value of his or her portfolio. An investor's risk tolerance varies according to age, income requirements, financial goals, etc. For example, a seventy-year-old retired widow will generally have a lower risk tolerance than a single thirty-year-old executive, who generally has a longer time frame to make up for any losses she may incur on her portfolio" (www.investopedia.com).

An asset allocation model is in its simplest terms, "the practice of dividing resources among different categories such as stocks, bonds, mutual funds, investment partnerships, real estate, cash equivalents and private equity. The

risk tolerance:
The degree of uncertainty that an investor can handle in regard to a negative change in the value of his or her portfolio.

asset allocation:
A strategy to reduce risk by dividing one's investment portfolio among different categories such as stocks, bonds, mutual funds, investment partnerships, real estate, cash equivalents, and private equity.

theory is that the investor can lessen risk because each asset class has a different correlation to the others; when stocks rise, for example, bonds often fall. At a time when the stock market begins to fall, real estate may begin generating above-average returns. The amount of an investor's total portfolio placed into each class is determined by an asset allocation model" (Joshua Kennon, http://beginnersinvest. about.com/od/assetallocation1/a/aa102404.htm).

The financial pundits teach us to "invest" in mutual funds, that net worth is the best indicator of wealth, and that we need to sacrifice our current desires and potential to achieve some far-off, imagined goal. In theory, we are saving so that we can actually enjoy our assets, but often the impulse to hoard money takes over, and we don't even think about why we are stashing our resources away. A big bank balance gives us an erroneous feeling of security, as though nothing can touch us, even though the money is just sitting there and not actually benefiting us in any way.

The accumulation theory poses a dilemma, as do all myths. It tells us to accumulate as much money as possible and let it sit stagnant in a 401(k) or mutual fund for years, increasing at a glacial pace if at all. But why are we accumulating money, if not to use it? We put off the moment at which we dip into our rainy-day fund for as long as possible, afraid it will run out and we'll be left with nothing. Even when we finally want to use it, we're afraid to—afraid to risk our nest egg, our net worth, our security. The irony is that if we don't use the money, we have hoarded it all these years for nothing. We end up feeling like we're damned if we do and damned if we don't. Although myths create dilemmas, these dilemmas are easy to work through once we educate ourselves to see the truth of the situation and realize that we have infinitely more options than we've been told.

What good is money if we don't use it? Utilizing money—that is, putting it to work and using it to provide services to ourselves and others, rather than simply accumulating it and putting it into so-called safe investment vehicles—is the most direct way to achieve our goals, increase our happiness, provide value to others, and realize all of the options we have to increase our true wealth. Rather than believing in the myth of throwing money into investment accounts and hoping that it will realize a return after a long waiting period, we can utilize our assets to immediately provide as much value for as many people as possible. Utilization means we stop waiting for financial freedom to come to us and instead become proactive in creating it ourselves, right now. Utilization is also about our own immediate enjoyment of life, as well as creating favorable conditions for long-term enjoyment, rather than locking up our assets for fear of losing them.

In this chapter, we'll explore how the theory of accumulation has been propagated, why the myth is so destructive, and powerful ways to transcend this myth, including learning the differences between utilization and accumulation, understanding the velocity of money, and learning how to turn net worth into cash flow.

The Destructive Nature of Accumulation

Why is the accumulation approach so wrong and so destructive to living our Soul Purpose or building our human life value? In short, because the "wisdom" that is taught is, more often than not, at direct odds with what is actually in our best interest. The fear the accumulation theory perpetuates keeps us from putting our own resources to use and keeps us chained to financial institutions.

The theory of accumulation is dominant in the financial industry and is based on the assertion that wealth can be measured as the monetary value of investments, so the more investments you accumulate—as stocks, bonds, mutual funds, basic savings, or other financial instruments—the wealthier you are. This theory is rooted in the business realm and the accumulation of capital, which is usually defined as assets invested for profit. While capital accumulation is a beneficial business concept that can help analysts determine the value of an enterprise, analysts value it because the assumption is that the business is utilizing the capital in the most efficient way to produce the greatest profit. Business capital is productive, not stagnant, as is most of the wealth accumulated by individuals. While accumulating capital can be beneficial to us as individuals and enhance our wealth, it will only do so if we utilize the capital in the most efficient and productive ways possible, and that is not what most financial institutions and retirement planners teach us to do.

Just as you usually have your own interests in mind when you take action, so do financial institutions. Robert Castiglione, the founder of the LEAP (Lifetime Economic Acceleration Process) system of financial engineering, teaches that financial institutions operate under four rules:

1. Financial institutions want our money.
2. They want it on a regular, systematic basis (preferably through automatic withdrawal).
3. Once they have our money, they want to hold on to it for as long as possible (hence early withdrawal restrictions).
4. If they have to give it back, they want to give back as little as possible.

Does this make the business practices of financial institutions unethical? No. The point isn't to criticize them for operating this way, but to clarify that their operations are based on their *own* interests—which often do not coincide with ours.

The fallacies of the accumulation theory are exposed when we understand what the financial institutions do with the money that we give them—the precise things that we're taught are "risky" and/or too "complicated" to do as individuals. We are told to invest regularly, as much as we can afford to; to never touch what we've put away before retirement; to expect single-digit or at best 10-percent rates of return; and to understand that any investment that might give us higher returns is likely to put our principal at risk. Do you think that a bank views a 10-percent annual return as a good, safe, sustainable rate? Not on your life. They convince us that we're lucky to get 10 percent through a mutual fund, and that it's safer to put money in CDs, savings, and money market accounts, earning at best 5 percent per year—then they turn around and lend out that same money at much higher rates than they are paying us. This is how banks make money using our money.

Banks operate under completely opposite rules than do most individuals, and they rely on that fact to stay profitable. While individuals are accumulating and hoarding, banks are utilizing the money we give them in far more productive and profitable ways. While individuals are hoping for a 10 percent annual return, banks are mitigating their risk to near zero and guaranteeing themselves healthy double- and sometimes even triple-digit returns. For example, if I buy a hammer for $3 and sell it for $6 at a yard sale, I've just made a 100 percent rate of return. Banks do this daily by paying us 3 percent on the money we give them and then lending it out at 6 percent. While individuals are more than happy to use their own money for their investments, banks use other people's money. While individuals think it is wise to lock up money for thirty years or more, banks keep their money liquid and in constant motion.

It's clear why financial institutions try to access our money: for their own profit. But why do retirement planners continue to propagate the myth of accumulation? If you were to meet with a retirement planner today, chances are that the "planning" process would generally go as follows: The planner would find out what monetary assets you currently have, ask you how much money you would like to have at retirement age (or make an arbitrary recommendation about what they think you should have), and make some assumptions. She might even use a snazzy questionnaire to determine your tolerance for risk—or how much of your nest egg you can stomach losing if it offers you a possibility for higher returns. Then, using mostly mathematical guesses and opinions, the planner would calculate the numbers with planning software that would tell you how much you "need" to save per month, and for how many years, and at what interest rate, and using what tax advantages. The advice seems authoritative and credible, so you take it.

The magic pill that the entire financial planning industry is built on—and that most of us are swallowing whole—is that financial success comes from investing in the right products, employing the right strategies, and basing calculations on countless unknown variables. This, despite the fact that it's not working for anyone. The dismal statistics speak for themselves. A Gallup sur-

75%
of workers want
to retire before
age 60.

only
25%
think they
actually will.

vey showed that 75 percent of workers want to retire before age sixty, yet only 25 percent actually think that they will. According to a study conducted by the U.S. Department of Commerce, only 5 percent of all Americans are financially independent at age sixty-five. This study further indicated that 75 percent of all retirees are forced to depend on family, friends, and Social Security as their only sources of income. An article in *USA Today* showed that the number-one concern for American retirees is the fear of running out of money. Fifty-one percent of retirees today have incomes below $10,000 per year. In a world filled with financial advice, few actually enjoy financial success.

I was able to see past the surface of the conventional industry because for the first few years of my career, I bought into it, believed it, and lived it until the limitations and flaws began to be very apparent in my own life. I was saving most of my income, I lived in an apartment when I could afford a home, and I based my feelings of success not on whether or not I was living up to who I was, but rather on external factors such as how much money I had in the bank, what rates of return I was getting, and how my products were performing. I was doing everything right according to the accumulation theory, yet I felt unfulfilled, and I knew that there had to be something more, something deeper to prosperity than numbers on paper, products, and investment returns.

Here's what I've discovered that the accumulation theory never takes into account: It's far more productive to base our investment and planning for the future on our Soul Purpose and human life value than our minimum requirements or our tolerance for risk. These two concepts are the foundation of true success, as measured in our prosperity and the fulfillment we get out of life.

In short, Soul Purpose is the mission that you were born to fulfill, and every individual was born with a unique and powerful Soul Purpose. You can recognize yours by identifying what you would do all day long whether or not you got paid to do it. When you find something this fulfilling that you can deliver as value to others, then you are living Soul Purpose. Not only will you get to do what you love, but you'll get paid for it, and you'll be very successful. You'll be doing something that only you can do to that level, which makes your services and products valuable indeed.

Human life value is the knowledge, skills, abilities, ideas, and relationships that you have, the qualities that let you produce value for others and the most important source of wealth. Applied human life value is the source of all money, prosperity, and progress. The more you increase your human life value, the more value you will provide for others and receive in return.

These two principles are the foundation of all wealth and happiness. Without these principles behind our actions, we'll remain stuck in the grip of accumulation and consumerism.

As long as we buy into the deceptions of the accumulation theory, the financial institutions have our money; they have it on a regular, systematic basis; they get to keep it for as long as possible; and they can give as little back as possible. In short, our money builds profits for banks, fund managers, and the government instead of for ourselves.

Meanwhile, our production is decimated through the faulty theory because accumulation is based on a construct of scarcity and is a recipe for fear-based hoarding. I have yet to meet anyone who teaches or practices the accumulation theory of wealth who does not live his life in scarcity. The advice we hear coming from the accumulation camp sends the message that spending and utilizing money is bad and that the highest ideal is for us to have a large "nest egg," so we can sleep at night knowing that we are "secure."

The underlying tenet of both scarcity and accumulation is fear of loss and a misplaced sense of security. Accumulation theory teaches us to hoard our money rather than to be immediately productive with it. We're even taught that if we save enough money, we will generate enough interest income to cover our expenses. Of course, in order for the 5 to 10 percent "safe" rate of return to serve as our main source of income, we need a massive amount of principal, which according to accumulation theory we can never touch. What I've found in my financial services practices is that the (very few) people who actually do accumulate such large amounts of cash spend their retirement years living like they are broke, in scarcity, suffering from the constant fear of loss. It took them so long to accumulate their nest eggs that their constant thought is to preserve it at all costs. Ironically, even when people "succeed" using the accumulation theory, the scarcity that led them to gain a lot of money is perpetuated as they hoard and preserve it. Sadly, many strategies exist that allow people to fully utilize their assets during retirement, live much fuller and happier lives, and eliminate virtually all risk of losing their retirement assets and income, but relatively few know about them (see chapter 8).

 Our doubts are traitors, and make us lose the good we oft might win, by fearing to attempt.   —**William Shakespeare**

The accumulation theory often creates the proverbial "broke millionaire," a person who has millions of dollars and yet lives like a pauper because of fear of loss. Where did the belief arise that the purpose of our existence is to scrimp and save for thirty years, then spend the next twenty in scarcity, afraid that we're going to lose all that we accumulated or just outlive our resources? Why do we buy into this kind of thinking? Why do we think that this is financial freedom? Truthfully, it is the opposite of freedom; it is a subtle yet powerful form of bondage. It causes us to be constantly worried about interest rates, inflation, and taxes because we're so worried about protecting our hoarded money.

The accumulation mindset severely limits productivity by making us believe that we can't afford to enjoy life before retirement; it is based on the misguided hope of futurism rather than maximizing the present, creating a dilemma that leads to inaction, or at least limited action. The belief that the purpose of our lives is to work hard and save until we turn sixty or sixty-five and *then* start enjoying life ends up destroying our potential. The irony of the theory is that it's designed to provide for our retirement—and yet what do most people do when they reach retirement age, when they are completely dependent on their accumulated money? They refuse to utilize and enjoy it because their worst fear is that they will lose the nest egg they worked thirty years to accumulate. How could we spend so many years in scarcity and hoarding mode, and then suddenly go against ideas that have been ingrained into our thoughts and habits throughout decades? It's highly unlikely that after spending our whole lives being cheap and frugal we could break out of that mindset overnight. And at the 70 percent of our former earnings retirement planners advise us to allot per year of retirement and lack of any other income, we wouldn't truly be able to break free of scarcity in any case. Of course, some of us won't live long enough to try.

THE MYTHS IN REALITY:

Postponing Your Dreams

With the right knowledge, approach, process, and tools, people can unlock the productive potential of all their resources, have greater enjoyment immediately, and still be much more prepared for retirement. One couple I worked with had a lot of money: both the husband and the wife made six-figure incomes. Yet they couldn't decide how to plan and what to do with their money. When I met them, they were meeting with five different retirement planners, and all five of them were telling them the same things: buy these products, save this much for retirement, use these strategies, etc. They were presenting the couple with illustrations and selling them on products and potential returns, rather than ascertaining what their lives were really about, and getting to the heart of what they wanted their money to accomplish for them.

I took a different approach: I simply asked questions. I dug deep to figure out who these people were, what their dreams and aspirations were, what their life purposes were. I knew that I couldn't prescribe products and strategies until I knew what they wanted from life. One thing that came out of the interview was that they had always wanted to buy a motor home. When I asked them why they hadn't done it yet, despite the fact that they had plenty of money, they replied that it all came down to money, that they didn't want to reduce their net worth.

After discovering this, I was able to help them with a series of strategies that unlocked the potential of their existing resources and helped them to immediately purchase a motor home so that even after the purchase they were still in a much better position financially. They took multiple trips in the motor home with their family and created cherished memories that they had been putting off for later. A couple short years later, the husband, then in his early fifties, unexpectedly died. Because of the steps we had taken together, they were able to enjoy their family like they had envisioned before the husband's death. But even so, the wife is doing incredibly well financially, her cash flow has increased, her money is even more liquid than it was before. This couple planned for the best and prepared for the worst and were able to live life to the fullest as a result. They were able to realize that they didn't have to wait to achieve their dreams, and that living their dreams didn't have to come at the expense of their financial future.

For more information and examples, go to killingsacredcows.com

As long as we're waiting for some magic number to appear on an investment account, we're not focusing on how we can develop our human life value in the now. Accumulation puts too much emphasis on cutting expenses to build our nest egg as opposed to increasing productivity and creating value in the present—for ourselves and others. In other words, it magnifies *frugality* to the exclusion of and at the expense of *productivity*.

The accumulation mindset distracts us from any effort to produce and create value. It replaces the critical values of education and individual responsibility with misguided faith in financial institutions, corporations, or the government. Those who live according to the accumulation theory routinely hand over their money to so-called experts, then cross their fingers and hope and pray that everything will turn out well. They fail to take responsibility for their own productivity and their human life value. They neglect the crucial discipline of stewardship, which means taking ultimate responsibility for the care and maintenance of all their resources. By doing so they significantly diminish their productivity and fail to find and realize their Soul Purpose.

The accumulation theory fundamentally requires an abdication of responsibility. It requires people to stop thinking, to accept social norms and clichés unquestioningly, and to quietly consent to their lot in life while allowing external circumstances to dictate their success, all in the name of achieving financial security. Yet the way to provide for security is to cultivate the ability to produce value in the world under any set of circumstances. The way for you to get what you want is to give others what they want; to make yourself valuable to others. When you create value for others, and they find it more beneficial to live life with you than without you, you create a true sense of security based on personal production, rather than on external, uncontrollable factors. Now many look to the government and corporations to provide security for them instead of turning inward to find and develop Soul Purpose.

Even worse than the blind trust the accumulation theory requires, though, are the effects of the fear and greed it inspires. Under the influence of the accumulation theory, we jump into markets at their peak because of greed, then when they drop we jump out because of fear. We chase markets because we have no understanding of how we are creating value, and so don't know what will increase our prosperity and what will decrease it. This is just a form of gambling, not investing.

Most people who place money in the stock market have no idea what their money is doing, no idea what kinds of returns they can expect, no mechanisms for reducing risks, and no idea of how they are creating value in the world. The way most people "invest" is like someone who, after playing craps at a casino, makes bets based on how he has seen other players win. Yet the financial pundits continue to refer to these people as "investors"—and the "investors" continue to feel good because they're doing what everyone else is doing and don't have to think much about it.

Anything that involves such a high degree of risk and uncertainty is nothing more than gambling. I define investing as anything we do that we can control, of which we have intimate knowledge such that risk can be mitigated to near zero, and which will safely yield a profit. When we invest by developing our Soul Purpose, we are in no danger of simply following trends, because we understand where the value comes from and what to do to create more. The stock market and mutual funds are not inherently wrong, and for some they do offer true paths to success, as long as those people possess an intimate knowledge of how they work, who is operating and benefiting from them, and how they are creating value in the world. But is the average consumer who has money in mutual funds investing or gambling? I believe the answer to that is unequivocally gambling.

 The darkest hour of any man's life is when he sits down to plan how to get money without earning it. —**Horace Greeley**

Unless we understand and practice the principles that underlie economic prosperity (developing our Soul Purpose and maximizing our human life value), there is no escape from the mental trap of accumulation. Even those with a lot of money fear the loss of their hard-earned stash. Fear, doubt, and worry are mental viruses that originate from a scarcity paradigm, which itself arises from an ignorance of prosperity principles. Fear evaporates when we alter our perspective and begin to consider what other people want and how we can create value for them. Ironically, this shift in focus away from self results in the greatest personal rewards, both in terms of wealth and happiness.

Replacing Accumulation with Utilization

It's time that the accumulation theory of wealth be questioned, challenged, and replaced. It is destructive to human life value because it limits our happiness and utility. It blinds us from seeing the unlimited possibilities that surround us—we do not engage our natural creativity due to this blindness. It is a recipe for mediocrity.

If we want to maximize our potential human life value and live our Soul Purpose, we must learn to see through the deceptions that hoarding our money will help us achieve true wealth; that security can be found by denying our passions; and that financial institutions can take better care of our money than we can. We have to take responsibility and utilize our assets now to create value for ourselves and others. Achieving true financial freedom requires courage and boldness. It requires that we see through destructive and limiting social norms. It requires that we follow our passion instead of following the crowd. But it's worth it. It's worth it to realize our potential, to live our Soul Purpose, and create a legacy with the gifts that we have been given. It's worth becoming who we were meant to become.

The way to overcome the accumulation myth and start utilizing our assets to their fullest advantage is to understand the following:

> How to seek value creation rather than practice frugality

> The difference between producing in the present and deferring life to the future

> The velocity of money

> Cash flow versus net worth

Value Creation

One of the key problems associated with following the accumulation theory is that it leads us to believe that money is power, and that we should place our faith in money, rather than in the things that create money. But in a world of cause and effect, value creation is a cause, and money is an effect. Money is not power; it is merely a representation of value. Money is never manifested and exchanged until value is created, and thus is an *expression* of value creation.

The accumulation theory teaches us to focus on the *byproduct* of value creation (money) and not the *source* (human life value applied in the service of others). I define value as something of worth or service that, when provided to another, creates joy for both parties. Value can come in many forms. Some value physical gifts, others value kind words, while still others may value acts of service more than anything else.

value:
anything of worth or service that, when provided to another, creates joy for both parties.

Focusing on accumulating money is like wanting to harvest the fruits of a tree while ignoring the roots. As we accept the accumulation theory, most of us become frustrated with the lack of fruit on our tree—or the lack of money in our bank accounts. And what do we do to solve this problem? We focus on the fruit *only*, rather than tracing the fruit to the branches, then to the roots. The real solution is to nourish the roots; then the fruit will naturally follow. This is the principle-based, rather than strategy-driven, approach. Value and dollars follow value creation. Dollars are the effect; value creation is the cause.

Because we are so focused on money as the end goal and not on value creation, we use illogical approaches to increase our hoarded dollars, with the worst being an excessive emphasis on decreasing expenses, living within our means, and having just enough to fulfill our needs. This is what I refer to as the "Ebenezer Scrooge" method of finances. It seems so illogical to me that the road to wealth could ever be to reduce expenses. Is not the concept of wealth itself all about what we use money for, rather than just having the money?

Now, I am not saying that cutting expenses is inherently bad, or that it isn't useful in the proper context. For some people there are principled reasons to reduce expenses. For example, people who consistently spend more than they make, and therefore borrow to consume, should realign their spending habits. But to enjoy better results in the present, instead of asking "How can I cut my expenses," we should ask "How can I create more value in this moment?" Almost universally, we can focus on creating value and increase our income and productivity rather than reducing expenses. In fact, there are even times when borrowing money can be the most productive thing a person can do (see chapter 8).

One oft-heard piece of advice is to "live within your means." Most of us automatically assume that this should translate into cutting expenses. But what about increasing our "means" instead? Why is this so rarely considered? Are expenses inherently bad? No. In fact, there are many expenses that, when understood and properly applied, can actually increase income (more on this in chapter 9). Don't misunderstand me: I'm not saying that we should become overly consumptive or do everything we can to consume more. What I am saying is that we should produce more than we consume.

For example, what if instead of spending thought, time, and energy on finding ways to cut monthly expenses by a hundred dollars we chose to redirect that focus toward figuring out ways to increase our monthly incomes? Time and energy spent focusing on cutting expenses can never be retrieved. But time spent focusing on productivity rather than on cutting expenses increases our value to the world, which ultimately impacts our personal wealth.

I know how fruitless it is to focus excessively on decreasing expenses. I once went through a phase when I thought cutting expenses was the way to go, so I began to study my finances in depth. It took me ten hours to cut $240 from my monthly expenses, a tiny fraction of my monthly income. Ironically, half of the expenses I cut ended up coming back a few months later anyway because they were things I really wanted. Afterward, I wondered how much income I could have produced in those ten hours had I focused on productivity instead.

It's much more effective for our financial success to spend the time that we would have spent thinking of ways to reduce expenses on thinking of ways that we can create more value. Many times sensibly and strategically increasing our expenses can be conducive to developing wealth and prosperity (see chapter 8). Because people fail to see themselves as their most important asset, they focus on sacrificing and cutting back as opposed to increasing productivity by investing in themselves.

To use the analogy of the goose that lays golden eggs, practicing the accumulation theory is like neglecting the goose and expecting to get more eggs. We're taught to feed the goose as little as possible, to get the "best deal" on food and shelter (translation: the cheapest) for the goose, and then to hoard the eggs when they emerge. The utilization approach teaches us to give our goose the best care, focus less on price and more on value in lodging, and immediately utilize the golden eggs as they emerge to produce value for ourselves and others. The lesson is that we are the geese that lay golden eggs, and if we want more golden eggs (or money), we must focus more on developing our human life value and our ability to create value for others and less on the actual dollars.

I often hear frugality referred to as a virtue and used as an excuse for not being wealthy. We hear people say things like, "I don't *need* a lot of money," or "I don't *need* to live in a big house," or, "I'll retire when I have *enough* money." The fact that those who say these things are focused on their own needs alone is evidence enough that they don't understand their own Soul Purpose and the ultimate benefits of value creation.

Being prosperous and financially free isn't about whether or not *you* need a big home, a nice car, or a high income. Having enough money and resources to fulfill your desires is no excuse to stop creating value for others. As long as we're focused on our individual needs alone, we will never be able to contribute to the world in a meaningful way. Finding and living our Soul Purpose is the process of looking beyond our desires to see what people around us want and then providing it for them in such a way that it also provides us with the highest levels of joy and fulfillment.

What many people attempt to pass off as frugality and wisdom is actually selfishness or shortsightedness. It may be true that your desires are relatively basic, but what do other people desire that you can provide? How is your small thinking negatively affecting others? The fallacy of "enough" allows us to think small, limited thoughts and prevents us from thinking and dreaming big. When we are working to provide value for others and realize our potential, we're not driven by greed or consumption, and we can use greater resources to create more value.

The best way to overcome the accumulation theory's effects on our thoughts in terms of reducing expenses versus creating value for ourselves and others is to remember that what we focus on grows. When we focus mainly on cutting expenses, we nourish the roots of a scarcity/accumulation paradigm that will continue to grow until we uproot it and replace it with an abundance/utilization paradigm. We may build a bigger bank account over a long period of time, but we probably won't be living our Soul Purpose or maximizing our human life value, and our joy and happiness will be limited.

Productivity in the Present

Why is it almost universally considered to be a virtue to defer happiness and enjoyment? Is there any truth to the cliché "All good things come to those who wait?" Granted, patience is a virtue in the right context, but this is not what I see being taught in the financial arena. We're taught that we should spend thirty years in scarcity, deferring our happiness, working in jobs that we don't enjoy because we have an employer match on a 401(k), clipping coupons, and generally living lives of mediocrity. Rather than living in the now and maximizing our immediate happiness and value creation, many sit around waiting for good times to come. Why not have them now? Why not

ACCUMULATION THEORY

> Tends toward **scarcity** in that those who practice it develop the scarcity mindset through years of **frugal saving**, always in fear of losing their accumulated money.

> **Compound interest** is the key.

> Wealth is determined by **net worth**.

> **Do-it-yourself**, reduce expenses, wait for the future.

> Invest in **material things**, products, and strategies.

> Security is derived from **accumulated money**.

> Investments are **unsecured and uncollateralized** (money in mutual funds and qualified plans can disappear with nothing to show for it).

> Higher risk equals higher returns.

> **Retirement**.

> **Diversify**.

UTILIZATION THEORY

> Tends toward **abundance** in that practitioners learn to constantly be seeking ways to maximize their usefulness to the world, rather than waiting for retirement.

> **Velocity** is the key.

> Wealth is determined by **cash flow**.

> Utilize the abilities of others interdependently, increase production, and act in the now.

> Invest in the people behind products and strategies and in clear value propositions.

> **Security** is derived from human life value, knowledge, experience, and practical application.

> Some investments are secured and collateralized (if the cash flow stops, the physical asset can be sold and/or leveraged).

> Mitigating risk to near zero equals higher returns.

> **Soul Purpose**.

> **Focus**.

break through the stifling, disempowering myths and create incredible lega-
cies of our lives?

What is the value of a dollar unspent during a lifetime? What is the
return on money that is never utilized to its fullest potential? People may feel
good about passing money to heirs, but assets that go unutilized during a
person's lifetime amount to the worst and most expensive kind of life insurance, particularly when you factor in the estate and income taxes that your
heirs might have to pay upon your death.

The table below shows the tax rates used for estate taxes. Like income
taxes, estate taxes are a graduated tax. As your estate's value increases, so does
the tax for that portion of your estate.

Estate Tax Rates 2008		
Estate Amount Exceeding:	Up to:	Is taxed at a rate of:
$1,000,000	$1,250,000	41%
$1,250,000	$1,500,000	43%
$1,500,000	$2,000,000	45%
$2,000,000	or more	45%
Please note that for 2008 there is an exemption of $2,000,000 for estates (unless you have used a gift exemption). Under normal circumstances you will owe no taxes on estates of $2,000,000 or less. The value of your estate over $2,000,000 would be subject to a 45% tax.		

In the movie *Dumb and Dumber*, the characters played by Jim Carrey
and Jeff Daniels spend a bunch of money that they find in a briefcase and
then replace it with a bunch of handwritten IOUs. The IOUs are worthless,
of course, but the characters are pleased that they made sure each dollar was
accounted for with a worthless piece of paper. This is what I liken 401(k)s
to. Qualified plans seem like a tax savings, but they are deceiving; the only
way they work is for you to give up a portion of your income in the here and
now. In other words, it's not a tax savings—it's an income deferral. You pay
less in taxes when you contribute to a 401(k) because you earned less money
after the so-called deduction. Furthermore, if you never spend the money out
of your 401(k) or only spend a fraction of it because you're concerned with

preserving your nest egg, what good does it do you? What good does it do your heirs if they have to pay hefty taxes on it after your death? And further still, what will it actually be worth after inflation erodes it? It might as well be a handwritten, never-collected IOU.

Of course, many people believe in 401(k)s and other income deferral plans because one of the ways that the myth of accumulation is marketed is by glorifying compound interest. Retirement planners like I once was show us graphs of what can happen if we just put our money into an account and watch it grow over thirty years (of course, it has to be that long, because compound interest doesn't look very exciting in five- or ten-year increments). Of course, there's no consideration at that point about downturns in the market or disappointing returns. And what the graphs don't show is that while we're accumulating and compounding, the financial institutions that hold our money are utilizing and velocitizing.

Compounding interest is used to convince people that the best thing they can do with their money is to put it away and let it sit for many years and grow on its own "automatically." This is a problem because it causes us to stop creating value directly, to shirk stewardship, and to depend on external factors for some indefinite future financial success. Even if a person does practice the theory of compounding interest and sets money aside to grow at a very young age, once she has conditioned herself to live in scarcity mode and sacrifice everything to "provide for the future," it will be extremely difficult to actually use the money she's accumulated. Under the accumulation paradigm, to stop saving and start using one's

To my knowledge no strategy exists to avoid taxation on unused qualified plans (e.g., 401(k), 403 (b), TSA, SEP IRA, etc.) at the time of a person's death. The investor's heirs are unable to access it without severe tax penalties.

money is tantamount to preparing for death—the only situation in which the "security" of the nest egg isn't needed.

A more productive way of thinking begins by asking the questions, "What can I do *today, right now* to increase my productivity?" "How can I immediately be the most productive with my current resources?" "Where is there discontentment in the world that I have the ability to alleviate in this moment?" "How can I be the steward of my money instead of turning it over to someone else and abdicating my stewardship?" "How can I use my assets to live my Soul Purpose and increase my human life value?"

Escaping the 401(k) Trap

Suppose a person has $100,000 in a 401(k) that has been accumulating for ten years. She has contributed $50,000, her employer matched 50 percent ($25,000), and the money has grown another $25,000. There is plenty of financial advice that says to leave that money under lock and key, letting it sit and accumulate, until the contributor is at least age fifty-nine and a half. But let's challenge this advice and offer an alternative.

Suppose that this person realizes that she isn't being as productive with this resource as she can be and withdraws 100 percent of it. The penalty will be 10 percent immediately, for a cost of $10,000, and assuming she is in a 25 percent tax bracket, she'll also pay $25,000 in taxes (in April), for a total cost at tax season of $35,000. (Keep in mind that this is an example only and circumstances are different with every individual in real life). So she withdraws $100,000 and ends up with $65,000 that will not be going to the IRS, and she then puts it toward buying two real estate properties that together bring in $1000/month in positive monthly cash flow. Was it worth it to take the hit on penalties? I would argue that it was an excellent move. She's just converted an uncollateralized asset that was contributing nothing to her cash flow into a collateralized investment that has added $1000/month to her monthly cash flow. Now she can use that $1000 per month in other productive ways to further increase her cash flow and to continue to create greater value for herself and others.

This is how people think when they utilize rather than accumulate. This is why I believe that 401(k)s are the ultimate sacred cow. Plenty of advice leads us to believe that they are untouchable and so they sit in the form of unrealized potential—they don't produce any value until the money is actually put to use.

At one of my speaking events, a woman presented her situation to me and asked for advice. She told me that she had an amazing gift for teaching children, and a brilliant business plan to use her gift with an educational system she had created, but that she couldn't implement her plan because she didn't have enough money to fund the project. Upon further questioning she told me she had $200,000 sitting in a 401(k) that hadn't increased at all for a few years. I recommended that she withdraw that money and use it for her Soul Purpose. Her first reaction was, "But what about the 10 percent penalty?" I asked her if she thought she could make more than 10 percent with her business concept and educational system, and she immediately responded, "Yes, for sure."

Then why the concern about a relatively small penalty? Because we're trained to assume that qualified plan money is taboo, meant to fund a golden age of retirement when we can finally do what we want to do. But many of us give up the lives we want to live now because we are so concerned about building our retirement funds. To me it's all about the difference between price and cost. Sure, for this woman the *price* of withdrawing her money was 10 percent or more, but what was the *cost* of *not* doing it? More importantly, what value did she gain from doing it? To fail to embrace Soul Purpose because of a 10 percent penalty strikes me as senseless. (Granted, there are also taxes to consider, yet various strategies exist to offset them as well and every situation is different.)

What is the real penalty, 10 percent or living without Soul Purpose? There are many loans that cost more than 10 percent and yet people use them all the time. Furthermore, there are countless ways for people to earn greater than 10 percent on their money to more than compensate for any penalty. I think that the word *penalty* helps deepen our reluctance to touch a 401(k). If you viewed the 10 percent hit as a cost instead of a penalty, would it change your view?

The predictable criticisms of the utilization approach that we hear regarding 401(k)s are that it's risky and that it's downright stupid to willfully lose so much money in early withdrawal fines. Yet if we automatically discount

penalty:

the suffering or the sum to be forfeited to which a person agrees to be subjected in case of nonfulfillment of stipulations; disadvantage, loss, or hardship due to some action.

cost:

the amount or equivalent paid or charged for something; the outlay or expenditure (as of effort or sacrifice) made to achieve an object.

Source: *Merriam-Webster's 11th Collegiate Dictionary*

touching a 401(k) to avoid a 10 percent penalty, despite the potential to use the money more productively and in ways that will bring us greater joy, greater benefit, and greater prosperity, we risk denying our Soul Purpose and wasting our human life value. These are risks that aren't even considered by those who encourage us to contribute to a 401(k); the costs of this lost potential cannot be calculated.

Life is to be enjoyed and we were born to be happy. We don't have to wait years for happiness and financial freedom; we can achieve them now.

For more 401(k) info see killingsacredcows.com

Velocity of Money

The velocity of money is essentially how productive it is or how much benefit (profit, revenue, value) is produced with a given amount of investment. On a national macroeconomic scale, the mathematical equation to describe velocity is gross domestic product divided by the money supply. Applied individually to personal finance, the equation is simply output divided by input.

For example, suppose you have a lump sum of cash ($100,000) earning 10 percent. If you take the interest earned and purchase a mortgage for a rental property, you would then have a stream of rental income as well as possible tax benefits. If you then used the rental income to invest in another account (e.g., permanent insurance), you could build future cash value. In this way, you are increasing your velocity by increasing the productivity of your money.

Simply put, velocity is increased by keeping input at a minimum while increasing output. The goal, then, is to put continually *less* time, effort, risk, and money into something (input) and have it bring continually *more* productivity and value (output). For example, in my financial services practice, I started out by meeting with one client at a time in my office. I have now put systems in place so I can meet with anyone at any time through remote videocast/web meetings. Furthermore, through similar technology I do online seminars where I can teach multiple people at the same time. For the same amount of effort (if not less) I can now impact far more people than ever before, and my personal cash flow has also risen substantially.

This book is yet another example of how I am increasing velocity. Much of this content comes from topics that I teach in my national seminars. But I have only so much time to do individual seminars, even though I may speak to hundreds of people at each one. By publishing this book I can essentially be in thousands of places at one time, using the same content that I have already been using. The output I receive is exponentially greater than the input in money, energy, and time of getting the book written and published. By increasing velocity I end up impacting far more people than I have ever been able to, and infinitely more value is created for both those I impact and for myself.

The Velocity of Money

On a national macroeconomic scale, the mathematical equation to describe velocity is gross domestic product divided by the money supply. Applied individually to personal finance, the equation is simply output divided by input.

$$\text{Velocity} = \frac{\text{GDP}}{\text{Money supply}}$$

$$\text{Velocity} = \frac{\text{Output}}{\text{Input}}$$

Through the use of technology, markets, and various distribution channels, and by building more and better relationships with people (thus tapping into and leveraging the Soul Purpose of others), anyone can increase output without dramatically increasing input. On their CD *Piranha Marketing*, Joe Polish and Tim Paulson tell a story of a couple who owned and operated a carpet-cleaning business. Using automated voicemail technology, they recorded a telephone message advertising a 20 percent discount, then sent it to all of their customers. An investment of eighty dollars gave them about eight thousand dollars of income, and it only took them a short time to create the message and push a few buttons to send it out.

My friend Garrett White used to get people to his events the hard way: every member of his team would make personal phone calls to all of their clients to give the invitation. It took a lot of time and effort that could have been spent doing other things. He then connected with a company called Hello World (www.helloworld.com), which allowed him to film a three-minute video invitation to an event, which was then emailed to all of his clients. The event triggered the same response as before, but with dramatically reduced time and effort.

There are two ways in which the velocity of money can increase:

> The more exchanges made with the same dollars, the more wealth is created.

> The more simultaneous uses we find for each individual dollar, the wealthier we become.

Velocity Through Exchange

As described in the previous chapter, through the process of exchange, every individual dollar in an economy can be used infinitely. If I give you a dollar in exchange for something that I value more than the dollar, is that the end of the value of the dollar? Of course not. You can exchange it with others for something that you value more, and then they can exchange it, and so on. The more quickly the dollar is exchanged, the more velocity it has, and consequently the more productivity and profit are created in the economy.

Suppose I found risk-free, productive ways to lend money. If I lend $10,000 at a 10 percent interest rate (in the mortgage industry we would call this ten "points") but with the principal and interest being due thirty days from the time of the original loan, and then I repeat the process for every month out of the year, what is my actual interest rate? On every individual loan, the interest rate was 10 percent, but my actual annual return was 120 percent. Why? Because I increased the velocity of the money. I moved it quickly and repeatedly. Every time I exchanged the same dollars, I created more wealth. This is what banks do—the same banks that tell us to put our money in one spot and sit on it for thirty years. (In fact, it's actually our money they're loaning out.)

To offer a more concrete example, I increased the velocity of the money invested in this book by pricing the book at $21.95. If I were to charge $100 for this book, there might be people who valued it that much and were willing to pay for it. Selling the book for $100 would give me a high profit margin, or rate of return, but the turnover, or incidence of exchange, would be slow at best, which would greatly reduce my total profit and decrease the velocity of the money invested. Selling the book for $21.95, the profit margin on each unit sold is lower, but the actual difference in returns is more than made up by the greater number of books I can sell. The more books I can sell the more my actual profit is impacted and the greater the velocity of the money invested in the book. This is how we have to examine every use we put our money toward.

Velocity Through Simultaneous Use

If I place money in a mutual fund for long-term growth, every dollar that goes into the fund serves one purpose (at least in terms of my personal goals)—to gain a return. But suppose I could find an investment where each dollar simultaneously served two or more of my goals for my money: control, flexibility, rate of return, risk mitigation, tax protection, liability protection, disability protection, and death protection. By investing my money in a way that helps me achieve more than one of these goals, I've automatically increased the value of every individual dollar that flows through my plan.

For instance, I have recently invested in a great office building in Sandy, Utah. I've immediately increased the velocity of each dollar that went into the project because each dollar now serves multiple purposes:

> It increases my cash flow.

> It decreases my risk (because now my investment is collateralized, meaning that I'm now the owner of a tangible, physical asset that can be utilized and leveraged if I lose money).

cash flow:

the combination of the amount of net income a person receives, how that income is produced, and how sustainable it is.

net worth:

assets minus liabilities. A person could have a net worth of $1 million and have no income.

> It can create tax deductions through various strategies.

> It fosters a business environment for many of my companies.

> It can appreciate.

> It can provide liquidity (via a buy-sell in my business) upon my death and transfer equity to my heirs.

With an investment like this, my productivity is instantly increased—not because I have more money, but because I have increased the efficiency of money that was previously dormant or contributing to only one goal.

If we can devise financial strategies that help us unlock previously unused dollars, we can then use those dollars for other investments without sacrificing the first investment. This can be accomplished in a number of ways, including saving money on taxes through tax strategies, recovering lost insurance premiums (see chapter 7), or increasing the efficiency of current investments. Again, the goal is to increase our output without significantly increasing our input.

For more information and examples, go to killingsacredcows.com

Cash Flow vs. Net Worth

When it comes to monetary prosperity, cash flow, *not* net worth, is the single most important indicator of our financial health and success.

Cash Flow: the combination of the amount of net income a person receives, how that income is produced, and how sustainable it is. Healthy cash flows are created by investing in tangible assets such as real estate, or even more abstract assets such as intellectual property, which produce high and sustainable income. This can be measured on an income statement.

Net Worth: assets minus liabilities. Net worth is removed from income in that a person could theoretically have a net worth of $1 million and have no income. Net worth is a function of a person's balance sheet.

This doesn't necessarily mean that the more cash flow I create, the happier I become; it just means that I'm effectively utilizing my assets, and hopefully I'm utilizing them in a way that contributes to my overall happiness, my ability to live my Soul Purpose, and my achievement of my human life value.

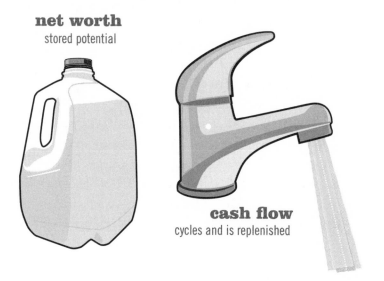

net worth
stored potential

cash flow
cycles and is replenished

We can think of net worth as potential energy, like a boulder perched on top of a hill. It can release a lot of energy when it is deployed, but only once before it's gone. Cash flow, on the other hand, is like a hydroelectric dam in which energy is constantly being generated without depleting the source.

Consider the case of someone of modest means who owns empty land in a developed area. The market value of his land may be $1 million, but unless he utilizes it in some way, it doesn't contribute any value to him or his income. How useful is it to him? Property assets have zero utility until they provide cash flow or are physically utilized—in fact, they increase the taxes we have to pay. It might make the landowner feel good to see big numbers on a piece of paper, but that's the extent of the land's usefulness. In this scenario, the landowner is technically a millionaire, but a poor millionaire living in scarcity.

The trouble with unutilized assets is that they can increase our potential losses without providing us any more security than we would have without them in a pinch. I have seen situations where people have equity in a property—increasing their net worth—but due to financial problems, a disability, or the loss of a job, they are unable to tap into it or use it and in some cases even lose their homes. How valuable is net worth in that situation?

Financial institutions know this principle and apply it liberally. For example, I know a man who inherited a fair amount of land when his father died. The land was not being utilized, but the market value was approximately $750,000. The man also owned half of a $200,000 home he had purchased with his first wife, who was still living in the house. He and his new wife were trying to purchase a fixer-upper home for a fairly small amount (about $100,000), but he could not get approved for a mortgage with a decent interest rate. The bank explained that although his net worth was high, his cash flow from his assets was limited or nonexistent, so they couldn't approve a low-interest mortgage. His wife, who had little net worth, but a good job and a decent credit history, had to apply for the mortgage as an individual in order for them to get a good interest rate on a small mortgage.

Best-selling author, speaker, and consultant, T. Harv Eker says, "Net worth is the ultimate measure of wealth because, if necessary, what you own can eventually be liquidated into cash." But I would argue that anyone with a cash flow that exceeds their expenses will never have need to liquidate assets. What they own will *already* be providing them with cash. When it comes to financial success, one of the most important things to understand—and one of the most overlooked by the financial industry—is that learning to convert net worth to cash flow can bring you more financial success than all of the books, magazines, and TV and radio shows on personal finance combined. It's that simple.

Converting net worth to cash flow requires that we use net worth assets to create value for others in such a way that people will pay us on a regular basis for the use of the asset. For example, if I own a piece of commercial land that isn't generating any income, I can lease the land to a development company who will put an office building there. They pay me when businesses rent the office spaces. If I just sell the land, I haven't yet converted the net worth asset into cash flow; all I've done is convert the form of the asset (from land to cash), but it's still just net worth and not cash flow. While the cash may be more portable and useful in my particular situation, if I spend it, I'm spending down my net worth without creating a corresponding cash flow to replace it.

Real estate gives us a tangible example, yet it works for cash and other net worth resources as well. A friend and associate of mine, Philip Tirone, struggled with this concept, but when it clicked for him, his business and income exploded. Philip is the creator of 7 Steps to 720® Credit Score (www.7stepsto720.com), a business that helps people raise their credit scores. For a long time, he wanted to create an infomercial advertising his products. The problem was that it was going to cost him $500,000 to produce it, and even though he had the money, he didn't want to reduce his net worth, for fear of losing his 'nest egg.' He finally made the choice and produced the infomercial, and it has paid off for him in many ways, and not just by selling products. Now that $500,000 that previously sat dormant has been converted into an income-producing business, which has far exceeded the initial investment from his net worth. More clients now pay him for his services on a regular basis, he's gained access to many more speaking events, and he receives referrals constantly. In addition, he's also gained other side benefits such as high-profile clients contacting him for work. Had he not make the decision to convert his net worth asset into cash flow, his business would be much less viable, make less of an impact, make less money, and be much less sustainable in the long term.

Net worth is only potential value—it is worthless until realized, just as a person's potential is worthless until it is realized through serving and creating value for others. The way to bridge the gap between the potential of net worth and the productivity of cash flow is through creating value—finding ways to meet the perceived needs and wants of other people. To be financially successful, we must stop focusing on accumulating net worth and focus instead on providing goods and services that other people value.

When assessing our cash flow and opportunities to make productive use of our assets to create value, there are five things we must consider:

1. Whether or not we must be physically involved in making cash flow to us
2. How often money comes to us

3. In what amounts and what forms it comes
4. How long it will flow without our direct involvement
5. What steps or processes should be employed to monitor and contribute to the sustainability of the cash flow

Those who focus on these aspects of cash flow instead of on building net worth become wealthy. Those who focus on net worth might have an impressive number from their CPA to show off, but if they are unable to convert net worth to cash flow they will still live in scarcity and will still have to work to keep accumulating. They will limit their potential, their human life value, and the impact that they could have had on others.

The accumulation theory takes advantage of our innate desire to feel secure, but it promotes a false sense of security—a security that is at direct odds with freedom. Much of typical financial planning is based on the assumption that you and I don't have the time or the inclination to educate ourselves and become wise stewards of our own resources. Sadly, this is probably true. I would argue, however, that it has *become* true because so many of us labor under the false beliefs taught by the accumulation theory. Myths and neglect go hand in hand. However, in the following chapters, we'll learn how to shake off these myths and replace them with productive thinking.

* * *

One of the best ways to break through the stronghold of popular myths is to make our purpose bigger than what we think we are at that particular moment. We must start dreaming and thinking big again, the way we used to as children. We must spend time in the realm of possibility, then strive harder to bridge the gap between our vision and reality. Deep down, all of us know we were born to do so much more than accumulate a million dollars and retire after thirty years of an uninspired and uninspiring career. In the words of Marianne Williamson, "Our deepest fear is not that we are inadequate; our deepest fear is that we are powerful beyond measure. We ask ourselves who am I to be brilliant, gorgeous, talented, fabulous? Actually, who are you not to be? Your playing small does not serve the world. As we are liberated from our own fear, our presence automatically liberates others."

MYTH
3:

{ **It's All About the Numbers** }

Whatever your income, how much should you be worth right now? Multiply your age times your realized pretax annual household income from all sources except inheritances. Divide by ten. This, less any inherited wealth, is what your net worth should be.

—Thomas Stanley, "How to Determine if You're Wealthy" in *The Millionaire Next Door*

The financial industry has us trained to make decisions based on numbers on paper. They would have us believe that prosperity can be reduced to and quantified by math. Retirement planners use our misguided faith in numbers to pitch products to us. More often than not, whoever has the guts to show the highest returns on an illustration gets the business. We might be faced with making a choice between two retirement planners, one who has a proposal that makes the best economic sense for us, and another who proposes things that will, in reality, be very harmful for us in the long term. Yet if the second proposal shows higher numbers we're automatically drawn toward it and away from the first.

The subject of personal finance has become almost completely removed from sound economic theory, reasoning, and application. As Frédéric Bastiat, Henry Hazlitt, and others have explained well, the art of economics is learning to see what the eye cannot see, and to anticipate the indirect consequences of all our theories and actions. Of course, it's impossible to factor in every consideration because of our limited knowledge. But a healthy percentage of the battle to create wealth is simply learning to look and see what most people don't see. It's training our minds to instinctively search deeper than the surface level. It's learning to see beyond numbers. It's learning to view our finances on a macro, not a micro level. It's about seeing through subtle forms of deception and developing an understanding of the realities underneath the numbers.

A majority, an average—they are not anything real! They are real only for the abstract intellect, which is to say for the manipulation of the masses—by which I mean, for the manipulation of their unconscious minds . . . It seems to me that we live by nothing but numbers, and that we endow each one with the privileges of a god. What a strange mythology is ours! If only we realized that it is a mythology, and a very primitive one at that!

—Jacques Lusseyran

This chapter questions the fallacies that arise when we view numbers and quantities in the wrong way, especially when it comes to money and financial decisions. It explains how destructive it can be to equate numbers with prosperity. It challenges the belief that the products that deliver the highest returns are what matter most. I'll discuss the differences between quantity and quality, and why quantity is a poor reflection of reality. I'll finish by presenting empowering ways to see through and overcome the myth, and how to place the numbers in their proper context.

The Destructive Nature of Numbers

The myth that prosperity can be reduced to and quantified by math destroys our human life value because it is focused on the effect, rather than the cause of prosperity. It prevents us from considering the unseen factors in our financial decisions. It causes people to work for money and to pursue a number on their bank balance or a calculation of net worth instead of creating value, and it leads us to make unwise decisions regarding money.

In a world of cause and effect, money is an *effect* while creating value for people is the *cause*. The myth that numbers define prosperity is fundamentally based on an ignorance of this truth. Typically, when retirement planners give proposals and show us ending up with a big, magical number at the end of thirty years, the underlying implication is that what matters most are the strategies and products that the proposal is based on. Retirement planners spend a lot of time manipulating numbers and figuring out mathematical calculations, and very little time teaching clients the real ways to increase their income and maximize their wealth. Rarely do they say anything about ways that individuals can increase their human life value and become more responsible and productive. The entire process undervalues people and overvalues financial products and calculations.

However subtly, typical financial planning teaches people that their future financial freedom is almost entirely dependent upon picking the right stocks, or buying the right products, or employing the right strategies. A large part of the reason we believe these subtle lies is the importance that we have come to place on numbers. We want to base our financial futures on some magical numbers, so we become enamored with fancy software programs and false promises instead of seeking out our own paths to prosperity.

Any intelligent fool can make things bigger, more complex, and more violent. It takes a touch of genius—and a lot of courage—to move in the opposite direction. **—Albert Einstein**

What we don't see because we're blinded by hypothetical numbers is what our unwise decisions are costing us, not only in dollars, but in happiness as well. There's no way to put a number on happiness, yet the whole purpose of financial planning should be to create favorable conditions for the highest levels of happiness possible. If all we can see are the easily apparent calculations of what amount it would take to maintain our current standard of living in the years to come, we're ignoring the more critical unseen factors that render the seen factors virtually irrelevant.

Can you quantify what it's costing you to stay tied to a miserable job because it has good "benefits" and maybe even pays well, rather than finding and living your Soul Purpose? Is there any way to assign a number to what the world is missing out on because one person sacrifices Soul Purpose to a false sense of security? It's impossible. And numbers on paper can't help you understand the opportunity costs of the financial and life decisions you make. Opportunity costs are the paths not taken, the opportunities we lose when we choose a particular course of action—what our money could have been, or the experiences we could have had, or the jobs we might hold had we made different choices. When we place too much value on the numbers on our balance sheets and in our retirement accounts, we run the risk of staying in miserable and limiting situations because the numbers dangle in front of us like the proverbial carrot. We make decisions based on how much money we can make, rather than focusing on how much value we can create, for others and for ourselves. Can you quantify the burnout that eventually hits people doing things that make them miserable, even if they make good money? Furthermore, can you quantify the lost production that comes from people working for money, instead of working to create value?

 Do what you love and the money will follow.   —**Marsha Sinetar**

The more focused we are on our paychecks the less likely we are to find and live our Soul Purpose and to realize our full potential. The path to prosperity is value creation. Misery, heartache, and limitations on human life value come when people overemphasize the importance of numbers and deemphasize the importance of the unquantifiable factors of wealth, like where they live, who they work with, and whether they feel like they are contributing something worthwhile to the world.

The magnification of quantity at the expense of quality leads us to make unwise and costly decisions. When we get too caught up in thinking that money has intrinsic value, or that it means more than it actually does, we start ignoring sound economic reasoning and become less focused on more critical concerns, like value creation and happiness. When we're under the grip of the myths we prefer the seemingly solid *feel* of quantity, even though it's deceiving and takes us further away from the things that really matter in life.

Our perspective and all of our decisions are heavily influenced by the value that we place on abstract numbers. The burden of financial myths makes us choose courses for our future that we otherwise would never choose. It makes us ignore the unquantifiable considerations that, if explored and understood, would assist us in making far more productive and valuable choices.

Replacing Numbers with Real Prosperity

The more we confuse the cause and effects of prosperity the less likely we are to live up to our full potential. Productivity is the standard of value, not numbers. And money as represented by numbers is just a reflection of value creation, not actual value or prosperity.

Breaking through and overcoming the myth that prosperity is a function of quantities removed from qualities requires that we learn to do the following:

> Understand the difference between numbers and happiness, and quantity and quality

> Understand how the financial industry uses numbers

> Reject the common faulty calculations used to make financial decisions

> Focus on the unseen aspects of our financial decisions as much as on the seen

> Think like a personal economist

> See the differences between macroeconomics and microeconomics and act accordingly

> Base financial decisions on happiness, the only true indicator of prosperity

Quality vs. Quantity

The concept of quantity is relatively meaningless on two levels: (1) all material things have different qualities, and (2) each person values material things differently from everyone else. The idea here is to direct our attention away from a focus on quantity, which brings us toward placing more value on quality.

Pure quantities removed from qualities tell us nothing of reality. Quality is subjective and immeasurable, while quantity is measurement without accounting for individual values. To achieve true prosperity, we must begin to focus on quality. The concept of quantity does serve a valuable purpose, but it's critical that we realize that it also has drastic limitations. For example, can you prove to me that you love your spouse and children, or describe *how much* you love them using numbers? Is your love for your family a ten? Is it one hundred? How about one million? Numbers don't make any sense because your love is based on quality, not quantity. There's no way to quantify such an abstract, qualitative concept. If our end goal is happiness, numbers and math are no more use—would you like seventeen happiness, or $250 worth?

Love and happiness might seem a bit abstract when our topic is money, but counterintuitively, the same principle of unquantifiability holds for money. Why? Because nobody wants actual currency—they want what they can buy with it. What good is money without love, happiness, and fulfillment? Even simple material possessions are hard to assign dollar values for—since we all value different things, we value the same material things differently from anyone else, and we value things based on their qualities and not their quantities alone. Therefore, there's no way that we can base financial success on numbers alone, because the numbers tell us very little about how they can help us realize happiness. For a person to say that he "needs" $1 million to retire is almost as abstract and ridiculous as saying that he loves his wife twenty-nine and a half. I use the word *almost*, because there is a slight difference between the two. The difference is that people *can* exchange their currency to get the qualities that they value, so if they are able to accumulate $1 million they would have a chance of being able to convert it to something meaningful.

But don't associate prosperity with a number, as in, "I'll retire when I have a million dollars," or "He must be rich because his net worth is $1.5 million." The point remains that $1 million as a number says nothing about the realities of their lives and the qualities that they value. It's impossible to quantify prosperity. I know people who live in complete scarcity, yet they have millions of dollars (although you would never know it by looking at them).

Numbers can be valuable tools when we place them in the right context, but when we overvalue them they cloud our judgment and negatively influence our decisions. Numbers can be used to manipulate, overemphasize, and deceive. Remember: they are just one ingredient of the full equation.

I get frustrated with our fascination with the term "millionaire." It's often used as the benchmark for financial success and as the standard of wealth. We look up to the millionaires as the ones who have really "made it." What does it mean to be a millionaire? To have a net worth of at least a million dollars. But what does that mean? A number on a balance sheet that says $1 million

THE MYTHS IN REALITY:
The Broke Millionaire

The neighbor of one of my business partners was an executive at one of the larger tech companies and for many years was earning a six-figure salary. When he retired, his million-dollar home had no mortgage, and he had more than 1.5 million in his retirement plan, making him a multimillionaire in terms of net worth. But once he stopped earning money, he became obsessed with the possibility of losing what he had. Uncertain how long he would live and reluctant to pay additional taxes on his Social Security benefits, he only used the interest generated by his nest egg. The first thing he did every morning was check stock prices to see if any of his money had depleted overnight. He sold his nice car and bought a twelve-year-old model to save on payments. Then the tech bubble burst, and his stocks lost value and stopped earning interest. For three years, 2000, 2001, and 2002, he didn't touch his retirement money at all. The only income for his household was his Social Security and income from the part-time job his wife had originally taken to reduce his stress and support the lifestyle she had developed over the years. All this despite the fact that he still had more than a million dollars saved "for his retirement," a million dollars he wouldn't use even as it was endangered by the vagaries of the market, new tax laws, and inflation.

For more information and examples, go to killingsacredcows.com

Our goal
should never
be to become
millionaires;
our goals
should be based
on what will
bring us our
ideal quality
of life and the
highest level of
happiness.

is nothing but a quantity, and it says nothing about the quality of life of the individual millionaire. There are many poor and miserable millionaires in the world. I know individuals who have a double-digit net worth at best, but who are far happier than many net worth millionaires I know. In fact, my life in college is a perfect example; I was worth probably five figures on paper, yet I lived a very enjoyable, happy, and fulfilling life. I was prosperous and felt wealthy, despite what the numbers in my bank account showed.

Our goal should never be to become millionaires; our goals should be based on what will bring us our ideal quality of life and the highest level of happiness. Being a millionaire is worthless and purposeless if the millionaire still lives with a mindset of scarcity or ignores her quality of life. We routinely fall into the millionaire trap because we're trained to think that numbers have intrinsic value, and that they are the best indication of prosperity.

Numbers must be subordinate to the qualities that we want in things, and they should only be used after we've identified what we actually want. For example, if your goal has always been to be a millionaire, *why* do you want to be one? What can a million dollars add to your life that you don't already have? What would you do with it? How would it increase the quality of your life? What do you really want out of life? What would it mean for others if you were doing what you were born to do? What value would you create in order to become a millionaire? Identifying these more important considerations gives you the context to determine how to properly use numbers.

I can teach anybody how to get what they want out of life. The problem is that I can't find anybody who can tell me what they want.

—**Mark Twain**

How the Financial Industry Uses Numbers

Prosperity isn't about numbers; it's all about quality of life and happiness. This is why it's so ridiculous—if not downright unethical—for retirement planners to guide people based on numbers on paper. It's easy for anyone to gather some information, plug some numbers into a computer illustration, and tell you that you should purchase a variable life policy or a mutual fund because, based on the calculations, all you need do is save so many dollars, at an assumed rate of return, with assumed tax and inflation rates, and for an assumed period, and there you have a magic number that will give you peace and happiness.

If you torture numbers long enough, you can get them to confess to anything.

—**Garrett White**

First of all, nobody can ever make proper assumptions about future market performance, tax brackets, the rate of inflation, life expectancies, spending habits, or what a person really "needs" to retire. Second, for a retirement planner to create a plan based on numbers, and for people to make their decisions based on numbers, is a great recipe for financial confusion and eventual failure. Granted, many retirement planners would say that they make their calculations based on the qualitative data that they gather about what their clients want when they retire. Even so, their final calculations are still fundamentally based on quantities detached from qualities, and as a result, are removed from reality. There are so many factors involved in a financial plan that are indeterminate, so even if a planner is 1 percent off on one number it changes the entire picture, and usually quite substantially.

Let me use an example from my own life that may help illustrate my point. When I was a college student, I met with a retirement planner. After gathering some information from me, he presented an illustration for a variable universal life insurance policy that showed me accumulating $1 million by age sixty-five by getting a continual 12 percent rate of return. I took the bait and bought the policy. The problem with the entire scenario was that the retirement planner based the final number on a bunch of variables that were completely unknown and unknowable. Also, the $1 million was a number and a number only, without any basis in quality, and so it was essentially meaningless.

When I decided to buy, I was looking at that big number on a piece of paper. I didn't think about the fact that it was a completely uncertain proposition. I also never stopped to ask myself questions such as, "How will this decision affect the quality of my life?" "Beyond money, what do I really want in life, and will this product help me to achieve that?" "How does this one micro decision fit into the macro puzzle of my financial situation?" "Do I really want to wait forty-five years to get $1 million anyway, or are there other ways to do the same thing in less time?" "Will this product create real value in my life?" "If so, how?" "Will it increase my ability to create value for others?" My final decision was based almost entirely on an abstract quantity as opposed to matters of quality and value.

Where quantities really fail us is when we think that we can equate one thing to another based on quantity alone. Consider this: No one thing is equal to any other one thing. For example, is one apple equal to one orange? In terms of quantity, it's true that 1 = 1. But in terms of quality, apples and oranges are different and unequal. They taste different, they look different, they feel different, and they smell different. Even if we were to consider two Red Delicious apples, they are only equal in quantity, but not quality. No two apples can be exactly the same in terms of quality. They are composed of different matter, they exist in different places and times, or if they don't, they affect each other's value—how much do you value a second, seemingly identical apple after you've just eaten a first one?

Again, this may appear to be unnecessarily philosophical, but it's critical that we make a clear distinction between quantity and quality, realize that quantity alone tells us little about reality, and that quality is the most important consideration. If we place too much value in math, numbers, and quantities we start believing and acting as if some amount (or quantity) of money will make us happy. We begin to derive a sense of fulfillment from the number that shows up on our checking account balance. We develop a twisted sense of prosperity that is based on numbers instead of quality of life and happiness. Granted, some of us might feel happy to have "a lot" of money, but if our sense of happiness is based primarily on our amount of money it is an illusory and transitory happiness at best.

Quality and quantity are fundamentally different from each other, and one cannot be substituted for the other. The quicker and more fully we realize that, the better able we are to pursue real prosperity. If we can learn to focus more on quality and less on quantity, we will be more able to utilize and maximize the productivity of any amount of money that flows to us.

Faulty Assumptions and Calculations

To escape the focus on quantity, numbers, and accumulation over productivity and quality of life, we must question the assumptions and calculations of our retirement planners, institutions, planning software, and anyone else who tells us what we must do.

The primary faulty assumptions seldom questioned by retirement planners are average returns, inflation rates, market fluctuations, and tax brackets. These are huge pieces of a person's financial puzzle, but most planners just plug in assumed numbers into individual plans. These "ballpark figures" amount to nothing more than opinion, at best, and at worst, blatant deceptions intended to make a sale. Many retirement planners are simply doing what they think will get you to buy or defining what they think you can afford, rather than advising on what is actually best for you. Their game is neither efficiency nor productivity—it is sufficiency. Their calculations are needs-based (meaning they base their proposals on minimums, the least you could get by on if everything goes well) as opposed to planning for worst-case scenarios and maximizing productivity. With these limited and limiting methods, the only way for the plan to work is for numerous unknowable and unpredictable assumptions to turn out precisely according to plan—which, of course, is impossible. A retirement planner like this, however well-meaning, is a guide to disaster.

Average Returns

This is one of my favorite assumptions to expose. Consider the following analogy: Suppose I'm standing in a shower that has two spigots, each on opposite sides of the wall. Out of one of the spigots comes scalding hot water, and out of the other comes freezing cold water. The average temperature of the shower may be a pleasant 80 degrees, but how pleased do I feel? I'm absolutely miserable! The extremes of financial returns can be just as unpleasant, and averaging them does not take away the pain and make up for the losses.

Here's an example: Suppose I have $1,000 to invest in a mutual fund. I invest it in a fund that has an estimated 10 percent return and enjoy a 100 percent positive rate of return in the first year. Now I have $2,000. In year two, the market actually drops 50 percent, leaving me with half of my $2,000, or $1,000. Year three results in yet another 100 percent positive rate of return, so again I have $2,000. Unfortunately, year four brings 50 percent negative yet again, so I'm back to my original amount of $1,000.

$1,000 Placed in a Mutual Fund for 4 Years		
Year	% Return	$ Return
1	+100	$2,000
2	-50	$1,000
3	+100	$2,000
4	-50	$1,000
Average Return: +25%		
Actual Yield: 0%		

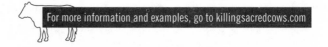
For more information and examples, go to killingsacredcows.com

The mutual fund company is pleased to announce a 25 percent rate of return on its prospectus for the last four years, but what does that mean for me? (Of course, this is an extreme example to prove a point. Mutual fund companies are much more subtle than this, because they would show the fund over a longer period of time so as not to high-light the wild variations in such a short period of time.)

My *actual* return, as concerns the fund alone, is $0 and 0 percent—or so it would appear. The situation is actually worse when we take into account inflation (which, generally speaking, is grossly underrated by most media), the capital gains taxes I paid in years one and three, fund expenses (because the mutual fund company gets paid even for bad performance), and lost opportunity costs. But let's look at just the fees and taxes for now. And keep in mind that this illustration does not even take into consideration inflation and opportunity costs.

$1,000 Placed in a Mutual Fund for 4 Years with Expenses
(1% Management Fee / 30% Tax Rate Total)

Year	% Return	1% Fee	30% Tax Rate	Total Amt.
1	+100	-$20	-$294	$1,686
2	-50	-$8	—	$835
3	+100	-$17	-$245	$1,407
4	-50	-$7	—	$697

Average Return: +25%
Actual Yield: -8.65%

Sometimes losses create deductions and other times they do not (see killingsacredcows.com for more information).

Even when we lose money in "investment" accounts in a down year, financial institutions glaze over the losses by saying things like, "You're in it for the long haul," "You're dollar-cost-averaging so you'll come out on top in the long run," or, "If we diversify your portfolio, we'll reduce your risk." My favorite one is, "If you just wait long enough, the

dollar cost averaging:
The technique of buying a fixed dollar amount of a particular investment on a regular schedule, regardless of the share price. More shares are purchased when prices are low, and fewer shares are bought when prices are high. Dollar cost averaging lessens the risk of investing a large amount in a single investment at the wrong time.

(investopedia.com)

Your Personal Rate of Inflation

Personal rate of inflation is defined by how prices for goods and services rise for each individual based on their unique propensity to consume, the types of goods they consume, and when they consume them. For instance, if the price of gas rises disproportionately and you have a thirty-mile daily commute, your personal rate of inflation is likely higher than the consumer price index rate.

Calculate your own personal rate of inflation at killingsacredcows.com.

market will recover." But does a person ever really recover lost time and opportunity? Of course not.

Rate of Inflation

The financial services industry does no better when it comes to inflation. Most retirement planners use the historical average rate of inflation, which has some significant inherent problems because of the real nature of averages. Also, few retirement planners differentiate between the government rate of inflation (as evidenced by the consumer price index) and a person's personal rate of inflation, or rising prices of consumer goods.

When it comes to personal finances, inflation considerations go much deeper than merely factoring the impact of fiat money printed by the government.

One's personal rate of inflation is impacted by such factors as the propensity to consume, planned obsolescence, and technological advances. For example, according to the consumer price index, the price of computers progressively lowers because the rate of technological advances outpaces the rate of inflation. On the other hand, more and better computers are being produced constantly, which then increases our propensity to consume. A comparable computer may cost half as much today as it did three years ago, but because we want the advanced models, we buy better machines more often. Individual computer prices are lower, but we may actually be spending more on them.

This is critical to realize because most accumulation-theory planners teach that you'll be able to live on 70–80 percent of your preretirement income when you retire. But people who buy into this dogma put themselves in a position of scarcity at retirement: more than likely they will not be able to purchase new products because when they planned for retirement they failed to take into account their personal rate of inflation. If their investments don't keep pace with new developments, they won't be able to enjoy their retirement, at least not as fully as possible.

Furthermore, most retirement planners fail to address the tax implications of trying to beat inflation, by which I mean that as people make more money to prepare for future inflation, their tax brackets increase and they keep less of the money than they had planned. The bottom line in the financial industry is that the rate of inflation is usually underrated.

HOW TO ACCOUNT FOR INFLATION

Have contingencies.

Maximize cash flow so you have a continual source of income.

Avoid planning a future of passive retirement—find and live your Soul Purpose.

Don't think 70 percent of preretirement income will be enough. Rather, do everything in your power to maximize, as opposed to limit by an arbitrary number, your future income potential.

In a tough spot, consider spending down principal of assets in retirement (see chapter 9).

Learn advanced strategies that deal with charitable giving to avoid unnecessary tax, create cash flow, and even coordinate ways to replace those contributions to heirs (charitable trusts).

Market Fluctuations

The first financial services firm I ever encountered attempted to convince me to put my money in a particular vehicle that was popular at the time. One illustration I was given showed a continuous +12 percent annual return. Why? Because the stock market has averaged +12 percent since 1929! The illustration, of course, showed me ending up with a fat nest egg at retirement age with relatively little monthly investment. The company also showed me

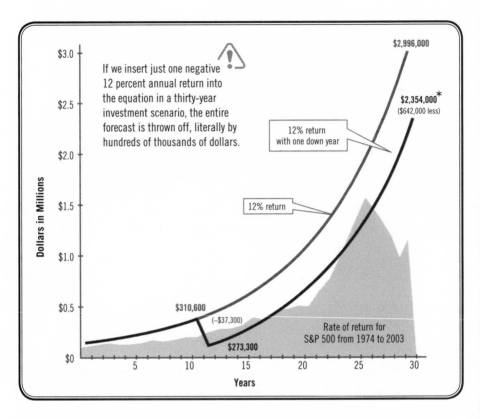

what I would end up with if I had a continuous 18 percent rate of return. They had to show me that on a separate calculator, apart from their company software illustrations, because industry laws prevent financial services firms from legally illustrating more than a hypothetical 12 percent annual return.

Aside from their illegal tactics, their approach was also fundamentally flawed. Along with the problems we've already discussed concerning average returns, financial services companies also overlook that if we insert just one negative 12 percent annual return into the equation in the time frame of the investment, the entire computation is thrown off, literally by hundreds of thousands of dollars. It gets even worse when we replace the continuous +12 percent with the actual historical performance of the stock market.

Why do retirement "planners" fail to consider and illustrate the possibility of negative returns? The answer is twofold: First, most of them are not trained to incorporate negative returns into their calculations and may not realize how dramatic the effects can be. Second, even the ones who do realize

---

*It takes 42.5% positive ROR the next year (then back to 12% for the remaining years) to make up for the -12% loss

this concept don't want to lose a sale by showing dismal numbers. Optimism, even unrealistic optimism, brings in more customers. Because most of us labor under false information and financial myths, we get excited about the positive numbers and tend to think these calculations actually represent reality.

Tax Brackets

One of the most destructive pieces of advice that is thrown around is to base decisions primarily on tax ramifications. Taxes should definitely be taken into consideration with any financial plan, but some people actually don't want to produce more because they're afraid of paying too much in taxes; they let the tax tail wag the dog. Whenever I encounter this, I ask the person, "Would you rather pay $1 million in taxes or $10 million?" The knee-jerk response for most people is $1 million. My answer is always $10 million, because it would mean that I made much more money than if I owed $1 million in taxes. Since

taxes are calculated as a percentage of income earned, higher taxes will never wipe out increased productivity completely, though they can dent it if poorly managed. My advice to deal with taxation is to earn more dollars rather than limiting productivity or settling for a lower income.

And in long-term planning, the effect is worse. Retirement planners routinely tell their clients that 70 percent of their preretirement income will be sufficient for their retirement years, and that living on this percentage will lower their tax bracket. First of all, no one knows exactly what future tax brackets will be. Tax rates are constantly changing; it's impossible to predict future taxation based on current or even historical tax brackets. Second, this unfounded assumption leads again to the problem of scarcity by implicitly telling clients to live even more cheaply than they have to in order to accumulate their retirement fund, with the knowledge that they'll have to live at 70 percent of their current standard upon retirement. Forget about travel or taking advantage of new opportunities or anything else that can contribute to joy and happiness.

For more information on tax history, go to killingsacredcows.com

One of three things must happen for people to qualify for a lower tax bracket when they retire:

1. They must have more tax deductions than before (which is unlikely because their kids are no longer dependents and, if they're living according to most advice, they're no longer running businesses or working in a career).
2. They must live on less income than before (which is hardly empowering when it comes to maximizing those years).
3. The government must lower the tax brackets (which could happen in theory, but is obviously not a safe bet based on the history of taxation in the United States).

Seen and Unseen Factors

Aside from the myriad misperceptions and faulty assumptions the financial industry uses, financial calculations also rarely include the hidden, unseen factors that play a much more important role in our financial lives than do the easily seen factors. For example, I've met many people who base all of their financial decisions on internal rate of return, which gets more marketing attention and distorts more people's thinking than almost any other number. The internal rate of return of an investment is the stated or marketed rate of return, without considering other, macro factors, like taxes, inflation, utilization, etc. In other words, the internal rate of return for a mutual fund is the percentage of growth (usually calculated annually) above what you put into it.

The external rate of return is the return generated (or lost) because of the indirect effect that the product has on every other piece of the financial puzzle, such as taxes, insurance costs, inflation, opportunity costs, etc. Internal rate of return matters, but it's a relatively minor part of the picture.

Basing our decisions primarily on internal rate of return is like choosing to get rid of your cell phone because it's a bad investment. After all, you lose every dollar that you directly spend to pay your cell phone bill. But is that the most important thing to consider? We have an intuitive sense that this is a complete joke, because we understand the value that having a cell phone provides us.

More important than the internal rate of return is the external rate of return. Can you even calculate the external rate of return on your cell phone? Can you quantify the amount of increased productivity it brings to your life?

What about your car? It would save you money to get rid of your car because you would no longer have a payment, insurance, title and registration fees, gas, and maintenance to pay for, right? Wrong. Can you even begin to calculate how much money it would cost you to get rid of your car because of decreased productivity? Of course, if you live in New York City it might be a different story, but the point holds true for most of us.

Think of a person considering a purchase of a $200,000 rental home that he calculates will only make him $1,000 per year. That's the internal rate of return for the property. However, there are many other factors to consider, perhaps far more important than the internal rate of return. Suppose he wants to make the purchase using $50,000 cash in the bank that he received from selling a cheaper home. If he doesn't roll that cash into a property of equal or greater value (what is called a 1031 exchange), he will have to pay capital gains taxes on that $50,000. By purchasing the new home, he avoids capital gains taxes. This is but one example of an external return, a return that the investment decision allowed him, but that came indirectly. Internally, the home is only producing $1,000 per year, but externally, it might create much higher actual returns.

One of the main reasons we buy into the fallacy about numbers is because we like the concrete feeling that calculations give us. It makes us more comfortable to make decisions when we feel that we have quantified our options. The elusive obvious truth of the matter is that *when it comes to our finances the most important considerations are not immediately quantifiable, if they can be quantified at all.* Can you quantify how much money you would lose in getting rid of your cell phone and your car, just in an effort to save money? Of course, you can make the attempt and come up with a few calculations based on known factors, but ultimately there's no way to assign a number to it because of all the unknowns.

The most important factors concerning our prosperity are unquantifiable, and this makes us afraid of them. We buy into the false and illusory sense of correctness that numbers give us, but we avoid our Soul Purpose and the future possibilities of our human life value.

Thinking Like an Economist

Only government can take perfectly good paper, cover it with perfectly good ink and make the combination worthless.

—Milton Friedman

The subject of personal finance has become almost entirely removed from the study of economics, both in theory and in application. We've come to think that economics is a topic reserved for college professors and experts, even though the origin of the word itself speaks more of personal finance than it speaks of things like gross national product and supply and demand charts.

The word "economics" comes from the Greek words *oikos* (pronounced ee kos) meaning "home" or "house," and *nomos*, meaning "name," "organization," or "management." To the Greeks, an "oikonomos" is a manager of a home. Economics isn't about charts, graphs, interest rates, and indexes. It's about what you do on a daily basis to create a profitable, thriving, and sustainable home life. The science of economics, then, is much closer to home than many of us think. Not only is it highly *relevant to* your personal finances, but it's also actually *based on* personal finance. A national economy is nothing but the reflection of individual and family economies.

 What is prudence in the conduct of every private family can scarce be folly in that of a great kingdom. —Adam Smith

Learning to think like a good economist is a critical step toward prosperity. In his book *Economics in One Lesson*, economist Henry Hazlitt writes,

The bad economist sees only what immediately strikes the eye; the good economist also looks beyond. The bad economist sees only the direct consequences of a proposed course; the good economist looks also at the longer and indirect consequences . . . The art of economics consists in looking not merely at the immediate but at the longer effects of any act or policy; it consists in tracing the consequences of that policy not merely for one group but for all groups.

When you're facing any financial decision, take your time and train yourself to consider the unseen factors beyond and behind the factors you see at first. For example, if you're shopping at Costco and come across what appears to be a good deal, stop and consider the lost opportunity costs that buying the bulk item will incur. It might appear that you're saving money, but more often than not you'll find that the unseen costs far outweigh the seen price. Consider also the people who drive out of their way to save a few cents on gas (and then wait in line at the pump), so the extra time and hassle far outweighs any benefit they receive from saving money on the price of gasoline.

When you're presented with a proposal from a retirement planner, look beyond the numbers on paper and do your best to calculate the hidden numbers and considerations. A perfect example of this is the fallacy that an employer match on a 401(k) is a "guaranteed" rate of return. How many times have you heard people teach that if the employer match is 50 percent, the employee has a guaranteed 50 percent rate of return before he even gets started in the market? When we do the math, we realize that this is misinformation. If I put $10,000 per year into a 401(k) and my employer matches 50 percent ($5,000/year), and assuming (after administrative expenses and fund fees) a 10 percent market rate of return, in twenty-five years I end up with a gross amount of $1,622,726. That's what we see. More often than not, what remains unseen is the fact that upon withdrawing that money to use for my retirement income, assuming that I'm in a 30 percent tax bracket (which again is an unknowable assumption), I actually end up with a net amount of $1,135,908.

401(k)s seem to have a "guaranteed" rate of return. This is a fallacy. But we cannot see it as such unless we begin to think like economists and consider the unseen factors.

Are you ready for the 401(k) challenge? Go to www.401khoax.com

When we do the math we find that my actual rate of return was only 12.51 percent—much less than the 50 percent return that was shown in the beginning. The match only impacted my earnings by 2.51 percent, not 50 percent. Furthermore, if I actually had received a 50 percent rate of return on my money, I would have ended up with over $2.8 billion.

The "guaranteed" rate of return based on employer matches turns out to be a complete myth. But this is something that we can never see unless we think like economists and consider the unseen factors. Think about it. When do most people actually get the money in a 401(k)? How do they know what's going to happen with the match? How do they know what the market is going to do to affect their contributions? When will they have access to their money? What will the purchasing power of the money be in the future? What will the tax situation look like with distribution? What laws governing the 401(k) will change as time goes on? How will it improve their lives? How do they plan on getting the money out of the plan? What happens when what's left is passed on to heirs at death?

Thinking as an economist means considering as many aspects of financial equations as possible, both the seen and the unseen elements, the primary and the secondary consequences. This approach gives you an entirely new perspective on your finances and opens up a wealth of opportunity, as well as helping you to avoid costly mistakes.

 In economics the majority is always wrong.   —**John Kenneth Gailbraith**

Macro vs. Micro

One excellent way to think like an economist is to understand the difference between macroeconomics and microeconomics. Macroeconomics is the study of how every part relates to and impacts the whole, and learning how to maximize and utilize specific parts in order to maximize the whole. It helps us to make holistic decisions based on how those variables affect the whole of our situation, not just a part. Microeconomics is the study of parts, unrelated to the whole. It's like studying the electrons within your body without knowing or caring how your entire body works. (Imagine where science would be if we ignored everything not seen with the naked eye. How would we explain gravity or disease, for example?)

An easy way to make this clear is to consider businesses. Suppose I own a tire shop, and tires have the highest profit margin of any of the items that I sell. Oil changes have the lowest profit margin. Viewed from a micro perspective, it might make sense for me to stop doing oil changes and focus on selling more tires. But a macro perspective tells me to consider the whole picture, rather than separate parts. What if my oil changes are my best form of advertisement, and one of the main reasons that people come into my shop in the first place? If I get rid of oil changes it initially appears as if my profit margin will go up, but by doing so I might actually lose a lot of customers.

Let's look at another example that is perhaps more universally applicable and closer to home. If I have money in a savings account, I may not be getting a good rate of return (if any), but by having savings I can raise my deductibles on my auto and home insurance, which effectively lowers my cost of insurance. The micro effect of my rate of return on my savings is poor, but it has a great macro effect when I consider other factors.

Another example I like to use to explain macroeconomics versus microeconomics is the idea of using only one gauge to measure my flight speed to fly an airplane. I'm so concerned about how fast I fly that I ignore all of my other indicators. Suppose I'm flying in clouds and my gauge tells me that I'm flying at three hundred miles per hour at full throttle. An hour later I'm out of the clouds and realize that I haven't gone anywhere. I was hitting a three-hundred-mile per

**macro-
economics/
micro-
economics:**
Macroeconomics is the study of how every part relates to and impacts the whole, and learning how to maximize and utilize specific parts in order to maximize the whole. Microeconomics is the study of parts, unrelated to the whole or without consideration of the whole.

macro

micro

hour headwind straight on, but I had no way of knowing that based on my flight speed gauge. I was taking a micro view of something that was drastically affected by other factors that I failed to take into consideration. Had I used my other indicators I would have realized my problem and been able to compensate for it.

So many people ask retirement planners questions like, "Should I pay cash for a car, lease it, or finance it?" The popular financial pundits are quick to answer with whichever one of those that happens to correspond with their opinions. I find this to be highly irresponsible. There's no way to adequately, accurately, and responsibly answer the question without knowing every factor involved in the decision. I never give people micro advice without knowing their macro picture, what their goals are, and what they're trying to accomplish. My answer to micro questions like this is always "It depends." It depends on their macro plan and how they're leveraging their human life value.

Prosperity = Happiness

Most—if not all—of us want to prosper, but do we even have a clear definition of what prosperity actually is? Is it a number? Is it an amount of money? Is it retirement? I submit that to prosper means that we are happy because we're doing what we were born to do. It's that simple: if people are truly, deeply happy, then they're prospering, regardless of the amount of money they have in that moment.

As I've said before, nobody wants money; they want what money can buy. Everyone wants to be happy, and it's that desire for happiness that drives all human behavior. Many people seem to think that happiness is a function of the amount of money that we have. But it's self-evident that money cannot bring us happiness. It can certainly facilitate the purchase of items that contribute to our joy in life, but money in and of itself has no intrinsic value.

Prosperity means to be truly happy, and to be free of worries and stress about money. I'm not talking about naiveté, carelessness, or ignorant bliss; I'm talking about real, lasting happiness. We can never find happiness through carefree, irresponsible consumption; and neither is it to be found through scarce-minded hoarding and fear-based accumulation. It comes from identifying what we really want in life, and then realizing that the best way to get what we want is to give others what they want, and then embark on a lifelong commitment to serving others by using our greatest abilities. It comes from living Soul Purpose.

Happiness and value creation are a function of service, not self-centeredness. I would argue that people can make far more money living Soul Purpose than they ever can doing anything else or anything less. *But even if people will actually make less money in the short run living Soul Purpose than they can make in a different career, they will still be happier for doing so.* If your focus is on the amount of money you are making, then it will override the infinitely more important concern of your happiness. Contrary to the myth, prosperity is a function of happiness, not numbers. We can have a lot of money and still be miserable. We can have no money and be miserable. We can also have a lot of money and be happy, or have no money and be happy. The point is to stop focusing on money and to start focusing on happiness. Since happiness cannot be quantified, it's ridiculous to base our happiness on hypothetical, magical numbers in the future. If we focus on happiness first, the money we need will naturally follow.

One of the most destructive lies that we can fall prey to is thinking that having more money will change us. Many people fear wealth because they think it will change them for the worse, and still others invite wealth because they think that it will make them happy. The amount of currency available to you does nothing but make you more of what you already are. If you are naturally generous, increased wealth will simply give you greater opportunity to be generous. If you are greedy, wealth will do nothing but manifest your greed even more clearly. A bank balance does not have the power to change people; only people can change their understanding of and relationship with their bank balance. If you're not happy without money, you'll never be happy with it. Money is important and useful, but if you think that money will fix your problems, that *thought* is the problem.

If you want to prosper, find out what it is that will truly make you happy. Seek , find, and live your Soul Purpose. Focus on the cause of money—creating value for others—and let the effect naturally follow.

MYTH 4:

{ **Financial Security** }

My highly educated dad always encouraged me to seek a good job with a strong corporation. He spoke of the virtues of "working your way up the corporate ladder." He didn't understand that, by relying solely on a paycheck from a corporate employer, I would be a docile cow ready for milking.

—Robert Kiyosaki, in *Rich Dad, Poor Dad*

Myth: Financial security means steady paychecks and benefits. We're entitled to protection and benefits from a corporation, the government, or someone else.

Reality: We are ourselves the only source of security in this life, but unlike those who depend on external forces, we can make ourselves truly secure.

T his chapter focuses on the belief that external factors such as financial products, corporations, the government, health and retirement benefits, or good fortune are the source of security. Successful people understand that the only true security we can find in this life is the security of responsibility and Soul Purpose. They know that the only things that they can control are the thoughts that they pay attention to and focus on, and their own actions. To believe anything else is to be trapped in a myth of false security.

The Destructive Nature of False Security

Why is the common belief in financial security from external sources so destructive and debilitating? For three main reasons: It is actually false security but we still come to depend on it as though it were real, which means we are susceptible to risks and dangers we don't even look for. It leads to an entitlement mentality, which means we expect more and produce less, destroying our human life value and our ability to help others. And it keeps us working in conditions that don't bring us happiness in the name of security, which not only means more time not living Soul Purpose, but does not even result in the security we desire.

The pursuit of false security leads to shirking our responsibility to produce and create value, and neglecting the stewardship of the resources we do produce.

It replaces the critical values of education and individual responsibility with misplaced faith in financial institutions and the government. Those who live under a false sense of security routinely hand over their money to so-called experts, then cross their fingers and hope and pray that everything will turn out well. They fail to take responsibility for their own productivity or become stewards of their human life value. By not doing so they significantly diminish their potential and fail to find and realize their Soul Purpose.

To be more safe, they at length become willing to run the risk of being less free. —**Alexander Hamilton**

Any time our sense of security is derived from sources outside of ourselves and we don't take responsibility for everything that happens to us, we're setting ourselves up for failure. We're deceived. We're delusional. We're betraying ourselves and our Soul Purpose. And any time we subject ourselves to any form of deception (especially self-deception), we're automatically crippling the development of our human life value. It's not good enough to say, after we've experienced a letdown because of our own mistakes, "But I didn't know!" I routinely hear people who made bad investments say, "But I didn't know the company was failing" or, "I didn't know that he was embezzling money." There are certainly situations where things can go wrong despite all of our due diligence, but usually people say things like this to imply that it isn't their fault, and that someone else should do something to fix their problem. Nobody is responsible for you but you. You are the one with the responsibility and the power to change anything about your life that you don't like. *You.*

What condition is more wretched than to live . . . with nothing to call one's own, receiving from someone else one's sustenance, one's power to act, one's body, one's very life? —**Étienne de la Boétie**

When we think that financial security comes from sources outside of ourselves, we feel entitled to those external sources, whether the benefits come from our company, our government, our community, or our family. After all, we all deserve to be fed, clothed, and protected by others, or so we've been led to believe. But we often fail to connect the dots between these benefits and the labor of other people. We forget, for example, that the government is We the People, and that every form of benefit we receive comes from the labor of another person in some form. We've come to think of the government as some detached and self-sustaining entity that owes us something. But if all of us were to wait around for the government to take care of us, who would be left to actually do the caretaking? Any time we depend on the government to solve our problems, we're actually expecting our neighbors to solve them.

This type of entitlement mentality also transfers to the corporate world. Those who feel that they are entitled to benefits are the ones who focus far less on how they can serve and what they can give, and far more on what they want to receive. They seek to provide the least amount of value possible in exchange for the greatest amount of benefits possible. They complain anytime their benefits are reduced, as opposed to going the extra mile to make themselves more valuable to their company.

This mentality is destructive because not only does it lead us to illegitimately confiscate the labor of other people, it also limits our own potential through selfishness. People with this mentality are so concerned about what they can *get* from others that they never think of what they have to *give*. It is precisely what we have to give that results in the development of our whole being. Our Soul Purpose and our human life value are all about what we have to offer to the world, not what the world has to offer to us. As long as we're more concerned with getting than giving, we will never find and live our Soul Purpose. And consequently, we will never receive what we have the potential to receive, because there is a direct correlation between what we give and what we receive.

If the only tool you have is a hammer, you tend to see every problem as a nail.
—**Abraham Maslow**

Another destructive aspect of the myth of security is that we are convinced that we must stay in jobs that make us unhappy in order to move up the ladder, retire with a good pension, take advantage of vesting, or just to keep getting that paycheck. There's a scene from the movie *Jerry Maguire*, starring Tom Cruise, that illustrates this myth perfectly. Tom has just been fired from his job, and as he's leaving, he asks everyone in the firm, "Who wants to come with me?" There's dead silence for a moment, then one woman speaks up and says, "I'd like to but I'm due for a promotion in three months."

How many people in America are working in a job that they tolerate at best, and suffer through at worst, because they can't bear to give up their benefits and their "security"? How many of us can hardly stand to get up in the morning, yet we do it anyway because we're like beasts of burden pursuing a carrot that's being dangled in front of us? We're lured by the temptation of pay and benefits to remain in companies and positions that result in continued misery, like fish chasing shiny objects only to get hooked and caught in the end.

 A ship in harbor is safe—but that is not what ships are for.—**John A. Shedd**

This myth entraps us because we place more value in security than we do in people, in living our Soul Purpose, or in developing our human life value. Golden handcuffs are one of the worst forms of false security and one of the most effective at keeping people away from Soul Purpose. For those entrapped in this security dilemma, their focus is not on immediate and lasting production and cash flow—they're focused on misguided hope in the future and fear of change in the present. What could be more destructive than this? Furthermore, what could lead toward more insecurity than this? How much more risk can we expose ourselves to than to never reach our full potential because we put too much value on false security?

We limit and actually destroy our own human life value and that of others when we remain in jobs and careers that bring us more misery than joy in order to collect a paycheck or get a match on a 401(k). As long as we're frustrated, despondent, and suffering we will never access our potential and become who we were born to become. And the concept of golden handcuffs perpetuates losses for both employers and employees. A company with unhappy employees is a company whose productivity is severely limited, because that company's

"They made little or no money investing."

In 1960, a man named Srully Blotnick began a study of 1,500 people representing a cross-section of middle-class America. Throughout the twenty-year study, they lost almost a third of participants due to deaths, moves, or other factors. Of the 1,057 that remained, 83 had become millionaires. When Mr. Blotnick's team interviewed participants at the beginning of the study, the most widely shared impression they found was that "great wealth can come to you only as a result of doing things you don't want to do." They also noted that from the start, most participants assumed that chance would play a decisive role in determining who became wealthy.

They found that the 83 successful people shared five characteristics: they were persistent, they were patient, they were willing to handle both the "nobler and the pettier" aspects of their job, they had an increasingly noncompetitive attitude towards the people with whom they worked, and their investment activities—aside from their main career—consumed a minimum of their time and attention. Writes Blotnick, "We originally expected the people in our sample to become wealthy by taking the money they earned at work and investing it wisely, in such things as stocks, bonds, and real estate . . . we thought there'd be no way for [them] to become rich unless they used their surplus income to generate more income . . . It didn't work out that way. . . . More often than not they made little or no money investing."

In short, what the study unveiled was that the main source of wealth for the successful participants was that they found something they loved to do and they did it well. "In case after case," says Blotnick, "they did increasingly well occupationally, while their pursuit of investment profits proved to be largely a waste of time. In the long run, it was their work which made them rich." Blotnick concludes that investing in yourself, what you do, and with whom you do it are the most important determining factors of wealth.

Source: *Getting Rich Your Own Way*, Srully Blotnick (Jove, 1982).

most valuable assets—people—aren't operating at peak capacity. Employees who stay in positions because of fear of loss and desire for benefits never produce great value in the world. Ironically, in an effort to avoid their greatest fear, they actually create the very thing they're trying to avoid.

People want financial security so badly that they expose themselves to the single greatest risk of losing financial security, and that is not living up to their full potential through living Soul Purpose, which can only be achieved through freedom.

If money is your hope for independence, you will never have it. The only real security that a man can have in this world is a reserve of knowledge, experience and ability.

—**Henry Ford**

Replacing False Security with Freedom

The contrast between freedom and security is important to discuss, not only in order to differentiate between the two, but also to be able to identify the counterfeits of each and arrive at the truths of both. The Founding Fathers debated heavily to find the balance between freedom and security. They understood that, in a governmental sense, security is at direct odds with freedom. They knew that a people can only choose security at the expense of freedom. Sadly, history shows that most people prefer false security, even the security of subjugation, to freedom. As John Adams wrote, "The numbers of men in all ages have preferred ease, slumber, and good cheer to liberty, when they have been in competition. We must not then depend alone upon the love of liberty in the soul of man for its preservation."

It's time for us to face the fact that there is no product, company, person, government, or retirement benefit that can ever replace responsibility, knowledge, human life value, and Soul Purpose as the elements of true security. We can only achieve real security by pursuing freedom, as difficult as it may be.

The time has come for us to face up to the consequences of our misguided beliefs and actions. It's time for us to be real, honest, and authentic with ourselves and with each other.

Security is mostly a superstition. It does not exist in nature, nor do the children of men as a whole experience it. Avoiding danger is no safer in the long run than outright exposure. Life is either a daring adventure, or nothing.

—**Helen Keller**

So the way to overcome the myth of false security is to look within ourselves. As Sir Thomas Browne wrote, "We carry within us the wonders we seek without us." We must

> Embrace freedom;

> Be responsible stewards of our value creation;

> Be producers, not consumers.

Embracing Freedom

The idea that we can find security outside of ourselves is a blatant and undermining lie. It's simply not true. Nobody will ever find such security. They may find the *illusion* of security—but never will they find true security. By buying into this lie, we limit our ability to reach our full potential and create maximum value in the world. Freedom is where prosperity is found. Exercising our ability to choose productively and responsibly is the highest and only real sense of security that we can find in this life. By embracing freedom we, by default, also choose responsibility. The oft-used cliché that "freedom isn't free" is truer than we may realize.

Once we roared like lions for liberty; now we bleat like sheep for security! The solution for America's problem is . . . in big men over whom nobody stands in control but God.

—**Norman Vincent Peale**

When we begin choosing freedom, we realize that we alone are responsible for providing for our wants. We stop looking for solutions beyond our control. We stop being victims of products, companies, other people, and natural disasters. We choose heroism. We choose accountability. And through these virtues come spiritual and material prosperity.

How do we find freedom on a day-to-day basis? One powerful way is to ask yourself the right questions. Who is ultimately responsible for your prosperity? How can you overcome your fears? How can you be less selfish? What do you really want out of life? What do you have to give that has not been given because of fear or other limiting factors? Who can you serve today? How can you increase your value to others? These types of questions are based on the implicit assumption that you are responsible for the outcome of your life, and in this frame of mind, you can embrace life as a choose-your-own adventure where you have ultimate control of your destiny.

These types of questions will also lead to changes in your goals and career. When you face the realization that you're responsible, and then precisely identify what you have to offer the world, you'll begin thinking of how you can bring your unique value to fruition. Perhaps that means you'll start a business. Maybe you'll quit your current job to pursue another. Maybe you'll write a book, adopt a child, start a nonprofit organization. The possibilities are endless. But the change begins by simply embracing freedom, and the privileges and responsibilities that come with it; as your consciousness changes, so will everything else.

We must be cautious as we pursue freedom, though, that we aren't pursuing a false freedom the same way we currently pursue false security. Just as there is a counterfeit of security that takes away from freedom, so are there also counterfeits of freedom that detract from our safety. Many people who embrace freedom in a dogmatic sense tend to expose themselves to much avoidable risk. They believe that in the world of freedom, there is no security to be found whatsoever. They are the do-it-yourself types who derive pleasure from pitting themselves against all odds without any form of protection. Unfortunately, they almost always lose eventually. They choose self-sufficiency rather than self-reliance, which is a problem I'll address in the next section.

Responsibility

Many of the financial myths we operate under—scarcity, accumulation, and particularly security—fundamentally require an abdication of responsibility. They allow for people to remain ignorant, accept social norms and traditional clichés unquestioningly, and quietly consent to their lot in life while allowing external circumstances to dictate their success, all in the name of achieving financial security. Yet the way to provide for security is to cultivate the ability to produce value in the world under any set of circumstances—to be responsible and free.

Financial freedom requires responsibility and wise stewardship, not self-sufficiency. There's a difference between self-sufficiency—doing everything yourself, without cooperating with, giving value to, or receiving value from others—and self-reliance, being accountable for yourself while providing value to and accepting it from others. Responsibility implies interdependence; a responsible person develops her human life value and exchanges that value with others in order to meet life's challenges. Responsibility and self-reliance come from a paradigm of abundance and lead to peace and cooperation. Choosing this path means making powerful choices in your life regardless of what has happened in the past without using excuses or placing blame; it's a recipe for heroism.

Self-sufficiency, on the other hand, is a product of the scarcity paradigm and leads to disunity and mistrust. It's a selfish way to ignore and reject the human life value of others by seeking to "go it on your own"; it ignores that exchange is the platform for wealth.

However, there's also a third option among our choices about how we relate to others financially and in productivity: it is also possible to become dependent on others and take no responsibility for oneself. This paradigm comes from the security myth, which teaches that we cannot provide enough for ourselves, and it leads to helplessness and a victim mentality.

In late 2001, it was revealed that one of the country's leading energy companies, Enron, had practiced fraudulent accounting to pay key executives exorbitant and illegitimate bonuses. When Enron collapsed, thousands of Enron employees and investors lost their life savings, children's college funds, and pensions. Enron executives had convinced employees to fill their 401(k)s with company stock, which became worthless after the scandal. All those involved were dependent on their pension and their company for their financial security, and they quickly and painfully learned how false their sense of security really was. The irony of this example is that these people thought that they were getting security when they signed up for the job and the pension plan.

In interviews and statements, the language of the Enron employees indicates a complete lack of responsibility. In an interview with Wolf Blitzer for CNN (January 20, 2002), former Enron employee Roger Boyce said, "It's really difficult to explain where our losses came from. But I believe we, as average Americans, shareholders, trusting in the system . . . Enron executives let us down, auditors let us down, Wall Street analysts let us down. And the lenders, perhaps using poor judgment and had unsecured loans, they let us down." The Enron employees did nothing to mitigate their risk—they had zero control over the performance of their money, they had zero collateral to support it in the event of loss, and the failure of their pensions came as a complete shock to them. After the failure, they saw blame and failings in everyone and everything—except for themselves. They blamed their executives, the corporation, the accounting firm, Congress, auditors, Wall Street analysts, lenders—everyone except for the only people who had ultimate control over their choices and their actions. They were so focused on things and events outside of their realm of control that they were blind to the possibilities of what can happen when people take responsibility, become self-reliant, and start thinking and acting as wise stewards.

I recently came across an interesting article that tells of an ex-Enron employee's efforts to find creative ways to turn the tragedy into a positive experience ("Dark Humour and a line in T-shirts from Enron victim," David Teather, *The Guardian*, January 22, 2002). John Allario set up Laydoff.com, a website providing a forum for Enron workers. John also started making T-shirts bearing messages such as, "My boss got a retention bonus, all I got was this T-shirt." At the time the article was printed, the site had received 18,000 hits, and John had sold 500 T-shirts.

What I liked about the article was a statement by John, who said, "I left feeling pretty angry but that can destroy you, so I'm trying to put it into something positive." Now, there are probably better ways for him to leverage the lessons he learned from the scandal, yet his mindset led him to take action in the right direction. He used his own talents and abilities to create humor out of tragedy, and he profited from his effort. This is the type of thinking required to recover from disasters.

The principled way to approach finances is to take responsibility for your life and thoughts without rejecting the value that others can offer you. In abundance, we use the knowledge and value of others, but it is in an *interdependent*—not dependent—manner. The more self-reliant we become, the more we realize that *we* are our most important asset.

Men are anxious to improve their circumstances, but are unwilling to improve themselves; they therefore remain bound. —**James Allen**

I think it's time for us to turn inward, rather than outward and upward, to focus on what we can control. The real tragedy of the Enron example isn't as much what the executives did as it is the fact that so many people depended on their pensions and corporations for financial security and forfeited education and responsibility. To some this will undoubtedly come across as being overly harsh, but truth is rarely easy to face. It's natural for us to find things outside of ourselves to blame and to attack when things go wrong. All of us do it or have done it. But if we are to be free and prosperous, we must stop believing that financial security is a result of things outside of ourselves or beyond our control. We have to take control ourselves: we have to commit to a life of stewardship of our talents and our resources.

Stewardship

stewardship:
the responsibility to take care of our resources to ensure that they are sustainably managed for current and future generations.

It's the concept of ownership that gives capitalism a bad name, and rightly so. Ownership-oriented capitalists exploit the earth and other people for their gain. Selfish ownership has given us polluted rivers and oceans, deforestation, exploitation of developing countries, and many of the other problems we face today. This is why we see reactionary environmentalists swinging the pendulum to the opposite direction, giving the impression that nature and animals are more important than human beings.

The balance between those two extremes is stewardship. Capitalistic owners think that they can do whatever they want with their property; extreme environmentalists think that we should use the earth as little as possible. Stewards understand that material resources can be used for their benefit and that of others, without exploitation, and in safe, sustainable, and balanced ways. They take care of the earth and their material resources in the same way that we drive cars that are not ours—with care not to damage them. Stewards are the types who plant two trees every time they cut one down. They leave everything better than how they found it. They focus on how they can ensure that others, including posterity, can enjoy the earth and our resources. And this type of caregiving only occurs in people who understand that things aren't theirs to do with whatever they feel like doing.

Implicit in the concept of stewardship is the idea that none of our material blessings ultimately belong to us. Stewards recognize that they come to this earth with no material resources, they leave with nothing, and everything they enjoy throughout life is a gift to be used wisely, and ultimately must be accounted for.

Owners will often say things like, "This is my house," or, "This is *my* business, I built it and I'll do whatever I want with it." Stewards, on the other hand, learn to submit to a higher rule, and with that submission comes increased responsibility for how they use their resources. Their focus is on using the material resources they have the temporary use of to create the most value for others, as opposed to exploiting their resources based on what's in it for them.

By living a life of stewardship, we become attuned to the call to greatness—the call to become equal to our potential. We have a responsibility to multiply our talents and to create as much value as possible in the world. In short, through stewardship, we awaken to our Soul Purpose and start living life at much higher levels.

Far better to dare mighty things, to win glorious triumphs, even though checkered by failure, than to rank with those poor spirits who neither enjoy much nor suffer much, because they live in the gray twilight that knows not victory, nor defeat. **—Theodore Roosevelt**

Part of stewardship is investing in things that help me increase my Soul Purpose. I don't look at investments in terms of products. I also don't look at money's value in terms of net worth and savings accounts. I look at what allows me to serve others at the highest levels, enjoy life to the fullest, and to be the most productive person possible. My education and my mindset are the most important things I could ever invest in. They offer me the very best return on investment that I could ever possibly make, because education and mindset are what allow me to be more productive and continue to live life to the fullest in every sense. I'm constantly reading and going to events, and engaging in things that bring my mind to a higher level of awareness.

We have to remember that the key to true financial security is investing in ourselves. Property value is created by people, more specifically, through a person's human life value. Human beings have real, intrinsic value, and property does not. Property merely comes as a result of deploying our own value in the service of others. The more we choose to increase our knowledge, our integrity, our creativity, our abilities, our faith, our humility, and our courage—our value—and the more we improve our relationships with others, the more material things flow through our lives. By focusing on our internal world, our external world is enlarged, enhanced, and improved.

One of the associates I work with, Dale Clark, lived a stereotypical life until he awoke to his own call to greatness and realized that he needed to be a better steward of his gifts. Dale grew up thinking that he should be a mechanical engineer, not because it was what he really wanted to do, but because he saw social proof that it was a good way to find "security." His uncle and others he knew were engineers and they seemed to make good money. So Dale worked hard, got good grades, earned his degree, and then for seven years worked with no passion as a mechanical engineer. He did everything right, he followed all the socially prescribed rules, including maximizing his contribution to his 401(k), yet he felt largely unfulfilled.

A few years ago, Dale attended one of my seminars, and the ideas he was exposed to challenged his prevailing beliefs. He realized that he had lived a clichéd life, and the discomfort weighed on him. He kept wondering, *Isn't there a better way? Can't I enjoy my life now without sacrificing my future?* He continued educating himself, read books, and attended more seminars. The more he learned, the more he realized he had to take immediate action and become a wise steward of his knowledge. He spent a year building a real estate portfolio, which he was able to do because he invested in himself through real estate courses.

Then, on July 4, 2006, Dale declared his independence from the job that was not aligned with his gifts and purpose, and started to live his ideal life, despite being only thirty-two years old. He realized that his passion and purpose were to help others go through the same process that had brought him so much joy and fulfillment. So he became an advisor with my firm, not because he had to for the money, but because it was his Soul Purpose. Now he works harder and longer because he loves what he does. He has much greater energy, spends far more valuable time with his family, and makes more money than before.

Dale focused on his internal world, gained knowledge, acted on that knowledge, and as a result, received greater responsibilities, as well as more privileges. His external world now reflects his increased stewardship. He realized the fallacy and limitations of seeking security in a job or financial products, and found true security by investing in himself and living his Soul Purpose.

> You are your greatest investment. The more you store in that mind of yours, the more you enrich your experience, the more people you meet, the more books you read, and the more places you visit, the greater is that investment in all that you are. —**George Matthew Adams**

The first step to increasing our human life value and committing to stewardship and personal responsibility is education. We must commit to further our education every day, through classes, discussions with peers and experts, learning new skills, or some other method of growth. This is a lifelong practice that increases our returns from each hour of our lives in value to ourselves and others and give us security in our abilities.

We must next take action on what we have learned, putting our lessons into practice and changing our habits to constantly improve ourselves. What we know and do not act on cannot help us.

The third aspect of increasing human life value is dedicating ourselves to finding and living our Soul Purpose. Soul Purpose is the answer to the question, "What would you do all day long whether or not you got paid to do it?" Finding the answer can be a lifelong journey for some, but there are some things you can do to get the process started. I suggest asking your friends and family what they believe is great about you, and what characteristics and attributes they have noticed to be consistent in your life. The sooner you can realize your Soul Purpose and transform it into actual value in the marketplace, the sooner you will be doing what you were born to do—and reaping the rewards that will follow your added contribution.

As our human life value increases, we begin thinking and acting much differently from most people. We transcend destructive myths and confining social traditions. We start reducing our risk and increasing our returns. We stop accumulating money for the future, and instead we start to utilize money in the present moment. This is financial security: Choosing to be responsible and accountable and embracing freedom and abandoning false definitions and perceptions of security.

Producers vs. Consumers

The goal of all this development, the effect of maximizing our human life value and living our Soul Purpose, is to become producers instead of consumers. I mean this on a much deeper, more comprehensive level than what we traditionally think when we hear those words.

In the most basic terms, producers are those who produce more value than they consume. Consumers are the opposite, those who consume more value than they produce. But this simple distinction has massive effects on our lives, our societies, and our world.

Because consumers focus on what they get instead of what they can give, they avoid responsibility, they depend on others for their happiness, and they rarely create real value. Consumers operate in scarcity, so they view the world through eyes that see poverty and limitations. They think there isn't enough to go around, so they should get what they can before it all runs out. They take and leave nothing in place of what they take. They often feel victimized by other people and external circumstances when they don't get what they think they should. They believe that material things, not people, have intrinsic value. Because they feel entitled to everything that is given to them, they are poor stewards and allow their human life value to degenerate.

> We have no more right to consume happiness without producing it than to consume wealth without producing it. —**George Bernard Shaw**

Security to consumers is based on things outside of themselves and their choices. It is anything and everything they can think of: the government, their bosses, their company, their parents or grandparents, their 401(k)s, etc. When things go wrong, nothing is ever their fault—they place blame and avoid responsibility. Security to them is the expectation that someone somewhere will always take care of them and make things right somehow. They believe in luck and misfortune, not choice and accountability. Consumers are either fearful to the point of enslaving themselves, or foolhardy in their love of freedom to the point of exposing themselves to much unnecessary risk. Either way, they depend on others because they don't know how to take care of themselves, nor do they want the responsibility of doing so.

Unfortunately, this desperate grasping for security ends in misery. Consumers never become what they could have become because they never take the sometimes excruciating yet empowering step of taking responsibility for themselves. Their potential lies dormant in a pool of self-deception.

In contrast, producers are the responsible, innovative, and creative people who create all of the products and services that we buy and use. They are more concerned with giving than with receiving. They practice enlightened self-interest, the belief that the way to bring ourselves the most happiness is to serve others. They are happy, wealthy, and successful, or they are on their way to becoming so. Producers lift, bless, serve, and contribute to everything good

A: Your answer—although it's not always easy to determine— is probably what you were born to do, your Soul Purpose.

in the world. Producers always leave things better than they found them, even if they weren't responsible for the destruction that they fix.

When I was ten years old, my father and I were on our way to go camping when he pulled the car off to the side of the road and started picking up garbage. I said, "Hey, what are we doing, why are we picking up other people's garbage for them?" He said, "Look, I don't care who made the mess, I'm concerned about making any community I'm around better because I live there, not making it worse." I thought about what my dad was saying, and I knew it was right. I committed to myself at that moment to be someone that always created more value than I consumed. I decided that I was going to take personal responsibility for making my community great, rather than to just leaving it up to others.

Producers know that people, not material things, have intrinsic value. They love people and use material things to serve others. They operate in abundance, and they view the world through eyes that see limitless possibilities for value creation. They are wise stewards over everything that they have been blessed with.

 Always make your contribution bigger than your reward.   —**Dan Sullivan**

Many people have vague feelings that this must be the best way to live, but shake it off as misguided idealism, afraid of someone taking advantage of them. But becoming a producer means creating value, and creating value means receiving value abundantly and without fear for "security." As my friend Les McGuire once wrote, "Producers are committed to creating maximum value in all situations, regardless of circumstance, and they manage their risk to near zero. Consumers think that risk means losing money; producers know that risk refers to lost production, whether created in the past or yet to be created in the future. Producers reduce both risks to near zero."

Producers apply their minds and education to learn which financial tools and resources will help them create maximum value in the world even if they are sick, disabled, or dead. These include such things as insurance, businesses, technology, and estate planning. Les McGuire died in a plane crash in 2006. Because he was a producer, he leveraged many such tools and resources to create a legacy, and therefore his actions are still creating value today, despite his death. His life insurance proceeds are being used to perpetuate the value that he brought to the world. His will and trust ensure that his assets are directed toward productive ends chosen by him. We have videos of him teaching seminars that people can still learn from. We have essays and articles that he wrote. All of these things remain because he deliberately planned as a producer; his main intent was to "create maximum value in all situations, regardless of circumstance." While his death was unexpected, he had prepared for it, and so his legacy, his teachings, and his value still remain and will be perpetuated through generations.

While a major concern for consumers is to reduce expenses at all costs, the primary concern for producers is to create maximum value. With these different mindsets come entirely different financial strategies and products. For example, a consumer will buy term insurance for the sole reason that it is cheaper, while producers generally buy permanent insurance; even though it may seem more expensive on the surface, it allows them to create exponentially more value, assuming that they know how to use it. This concept will be discussed further in chapter 7.

Whether they are entrepreneurs, self-employed, or employees, all producers find a job, career, business, or cause that invigorates them, that fills them with joy, that makes them excited to wake up in the morning. Why? Because when we're happy, happiness overflows into value creation for others. When we're miserable, we make people around us miserable.

To a producer, *security* is his personal ability to choose his response to anything that occurs in his life. Producers understand the truth spoken by

security:

To a producer, security is his personal ability to choose his response to anything that occurs in his life.

Freedom from danger, risk; safety. freedom from care, anxiety, or doubt; well-founded confidence. something that secures or makes safe; protection; defense.
—Source: *Random House Unabridged Dictionary* 2006

Viktor Frankl: "The last of the human freedoms is to choose one's attitude in any given set of circumstances—to choose one's own way." Viktor was speaking from experience, having survived a Nazi concentration camp. Producers understand that security is determined solely by their attitudes, their paradigms, and their choices. Security for a producer is the power to understand as many variables as possible, and therefore create favorable conditions for production. Thus producers live calm, productive lives with the assurance that nothing can ever make them a victim. Producers know that victimhood is a choice—not an event.

Aimee, a friend of mine, shared with me her journey from consumer to producer and the dramatic changes it inspired in her life. Aimee grew up in a typical penny-pinching "saver" household, and the scarcity mentality was instilled in her at an early age. Her father had gone through bankruptcy, leaving him fearful. Aimee and her family cut corners with everything they did, spent time clipping coupons, and generally lived a life of mental poverty. Aimee admits that her scarcity worldview permeated her life, including her relationships; she found herself critical and negative of others, quick to argue, and little inclined to service.

A few years after she was married, Aimee and her husband were introduced to a course on finance and prosperity that went against everything Aimee thought she knew to be true. Where before she only saw lack, she was now being taught of abundance, joy, and creativity. Like all producers, she found a turning point in education. She began reading books that she otherwise wouldn't have read, attended seminars, and associated with new people, and her views began to change. She says that she achieved her biggest breakthrough at one of my seminars where I taught that our beliefs determine our results, and this powerful truth resonated with her.

Aimee experienced a paradigm shift then that has fundamentally changed her life. She's happier, she's filled with faith, she no longer feels the need to argue with people, and her relationship with her husband and family is better. She's secure in her views, and with this security she's now able to focus on serving, rather than competing or arguing, with others. Every day, says Aimee, is an exciting adventure to be discovered, not a struggle to avoid or fear.

Consumer vs. Producer

There are two mindsets for every individual to choose between that determine his or her happiness and success, or lack thereof: the consumer mindset and the producer mindset.

The Consumer Mindset	The Producer Mindset
Money and material wealth are a person's ultimate ambition.	A person's ultimate ambition is to attain happiness for himself and others through dedicated, principle-based service.
Material things have intrinsic value.	People have the only true intrinsic value.
The demand for wealth and opportunity far outweigh the supply.	There is and always will be an abundance of opportunity and prosperity for everyone, and the supply far outweighs all demand.
Other people are viewed as competition for wealth and personal opportunity.	Other people are viewed as valuable assets, and we achieve prosperity through service to others.
A person's opportunities, choices, and prosperity are restricted to external circumstances beyond their control.	Personal happiness and prosperity are internal choices, and are therefore achievable regardless of circumstance.
People are used to obtain more money and material possessions.	Money and material things are used to bless and serve other people.

The Consumer Condition	The Producer Paradigm
Scarcity	Abundance
Win-Lose	Win-Win
Fear	Faith
Selfishness	Service
Dependence	Interdependence
Ownership	Stewardship
Accumulation	Utilization
Destruction	Creation
Luck	Accountability
Entitlement	Value Creation

For more information and examples, go to killingsacredcows.com

I use the label of "producer" to illustrate an ideal for us all to shoot for. Ultimately, every one of us has both producer and consumer tendencies, and by raising our conscious awareness of what it means to be a producer we can more easily transcend what I call the Consumer Condition. Consumers are not to be vilified; they are to be helped. They are not to be condemned; they are to be served. The more we can help each other rise above the Consumer Condition and get into the Producer Paradigm, the better our world will be.

This is the lesson: Producers are able to identify and embrace the true meanings of both freedom *and* security and discard the counterfeits. They operate in freedom while protecting themselves against risk in any endeavor. This is done through the combination of internal, human life value–based protection measures such as education, the development of character, integrity, and unique abilities; and external protection measures including insurance, wills and trusts, investments, business systems, and technology, to name a few.

* * *

Leading more people to the path of the producers is the main purpose of this book. I envision an ideal society of heroes, as opposed to a stagnant society of victims. I choose responsibility, and the more people who make this choice, the more free and prosperous all of us will be together. Freedom takes courage, though, so we must be prepared to overcome the fear that comes with venturing into a new territory by taking responsibility for the value we create for ourselves and others.

MYTH 5:

{ **Money Is Power** }

The extent of the power of money is the extent of my power. Money's properties are my properties and essential powers. Thus, what I am and am capable of is by no means determined by my individuality . . . If money is the bond binding me to human life, binding society to me, connecting me with nature and man, is not money the bond of all bonds? Can it not dissolve and bind all ties? Is it not, therefore, also the universal agent of separation? It is the coin that really separates as well as the real binding agent . . . the chemical power of society.

—Karl Marx in *The Economic & Philosophical Manuscripts of 1844*

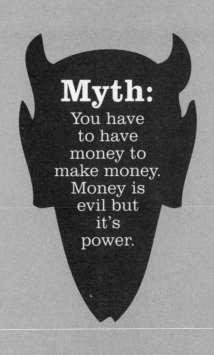

Myth:
You have
to have
money to
make money.
Money is
evil but
it's
power.

Reality:
Money is
nothing
more than an
expression and
byproduct of
value created
by people.

I would love to find the person who originated the myth that money is the source of power, of the abilities of people to achieve great things, of strife between people. I can't imagine how derisive that person must be of the accomplishments of our true creative nature and abilities. Dedication to this myth shows a complete lack of knowledge of what money is, where it originates, and what purpose it serves.

When we buy into this myth, we put our faith in money rather than in the things that create money. This misplaced faith supports all the other dominant myths: scarcity, accumulation, and security. But as I have said in previous chapters, money is nothing more than a representation of value. The creation of value is what we should all be seeking in order to create true prosperity. Value is something of worth or service that, when provided to another, creates joy for both parties.

There are various fallacies that relate to this myth. Some people believe that the only way to make money is to have money to utilize already. Others call money "the root of all evil." These ideas support the concept that money has intrinsic value and power, that it is the ultimate cause of our successes and failures. But money is none of those things. It is a tool or a representation of the things that people create or do.

They who are of the opinion that money will do everything, may very well be suspected to do everything for money. —**George Savile**

Instead of viewing money as power, we must recognize the power of value creation and how it promotes our own prosperity and the prosperity of others. If we stop avoiding our potential to be prosperous, happy individuals because we fear the power of money, we can maximize our human life value and lead productive, creative lives.

The Destructive Nature of Money as Power

When we believe that money is power we fall into two possible traps. We either believe that if we don't have money, we are powerless to develop wealth or value in the world, so we stop thinking creatively about how to make the best uses of our resources and sometimes simply rely on luck to achieve success, or we give up. Or we believe that anyone who achieves financial success will be corrupted by the power ("love of money is the root of all evil" paradox) and become paralyzed by our fear of pursuing money. Many of us believe both fallacies. We place ultimate value and power in material things or money rather than in people, which limits our human life value and theirs.

Often, people who don't have money believe that it's futile to even try to become wealthy. They think that the deck is stacked against them. They believe that they either need to win the lottery or be born into the right family to have a chance at prosperity. Even when they come across investment opportunities, they fail to act because they automatically assume that they can't make it happen without more money than they have. Without money, they feel powerless. Many times, they think

Famously misquoted as "money is the root of all evil," the correct quote from the apostle Paul puts the blame on the "love of money" not money itself for leading people astray.

THE MYTHS IN REALITY:
Million Dollar Ideas

My friend John has ideas every day, for a new board game, a restaurant chain, a business, but I've known him for ten years and he's still completely broke. He never pursues an idea for longer than a day or two. Sometimes he goes to a seminar or group to learn more about developing an idea. Afterward he says, "Wow, what great information," but doesn't take any steps. Instead of trying to find the people or the capital to carry through with one of his brainwaves, he starts to doubt an idea once he gets excited about it. So after ten years at least of a valuable idea every day, he's still broke and still just tossing around ideas. Ideas are potential value, not value in themselves. If you don't follow through on a good idea, it won't improve anyone's life, not even your own.

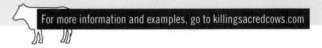

For more information and examples, go to killingsacredcows.com

that if their ideas were good someone would have already implemented them or figured them out, so they talk themselves out of taking action. Their faulty belief system shuts down creative thinking. It limits their possibilities. It's as if they're stranded on an island and a ship that could have saved them passes by, but they don't jump on board because they think it's a mirage.

When we believe that money is power and that power corrupts, we tend to view the pursuit of wealth or people who have money as morally bankrupt. This myth poses a paralyzing paradox to us—we believe money is evil, yet we want more of it. So we're either stuck in the misery of having none, or we're evil for wanting or having it. It puts us between a rock and a hard place, and the only way to get out of the predicament—or so it seems to us—is to resign ourselves to a life of limited resources, or toss our morals out with the garbage. But what if this belief is just wrong? What if it's nothing but a destructive lie that money is the root of all evil? Can you begin to see how empowering it can be to break through this myth?

Having the attitude that we shouldn't pursue wealth or prosperity because it is inherently bad or leads to corruption and exploitation limits the possibilities of what we can and should become through the pursuit of prosperity.

This attitude comes from a complete misunderstanding of what money is. Money is a representation of value creation for others. As long as you think that you shouldn't do everything in your power to pursue prosperity, you will never rise to your potential in serving others. Money isn't power, but it can increase your reach and your impact. If you shun the pursuit of money as greed or corruption, you hurt your purpose as well as yourself.

When people claim that they have transcended the base need for money, what they are really saying is that they have no intention to provide value to anyone but themselves. When they discredit the importance of money, or claim that money makes its owners shallow or corrupt or exploitative, they are essentially belittling the labor, talents, and commitments of others. And although many don't realize it, people who hold to the belief that there is some moral righteousness inherent in not seeking greater wealth or prosperity are ironically still valuing money over people, because by limiting these pursuits, they're limiting the value they create for others.

When we believe that material things have intrinsic value and that money is the source of power, the way we go about trying to help people, inherently a positive goal, is grossly miscalculated. We often believe that if we give people money, that will give them power, knowledge, and access to all of the resources they need to be prosperous. But that often is not the case. If we really cared about people, we would focus on really helping them, not thoughtlessly giving them material things. Material things may or may not help certain individuals, but if we start by focusing on material things we will almost always arrive at faulty solutions.

We've all heard the classic saying, "If you want to feed a man for a day, give him a fish. If you want to feed him for a lifetime, teach him how to fish." It really is true. We see so many political policies designed to help people, when in fact they don't do much more than perpetuate poverty. It's easy to hand people money, but more difficult, and much more charitable to reach into their lives, their minds, and their hearts to give them value that will actually help them to transcend their limitations and circumstances. We can teach them a skill, provide them with good books or other educational opportunities, give them responsibilities and guidance on how to fulfill them, or connect them with other people who may be able to help them. In short, we can give them the real value that lies beyond money, which is nothing but a representation of that value.

To relieve the misfortunes of our fellow creatures is concurring with the Deity; it is godlike; but, if we provide encouragement for laziness, and supports for folly, may we not be found fighting against the order of God and Nature, which perhaps has appointed want and misery as the proper punishment for, and cautions against, as well as necessary consequences of, idleness and extravagance? Whenever we attempt to amend the scheme of Providence, and to interfere with the government of the world, we had need by very circumspect, lest we do more harm than good.

—**Benjamin Franklin**

Ascribing intrinsic value to money is actually the root of the phrase "money is the root of all evil." But let's analyze the exact quote, which was given by Paul in the Bible. Paul never said that money is the root of all evil; he said that the *love of* money is the root of all evil. Adding two simple words gives the statement an entirely different meaning. Loving money means believing money has intrinsic value. When we love money, we ignore people. We come to worship something that is nothing but a byproduct. Placed in context, I believe that what Paul is saying is that money has no intrinsic value, and when we love it, we do so at the expense of what we should love instead—people.

Any material object is nothing but a reflection of value creation among people. When we're too focused on the material, we fail to see the originator of all utility: people. When we believe that material things, especially money, have intrinsic value, we ignore our own value and that of others to engage in materialist pursuits or to shut ourselves off from our potential to avoid them. We fail to develop Soul Purpose. The irony is that the less we think of materialism, and the more we think of serving others, the more material resources actually flow to and through us.

Replacing Money as Power with Money as a Symbol of Value Creation

To overcome the myth that money is all-powerful in our lives and that it dictates our ability to succeed or our ability to contribute positively to the world, we must develop an understanding of some essential truths about money and prosperity:

> Money is simply a means of exchange, a representation of value; it is not intrinsically valuable.

> Money does not control our lives or dictate who we are.

> Judgments based solely on money or materialistic mindsets are usually wrong or at least very limited.

> Prosperity is attained by putting our human life value to use and living Soul Purpose, not through the pursuit of money.

What Money Is and Is Not

Money is a byproduct of value creation, representing the exchange of value between people. It is an expression of our human life value as used in the service of others. In its most basic form, money is currency—a way to represent value that aids in economic transactions.

Currency is the paper and metal we use to exchange for goods and services. People created currency to aid the efficiency of economic transactions. It is not value itself—it *represents* value. It is a universally agreed upon symbol that aids the efficiency of market transactions.

Currency is like language. Language is nothing but sounds that we use as symbols for the purpose of communicating concepts deeper than the symbols we use. For example, we use the word "tree" in English to refer to a tree, but in Mexico, they use the word "árbol" to refer to the exact same thing. The important thing isn't the symbol, but what the symbol represents—that thing that has roots, a trunk, branches, and leaves.

Currency and language are both symbolic representations of the real things behind the symbols. A million green paper rectangles can't create lasting change in a person's life any more than language can. It's how we *use* the symbols that makes all the difference. And we use currency as a universal symbol to represent value.

If we didn't have currency, the only way to exchange would be the barter system. If I have wheat and you have pigs, and I want pigs and you want wheat, we can exchange wheat for pigs, and we both walk away from the transaction wealthier than before. I gave up something I valued less for something I valued more, and so did you. But what do we do when you don't want wheat, but I still want pigs? In that case, you and I have no basis for exchange, because you don't value what I have to give you in exchange.

Now put currency into the equation. If we agree upon symbols of value (ones that other people in our society also agree upon), I can give you currency instead of wheat in exchange for pigs, and you can use that currency to exchange with another person for something that you actually value.

So what does the currency represent? The value that each of us individually want. People choose what denominations of currency are worth to them, because they choose what they want to buy with the currency. The value is in the minds of people, not the currency. Money does only what we tell it to do, and the things we tell it to do are based on the things that we value and want.

To an imagination of any scope the most far-reaching form of power is not money, it is the command of ideas. —**Oliver Wendell Holmes**

To illustrate, let me pose a question. How much is a twenty-dollar bill worth? Most people would answer, "Twenty dollars." But this is exactly wrong. Because people determine value, not currency or other material things, a twenty-dollar bill carries a different value to every single individual on the planet. Why? Because every individual has different desires and different things that they want to do with that twenty dollars. Do you think that twenty dollars would serve a different purpose for Bill Gates than it would for a homeless person? Of course. *The value is not in the currency—it is in the minds of people.*

The fallacy that it takes money to make money becomes laughable when we view money this way. It's like saying that it takes the receipts for groceries to buy groceries. Money comes *after* one takes the action to make the money—it is merely evidence that a transaction has taken place, and it isn't the actual value in the transaction. Money is nothing but a representation of the real elements of productivity: applied human creativity and knowledge. Money isn't the root or primary cause of anything—it is an inert, inanimate object. It is not an actor; it is acted upon.

Money is, has always been, and forever will be value neutral. It is merely an extension of the purposes of its owner, and takes on the shape, character, and tone of its owner's intentions. But money itself holds no power for good or evil or intrinsic value of its own. Only people can have these qualities.

THE MYTHS IN REALITY:
Self-Employment Is too Risky

Monica Riedel, a friend of mine, has learned that self-employment is not too risky through an extraordinary journey. Just a few years ago, Monica was living in New York, got divorced, and decided to move to Utah with her three children. She arrived in Utah with literally no money, and nothing but her children and the contents of two suitcases to her name. She soon found a job working for a gift shop in the mall, and was able to provide for the basics; she created value first, and the money followed as a result.

But Monica knew she was capable of more. She was an amazing cook and loved everything to do with food and nutrition, and had always had a dream: to love people through food, as she puts it. She wanted to help people eat healthier, better-tasting food. However, her past experiences and associations had programmed her to think that being self-employed or starting a business was risky, that it would fail, and everyone around her gave the standard advice to get a good job with good benefits.

Fortunately, Monica didn't give up. She saw others doing what she wanted to do successfully, so she knew it was possible. She began changing her associations and investing in herself through education. She read books, attended seminars, listened to audio CDs and

Money Does Not Control Our Lives

I hope that this heading is as empowering to you as it is to me. However, there should be two more words in this statement to make it more accurate: Money does not *have to* control our lives. Unfortunately, we often let it. We do this by believing that it has power, that it holds intrinsic value (either good or bad), and that it represents solutions to problems.

Money does not dictate our actions or intentions. It does not dictate who we are. It is not power—people with money may have power, but only because they developed that power and money followed. Wise stewards of money have power because of their applied knowledge and human life value; they don't derive their power from money.

helpful radio programs, and began a daily journal to record insights and lessons learned. Her new education overpowered her old beliefs, and her new friends affirmed her belief that she could succeed. Slowly but surely, the trees of scarcity made way for new seeds of abundance, and her life began to change drastically.

She started by providing meals for individual clients, and I was one of her first. Because she did such an incredible job, word quickly spread and she created enough relationships and gained enough clients to quit her other job and focus on her dream full time. At the time that I recorded her experience, it had been one year from when she had quit her job, and she had earned in eight days her previous annual salary. In addition, she's written several articles for various publications on nutrition, she's been on the radio, and her prospects keep getting better and better.

Starting with literally no money, Monica has risen far above what she initially thought she was capable of, and is earning far more money than she would have ever thought possible, had she not learned the truth that money comes after value creation. By investing in herself and immersing herself in education, she transcended her limitations and was able to create substantial value for others, as evidenced by the money she now earns.

What our money does is reflect who we are. If we use our money to serve people, that's a good thing. If we use it to buy cocaine, that's a bad thing. It is the receipt that says that we have either created value for another person, deceived them into thinking we have, or coerced them into giving it to us anyway. Of course, deception and coercion destroy human life value, both our own and that of the people whom we deceive or coerce. The truth is that it's not the money that matters; it's the context in which it is used.

It's important to further explain here what happens to individuals and societies when deception and/or coercion are widespread. Societies with corrupt and overly oppressive governments, or with individuals and companies who are allowed to deceive others, create conditions for poverty because they stifle human creativity and the incentives to produce. If I'm trying to create a better life for myself and my family, but am stopped at every turn by thugs who steal my property, or a government who takes what I've rightfully earned, I will soon stop trying to maximize my production, and will instead live a small, poverty-ridden life, doing just the minimum to scrape by. I have no incentive to work harder than is absolutely necessary, because I won't be able to enjoy the fruits of my labor anyway. The same thing holds for deception in the marketplace. If I make investments based on promises of individuals or companies who are deceiving me, and lose money in the process, I become much less inclined to continue investing.

Furthermore, people who feel that the deck is stacked against them because of widespread deception and coercion soon turn to deceit and thievery themselves. Many do so not because they're liars and thieves inherently, but they simply feel they have no other option to provide for themselves and their families. Consider Jean Valjean, for example, the hero in Victor Hugo's classic *Les Misérables* who stole bread because he had no means of paying for it. He lived in a society that prevented him from enjoying the fruits of honest production.

So we see the power that coercion and deception have to prevent prosperity. This is why economic, political, and societal freedom is so critically important to prosperity. Deception and coercion are the opposite of freedom, and lead to poverty, misery, and dishonesty. The irony is that, because we believe money has power, we start using the force of government to "fix" things, which leads to increased poverty and less wealth for the majority, which in turn leads people to further believe that money has power because they experience life with less of it. It's a vicious cycle that can only be overcome by eliminating deception and coercion from the marketplace and from society. And this freedom is achieved by understanding that money has no intrinsic value or power.

Money Does Not Make Us Evil

So the belief held by many of us, even if only in some subconscious way, that money is the root of all evil is one of the worst aspects of the myth, and it's one of the ways we let money control our actions. It implies that any use of money is evil—including production. If this is the case, if it's really true, then the ultimate ideal for man is to be plunged back into worse misery than the Dark Ages.

That may sound overly dramatic, but really think about it. Money represents exchange and value creation. If it's evil, then we should stop using it altogether, including using it to serve others and provide them with the things that they want. Even if we were to do nothing but rid the world of the evil of paper and metal currency, wealth would still take the form of the products and services that we would barter with each other. So the only logical way to rid the world of the evil of money is to do away with every single type of transaction between individuals. By destroying the opportunity for exploitation, of course, we also destroy the opportunity for serving one another. Having no form of money results in having no form of exchange, and no exchange means limited relationships and lack of shared skills, which mean misery, poverty, and destruction. If we want to shut down a society quickly, all we have to do is shut down exchange.

We destroy ourselves and others when we believe that money, or any other material thing, is more important and has more value than people. To love money—an inanimate paper object representing an abstract concept—inspires us to want to get dollars without creating value, and this is a form of thievery. It's the destructive attitude of wanting something for nothing. Loving money causes us to ignore people at the least, and oppress them at the worst, in our pursuit to get more money. No material thing is inherently evil; people's thoughts, intentions, and choices determine if things are good or evil. And much of the evil and destruction in this world comes from people believing that material things have intrinsic value. The point, of course, is that the root of both our worst problems and our highest achievements is people. The only way to eradicate evil in the world is for us to stop placing blame on material things outside of ourselves, to face who we are, and start choosing good over evil. As long as we believe that money is the root of all evil, we're never facing the real problem, and therefore, are never arriving at real solutions.

Money Is Not a Prime Mover

This leads us to another major fallacy, which is that money is a prime mover. We think it takes money to make money because we think money is what makes the world go around. It's almost like we've come to believe that these green pieces of paper we walk around with have some type of magical quality that turns seeds into food, wood and brick into houses, plants and minerals into plastic and plastic into computers, and knowledge into books.

Nobody wants currency; they want the things that can be bought with currency. Deceived people who think that money is power want currency because those green pieces of paper or the numbers on their bank statements somehow make them feel better, bigger, more powerful, and more important. In other words, even these people don't want the currency—they want the prestige and image that they think comes with having money.

When I believed this myth, I wanted money to help me show the world how smart I was. This mindset was ingrained in me at a young age. When I was growing up, I had a "rich" uncle that I always looked up to and respected—not because of who he was, but because of what he had, according to my perception. He was an engineer, so I didn't even see him as being a powerful person; I thought that he was in a powerful career. To me, the power was in the money and the position, not in him as an individual.

After graduating from college, I saw a lot of older friends working hard for money, and I wanted to gain their respect; show them that I knew things that they didn't know. I thought that if I could figure out how to be a young millionaire then my friends and family would give me that respect. In other words, my focus wasn't on being a person of value, but rather on simply having a lot of money; I thought that the respect would come from what I had, not who I was. Money was the scorecard of my life.

The myths seem to tell us that we can throw money at any project and it will mystically become profitable—that if we have money, we will automatically

Are You Thinking of Starting a Business?

There may be some reading this who have an idea for a business that requires large amounts of cash to launch. To those, let me provide further clarification. Money is definitely useful, and even necessary in some cases. But the point is that you personally don't need money in order to launch your business; you don't need money to make money. The prime mover in this case is still you and your human life value.

If you need cash to start a business, you'll need to develop the concept, research, provide evidence of a demand in the marketplace, perhaps write a business plan, do as much implementation as you can, and then convince other people to give you the money you are looking for. Again, the prime mover still isn't the money; it's you employing your gifts to create value for others. You won't ever get that money unless you're able to show other people that it's more valuable for them to give you the money than it is to keep it or use it for something else.

make more. The ubiquitous examples of lottery winners who quickly squander their cash and go broke apparently isn't enough evidence to convince us otherwise. When we consider money from this perspective, it's so obvious how ridiculous it is to think of money being a prime mover, and yet we continue to act according to this belief. For example, we drain more and more money into our public school systems, thinking that money is the solution to our educational woes.

John Stossel produced a program on ABC News on January 13, 2006 entitled "Stupid in America" that showed how false this belief is. John interviewed Ben Chavis, a public school principal who now runs an alternative charter school in Oakland, California—a school that spends thousands of dollars less per student than the surrounding public schools. He laughs at other schools' complaints about money. "That is the biggest lie in America. They waste money," Chavis said. Even though he spends less money per student than the surrounding schools do, Chavis pays his teachers more than what public school teachers earn. Since he took over four years ago, his school has gone from being among the worst in Oakland to being the best. His middle school has the highest test scores in the city. "It's not about the money," he assures us. Ben explains how he maximizes the money his school is given through innovations like having students perform work normally reserved for janitors and other staff, teaching them valuable skills and responsibility, while also saving money. In other words, the effectiveness of their school is predicated far more upon the human life value of those operating it, and much less on the amount of money they receive.

The "solution" to put more money into things—with little thought given to strategic use and wise management—in an effort to make them more productive is evidence of a society that believes that money is a primary cause of action and production, that money has power, and that material things have intrinsic value. Oftentimes giving an individual, a company, or other institution more money for the sake of having more money develops a system of waste, misallocated resources, and entitlement.

As further evidence on this kind of thinking in the public school system, consider that between 1988 and 2003, national public school enrollment increased 15 percent, and spending increased 63 percent (adjusted for inflation). What happened to all that additional money? While it doesn't give all the answers, it certainly explains quite a bit to learn that over that period of time the school system increased administrator positions by 52.9 percent, while increasing teachers by only 25.9 percent (National Center For Education, www.nces.ed.gov). Meanwhile, we still hear continued cries for more money and more teachers, leaving us to wonder if any amount of money would ever be enough. What's needed in the school system is better management and more innovation—in other words, applied human life value—not more money.

I've even had occasions in my life where it was more productive for me to decrease money to either people or projects. For example, I had an employee running an insurance program on a salary basis, but I wasn't fully pleased with his level of production. The solution was to cut off his salary and place him on a commission basis. His production immediately increased because he was more responsible; he couldn't just rely on a regular paycheck regardless of his level of production. And incidentally, he started making more money than he was making on salary, because it came as evidence of his increased productivity.

When people or institutions claim that they need more money in order to be more effective and productive, more often than not what they actually need is better management rather than more money. This attitude of "If only I had more money, then . . ." permeates our society. But more money can never solve any problem in and of itself; the real solution is to increase human life value, leading to better stewardship over the resources that we already have, increased productivity, and ultimately, more resources, monetary and otherwise.

Discussing Money Doesn't Make Us Vulgar

It seems to be common knowledge that it's rude to discuss money, politics, and religion with people. Why is this so? Setting aside the last two for the purposes of this book, why do we have so many insecurities regarding money? What makes it vulgar?

I believe this reaction is partly because, even though we like to put up the façade that we know what we're doing, deep down we know how little we know about money. We don't want to look stupid by revealing our lack of knowledge, and as soon as we admit that we don't know something, it creates a breach in our understanding, leaving us intellectually stranded. Ignorance is one of the most uncomfortable feelings to deal with, yet truly scrutinizing our beliefs is key to our progression.

When it comes to the public discussion of money, sharing our finances or knowledge with others can make us seem prideful or shame us or others if handled poorly. Yet aren't there ways to discuss money respectfully, openly and honestly? While there may be legitimate reasons to not discuss money in certain situations, I don't think that the belief that money is vulgar should ever be considered a legitimate reason for not doing so.

There's nothing vulgar or tainted about money; in fact, there's no value to money whatsoever. We place our own value on money. If we view money as being vulgar, and if we think it's rude to publicly discuss money, then that says nothing about money and everything about us and the social agreements we labor under. If we are uncomfortable discussing money, then perhaps it's time to rid ourselves of the insecurities that come from ignorance, humble ourselves, and become open enough to begin our education.

Judgment and Exploitation

Maybe you have never *consciously* thought or believed that money is the root of all evil, but have you ever found yourself negatively judging people who appear to have a lot of money? Have you ever been engaged in conversations with people who have said things like, "Rich business owners should give more to charities"? Have you ever personally thought or said similar things? Have you ever seen a young adult driving a BMW and thought, "He must have gotten that from Daddy," or "I bet he stole it." Have you ever judged the owner of a mansion as being materialistic? Perhaps you have a "rich" uncle or sister, and you expect access to their time and knowledge because of the family connection. Have you ever felt guilty for wanting to be wealthy? Or have you heard or said something like, "I don't need money to be happy"?

Any time we have any feelings—however subtle—that people with money owe us or society something, or that we shouldn't want to be wealthy, we are falling into the trap of making judgments based on the belief that money or material goods have intrinsic value. But because material things have no intrinsic value, it is impossible for us to accurately judge other people based solely on their material things.

Different Soul Purposes require the utilization of different material resources. For example, Gandhi felt it useful for his mission to denounce all worldly possessions, yet this didn't make him poor by any means. His material possessions had no intrinsic value, but he did, and so his use of resources reflected his values and his purposes. On the other hand, I have a much different Soul Purpose than Gandhi, and so I find certain material things useful to accomplish that. If I were to get rid of my office building, for example, based on some irrational belief that my office building has intrinsic value, then I would dramatically limit my ability to produce value for others. My office is used as a tool of production, and by utilizing it, I'm able to impact more people for good.

But if someone were to compare Gandhi and myself based on our material possessions alone, they might make the mistake of saying that Gandhi is virtuous and I am not. Yet that is exactly what many of us do, and the judgments manifest in a variety of ways, the two dominant ones being that we assume that people who are wealthy exploit others, and we assume that people who aren't wealthy can offer no value to society. We find ourselves judging the rich for being wealthy, and judging the poor for being poor, and all based on their material possessions that we see with our eyes. But without actually knowing a person intimately, understanding his intentions, purposes, mission, and mindset, we have no way of accurately judging his life.

Are there people who use money to exploit others? Certainly. Are there people who use money to serve others? Of course. But the point is that we can't judge whether any situation is exploitative or benevolent based on the money involved in the equation. Just because Jane has more money than Bill, and Bill works for Jane's company, doesn't mean that Jane is exploiting Bill. In the absence of force or deception, both Jane and Bill are getting more than what they are giving up, according to their personal value determinations. Bill would never work in his position if he didn't value what he received from it more than the time and effort he spends on the position. Exploitation can only occur in an environment of deception or coercion. But again, we cannot find evidence of either in the amount of money that individuals have, since money is a byproduct, an aftereffect. The only way to determine if a situation is exploitative or beneficial to all parties is to know the people involved.

Furthermore, even if we really did believe that the way to determine the nature of an economic transaction was to look at the amount of money that the people involved have, money is the evidence of value creation. Therefore, if you believe a person engaged in free exchange has earned her money through honest value creation, her wealth is proof that she is helping, not harming, people.

The belief that money comes through exploiting others is a false conception that thrives in an atmosphere of scarcity. In abundance, every transaction, economic and otherwise, is a win for all parties involved. In scarcity, we believe that we can only win if other people lose. Hence, if we want to win, we've got to make other people lose.

People in the Consumer Condition target wealthy business owners as exploiters and point to the discrepancy between their salary and the wages of their employees. What they fail to realize is that, in the absence of deception or coercion, both the business owner and the employees are getting wealthier because of their relationship. Each employee values his paycheck more than he values his time and effort at work, and the business owner values paying the employee more than he values not paying him.

Remember the old saying that one bad apple spoils the whole barrel? This saying applies directly to how people view wealth and money. We find the most egregious examples of people who abuse their responsibilities and privileges, and then use those isolated people and incidents to make sweeping generalizations. We've already discussed the Enron scandal. What the executives involved did was shameful to say the least, and yet many people use that example as evidence of widespread corruption in business. The fact is, that scandal involved just a few people out of thousands in the company, and one company out of millions in the nation. Just because a few people or institutions are underhanded doesn't mean that everyone is. Nobody forces us to work for others; in America we choose that of our own free will. It's the height of irresponsibility to think otherwise and to blame others for our lack of opportunity and success. We have the freedom to create whatever life we deem to be the most ideal. We can become financially free through conscious, sustained, predictable action; none of us must be subject to chance or exploitation.

The other form of judging—which has the same consequences—is when we look down on other people because we have more expensive material things than they do. We feel better, more valuable, and more productive than others because we have more "stuff." We stop wanting to donate to charitable causes because we pontificate that, since we became successful on our own, everyone else should be able to do that also.

Just because a person doesn't have a nice house and car doesn't mean that she doesn't create a lot of value in the world, and neither does it necessarily mean that she's broke. People are assets, not material things. Material things are external reflections of what is going on internally in the minds of people, but this doesn't necessarily mean that those with little or no material things are poor, or that those with a lot are rich.

Pride and envy, then, are two aspects of our tendency to judge people based on their material possessions. They emerge in our lives when we place the emphasis on material things, not on people.

The truth of the matter is that, just like money, in a world of cause and effect, value creation is the cause and material things are the effect. Just because a person lives in a mansion doesn't necessarily mean that the person is materialistic, or that the person has his heart set on material things. As we mentioned earlier, we can earn money in one of three ways—deception, coercion, or value creation. The mansion in question isn't a cause—it's the effect of one of these three things. And until we know the person intimately, and know what was done to earn the mansion, we have no right or ability to judge the cause of a person's wealth, or judge what he should do with it once he's earned it.

There's another point to be made here, as concerns property and prosperity. Assume for a moment that we judge a person driving a Bentley as being materialistic. Even if it's true and the person really *is* materialistic, how useful is it for *us* to judge him? Judging without evidence automatically cuts us off from opportunities that could have been available to us had we been more willing to learn. Our pride gets in the way of our progress. For example, in *Rich Dad, Poor Dad*, Robert Kiyosaki writes that when he tells people about his methods of creating wealth, many people respond with accusations like, "You can't do that here," "That is against the law," or, "You're lying." Kiyosaki says, "I hear those comments much more often than, 'Can you show me how to do that?'" (*Rich Dad, Poor Dad*, 119) Everyone has something to teach us, but it takes an open heart, a willing mind, and productive, nonjudgmental thoughts for us to learn from every individual.

Turning Human Life Value into Prosperity

If we can understand the correlation between prosperity and human life value, we can pursue prosperity in healthy, constructive ways that place more value in people than in things. As Socrates said in his *Apology*, "I tell you that virtue is not given by money, but that from virtue comes money and every other good of man, public as well as private."

One of the most important lessons we can learn in our quest to prosperity is that we don't have to wait until we have money to be able to prosper. Prosperity is achieved by creating value, by maximizing our human life value. To refresh your memory, human life value is everything that we have to offer the world when we strip away all of our material possessions. It is our thoughts, our character, our ideas, and our unique abilities. We can create value now, and the more value we create, the greater our prosperity and the more money will come to us.

Avoiding Prosperity

Because many people don't understand the connection between prosperity and human life value or living our Soul Purpose, they tend to shy away from the pursuit of prosperity or wealth. They may believe that more money would change them. Having more money doesn't change our fundamental nature—it merely brings out more of who we already are. If we're charitable by nature, more money will give us more opportunities to be more charitable. If we're naturally greedy, more money will allow us to be more greedy. The point is that we must become our ideal selves in the present moment, regardless of the amount of money that we have. Money can neither save us nor damn us—that choice is up to us as individuals.

Often using the life of Jesus as an example, religious people sometimes hold the related belief that poverty is a virtue, and this makes them shy away from money and prosperity. But it seems to me that Jesus had everything imaginable he needed to be prosperous. According to himself, he was the wealthiest man that ever lived. He was the ultimate value creator. Many religious people who seem poor have every resource that they need to fulfill their particular mission in life, and they take advantage of those resources.

Wealth and virtue are not mutually exclusive. In fact, the most religious people in history have also been the wealthiest, meaning that they had every resource that they needed to fulfill their particular mission in life. Every one of us is born with a unique way to impact the world, and in order to do what we were born to do, more often than not we use material resources to do it.

Even if all a person wants to do is create shelters to help the homeless, that takes human life value and material resources. It takes wood and brick, clothing and food, bedding and health care. All of those things require some form of value creation by people. Remember what money is and what it represents. It doesn't take money to make money, and neither does it take money to help people. But it does take human life value, labor, thought, ingenuity, and creativeness, and money represents all of these things.

My belief is that if people are truly spiritual and want to help others, they should do all in their power to become as wealthy as possible; the wealthier they become, the more people they can help.

An even more common reason why people shy away from prosperity is because they attempt to achieve wealth, often through poor investments, and fail. This failure causes them to assume that any similar type of investment is unwise, and they immediately limit their options and potential. In the end they make sure that everyone they know is aware that the type of investment they tried is a bad investment. Instead of learning from their mistake and moving forward with increased knowledge and ability, they take one isolated incident to make broad judgments about all investments.

Even worse are the gossipmongers who haven't actually experienced something bad themselves, but still spread "Chicken Little" hearsay. They hear from their dad that real estate is a bad investment, and rather than researching it for themselves, they take his word for it, and spread the "information" to everyone they know. What they don't know is that real estate (or any other property value investment for that matter) is neither good nor bad—it is investors (people) who determine if real estate is productive or not. Real estate isn't the asset—what *you* do to create value for others *through* real estate is the asset, and a valid path to prosperity. For example, if I own a home that sits empty, it may appear as an asset on my balance sheet, but unless I use it to serve others, it will never create cash flow. I can rent or lease it out, or perhaps fix it up to make it more valuable to people. The people who pay me for the use of the home—and thus provide evidence that they value it—are the real asset, and not the home.

Prosperity Reflects Human Life Value

We can't touch, taste, feel, smell, or hear human life value; we can only see evidence of its existence through material symbols. This is one reason why

> If you want to prosper, you must stop thinking about **money** and instead start thinking of ways that you can create maximum **value** for as many people as possible.

understanding and appreciating human life value is difficult for people to grasp; we've become obsessed with materialism. We've bought into the destructive lie that material things have intrinsic value. In the midst of our dissatisfaction about money, we buy more and more things thinking that we'll be happy when we have a bigger home, a nicer car, or better furniture.

But if you want to prosper, you must stop thinking about money and instead start thinking of ways that you can create maximum value for as many people as possible. You don't need money to make money—you need human life value, and this is something that you can improve without money. For example, you can replace TV time with reading, exercise, seek advice from a willing mentor, and change your habits and your mindset, all without starting out with money. Yet as your human life value increases, the evidence will show in your increased prosperity in the physical world. Education is the first step to discovering and accessing your potential because it helps you overcome the myths and fallacies that hide your potential from you through fear and misinformation. This is why I constantly stress to people that they must always be reading good books, attending seminars, seeking out and engaging with mentors, working at certain jobs to learn specific skills, and doing anything else they can possibly do to increase their knowledge and awareness.

To overcome the belief that it takes money to make money, we must recognize that what we want is to increase our human life value and create value for others. And we can create infinite value for limitless people, *even if we possess no currency in our present moment.* If we find ourselves in a situation where we have less money than we want, the way out of that situation is to share our human life value with people. Do research for others and make phone calls. Educate yourself in a skill you feel passionately about that the economy is paying money for and use that knowledge to improve someone's life (as many people as possible). Turn your hobby into a business. Call the busiest people you know and offer your services to help get some things off their plates.

Even if you need money to start a business, the place to start is with increasing your human life value. Research your business and industry. Write a business plan. Implement small aspects of your business to show investors the demand. Practice your presentation skills and present to venture capitalists. The possibilities are endless. None of these things require you to have currency in order to make currency. They require YOU. They require your creativity and your initiative. They require your ability to get beyond short-sightedness and selfishness to see and fulfill the desires of other people.

It's also important that we are careful not to utilize our human life value improperly. The goal isn't to do whatever we can just so we can make money; the goal is to find and live Soul Purpose—to do those things that we are best suited for, that align with our core values, that create the most value in the world, and that bring us the highest levels of joy and fulfillment. Sometimes in order to get to this level we must take simple steps in the right direction and create value even if it's not our precise Soul Purpose at that moment. But we must always keep our eye on Soul Purpose as the ultimate end of our value creation.

Another important caveat is that, contrary to what often happens in the sales industry, we should never try to oversell, misrepresent, or push something onto others just because it benefits us. Yet neither should we hide the fact that we also want every transaction to be a win for us. We can be open about the fact that we want our service to be mutually beneficial, and still remain focused on the needs and wants of the other person.

It Doesn't Take Money to Make Money

The way to fix the statement "It takes money to make money" is to replace it with "It takes human life value and service to make money." Anyone can start right now, today, to create value. They can have nothing but the clothes on their backs and still make money. They can use their unique talents in the service of others. They can increase their knowledge through education, and then use that knowledge to produce more value in the world.

Success means we go to sleep at night knowing that our talents and abilities were used in a way that served others. —**Marianne Williamson**

If you still don't believe me, consider this: If it takes money to make money, then *whose* money does it take? How much money do banks make? Millions? Billions? And how much of the money in the bank is actually their own? They use *your* money to make money for *themselves*. They have the knowledge of how to make money without actually having and using their own money, because they have proven themselves to be wise stewards over money in general.

Every dollar we have comes from someone else's bank account. If we want people to give us money, all we need to do is convince them that their lives will be better for doing so. This is how banks make money without ever starting out with money—they've convinced all of us to give them our money. If it took money to make money, then no money would ever exist. How could it have materialized out of nothing? Money doesn't come from money—it comes from people.

Prosperity Through Serving Others

To prosper, we must relinquish our grip on selfish and shortsighted desires and serve others. The paradox is that the less we focus on our desires and the more we help others get what they want, the more we get of what we want.

> Being human always points, and is directed, to something, or someone, other than oneself—be it a meaning to fulfill or another human being to encounter. The more one forgets himself—by giving himself to a cause to serve or another person to love—the more human he is and the more he actualizes himself . . . self-actualization is only possible as a side-effect of self-transcendence.
>
> —Viktor Frankl

Since currency is a representation of value, the more value you provide for others, the more currency will flow into your life. But it doesn't require that you *begin* with currency before you can *receive* currency. Human life value is the cause; currency is the effect. Focus on the cause, and the effect naturally and inevitably follows. We all start with natural gifts and passions, but too often we focus on making money instead of developing our natural gifts. We want the immediate gratification that we think money can give us, and we don't always have the patience to take time to develop our productive capabilities long-term in the service of others.

What would the world look like if everyone set out to serve others instead of thinking only about their perceived needs? The more we serve, the more we will be served, and this is the key to creating the ideal world and to finding and developing our individual greatness. And the more we are served, the more prosperous we become, and the more prosperous we become, the more opportunities we have to serve more people.

People with true wealth are true value creators; they never intentionally deceive or coerce anyone. The only way to get more money to increase our human life value (and that of others) is to use our gifts in the service of others, to share our talents with people who value them and who are willing to provide evidence that they value our talents by giving us currency, or some other form of receipt.

It may be true that you don't "need" money to be happy, but why should you let your personal value determinations of what you "need" (which are probably based on fallacies and myths) stand in the way of your service to others, and stand in the way of your development as an amazing person who leaves an incredible legacy for posterity to follow? Do without the money if you don't value it, but never, ever limit your value creation because you don't care to enjoy the fruits of your labor.

John D. Rockefeller, Sr.
(1839–1937) revolutionized the petroleum industry and defined the structure of modern philanthropy. He became the world's richest man and first U.S. dollar billionaire and is often regarded as the richest person in history. His fortune was mainly used to create the modern systematic approach of targeted philanthropy with foundations that had a major effect on medicine, education, and scientific research.

Overcoming the Myth of Evil

Likewise, by breaking through the myth that money is the root of all evil, we can get over the "prosperity paralysis" that occurs when we think money is evil but want more of it; and we can start thinking creatively and overcome complacent attitudes in regard to money. When we realize that we, the individual people, determine what money does and what purposes it serves, we can focus less on the fruit and more on the root of prosperity: ourselves. We can correct our scarcity thinking, rid ourselves of shortsighted desires, and replace them with good, benevolent actions. Then we can use the money that results in the service of others.

God gave me money. I believe the power to make money is a gift from God . . . to be developed and used to the best of our ability for the good of mankind. Having been endowed with the gift I possess, I believe it is my duty to make money and still more money and to use the money I make for the good of my fellow man according to the dictates of my conscience.

—John D. Rockefeller

If we can break through the social programming that teaches us that there is something wrong, suspect, or even blatantly evil about money, we can then wholeheartedly embrace the fact that it's okay for us to prosper. We were born to prosper! Prosperity is the nature of the universe, and it is the nature of humankind. It is a destructive lie to think anything otherwise. Of course, prosperity comes with responsibilities attached, but that doesn't negate the fact that we were born to be prosperous.

If we can personally defeat the myth that money is the root of all evil in our own minds, we can then fully embrace prosperity. If we as individuals are good and productive, then our money will be used for good, productive purposes. By the same token, if we're destructive, we will use money in destructive ways. Production and destruction do not originate in money; they originate in people.

Nothing is good or bad, but thinking makes it so. —**William Shakespeare**

Prosperity Does Not Necessarily Equal Money

I believe that prosperity and happiness are synonymous. We become happy by serving others and overcoming our shortsighted and selfish desires, and the more we do so the more we prosper. Using this empowering definition of prosperity defeats the myth that money is the root of all evil, because we can't prosper unless we help people, and truly helping people is always good.

Can a person that has little material property be happy? Yes, assuming that she is living her Soul Purpose. Can a person with a relatively large amount of money be happy? Yes, again assuming that he is using his material wealth to find and live his Soul Purpose. Our happiness or misery doesn't depend on the amount of money we possess. There are miserable people with money just as there are miserable people without money. If we're not happy, then we're not prospering. Our happiness is the single best indicator of our level of abundance. Prosperity brings happiness and happiness brings prosperity. You can't have one without the other.

* * *

If we pursue our potential to be prosperous, we create maximum value for ourselves and for other people. Allowing the myth that money is power to influence whether and how we achieve wealth limits our potential in some of the most extreme ways. We must keep in mind that the opportunities for us to create value for others and ourselves are endless, and limited only by our misconceptions.

MYTH
6:

{
High Risk
=
High Returns
}

Over the years, an investor's financial objectives and tolerance for risk may change. An investor with a longer time horizon may be willing to take more risk for potentially greater reward than one with a shorter time horizon . . . All types of investments carry some risk, the possibility that an asset could lose some or all of its value . . . Generally, the riskier the investment, the greater its possible reward.

—Taken from a marketing piece of a leading financial institution

Myth:

Safe investments
yield low returns.
High returns
come from risky
investments.

Reality:

Investments
that support
or align with
one's Soul
Purpose have
less risk and
more return.

HIGH RISK = HIGH REWARD

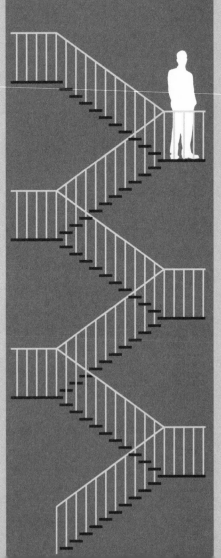

When you meet with a retirement planner, one of the first steps she will ask you to take is to fill out a risk tolerance questionnaire, asking questions about how long you have before you need the money, what you would do if the market declined, how much risk you are willing to take, if you can handle volatility, etc. The planner needs to know just how much risk you can handle, because according to many in the financial industry, the higher the risk you can handle, the greater returns you can get. In fact, it's drilled into us that we can *only* get high returns if we're willing to subject ourselves to exorbitant amounts of risk.

Let's just stop and think about this for a minute. They're essentially telling us that in order to increase our chance of winning, we must increase our chance of losing—and we're buying it! How does this make any logical sense whatsoever? Financial institutions have reduced financial success to a matter of gambling, pure and simple. Why do they want us to believe this? What's in it for them? And why do we swallow the bait and take on their risks, especially when the wealthy do the exact opposite of this? What is the truth of the matter? How can we get safe, sustainable, and high rates of return without high risk?

The philosophy that high returns necessitate high risk comes from relying on products, companies, and people other than ourselves. It's based on the crazy idea that to "invest" means that we throw money away in IRAs, 401(k)s, and mutual funds to buy shares in companies we know little or nothing about and have no hope of influencing. Then we hope and pray that we make money: this is what I call the "buy, hold, and pray" method of investing. By definition, it implies that individual investors can have little or no control over their rates of returns and the risk factors involved. It presupposes a dependence on the performance of everything *except* what the individual investor does.

But simply put, to increase our returns we must take responsibility for *increasing* our chances of winning and *decreasing* our chances of losing. This seems so logical, yet it is not what we are taught. The reality is that the best investments with the highest returns are, by their very nature, the lowest risk. The better we manage our risk, the higher our returns can rise. In this chapter, we will discuss how to increase your returns by mitigating your risk through wise investing. No responsible individual has to accept low returns as the price of "safety."

The Destructiveness of the Myth

This myth destroys our human life value and limits our potential because it leads us to avoid responsibility with our investment decisions. It keeps us from finding and living our Soul Purpose because it brings fear and worry into our lives. And it completely ignores the element of human life value because it's based on gambling and neglect.

If we buy into the faulty reasoning that to get high returns we must be willing to accept high risks, then we explain away our investment losses to the element of chance. We put money into high-risk investments (investments we don't understand and can't control), we lose money, and then blame our losses on everything but ourselves. We blame the market, crooked corporations, Wall Street, retirement planners, our human resources director who helped us to allocate our 401(k) funds—anyone and everyone other than ourselves, the so-called investors.

If we don't get upset over our losses, we treat them with an air of resignation, sighing, "That's just how it goes." But rarely do we stop and take a hard look in the mirror and personally accept responsibility for our losses. Furthermore, after we lose money, this ingrains the myth of high returns coming from high risks into our psyche that much deeper. We come to accept high risks as standard fare, something that we can't control that must simply be lived with and accepted, like bad cell phone reception or rush-hour traffic. Rarely do we stop and consider the fact that investing can and should be something we can control, and that there are numerous ways to mitigate risk while increasing our rates of returns.

There is a counterfeit of responsibility that many of us do engage in, however, and that is worry. We all want to make sure that we are fulfilling our obligations, paying our bills, making ends meet, and preparing for retirement. But every moment we spend worrying about these things is a moment that we are not thinking about producing value. Worry decreases our ability to fulfill our responsibilities. Wise solutions to problems are more difficult to find when worry over risky investments sucks our attention and drains our energy. To use a phrase from the movie *The Matrix*, risk is a "splinter in our minds" that keeps us awake at night and holds our focus on the very things that keep us from living our Soul Purpose.

Most of us don't care much for risk. We accept it because we lack the knowledge of how to mitigate it, but we don't like it. It exposes us to far more doubt, fear, and worry than we want in our lives. And as long as fear is our overriding emotion when we think of our finances and our futures, we will never live up to our potential. The essence of living Soul Purpose is replacing fear with faith and accountability. We can never become who we were born to become and make a significant impact on the world if we labor under false perceptions, constantly worried about our precious "nest egg," especially if we have exposed it to risky investments because we're not confident that we'll have enough money for retirement.

No man who continues to add something to the material, intellectual, and moral well-being of the place in which he lives is left long without proper reward. **—Booker T. Washington**

Most of us are gambling when we rely on financial myths to help us make decisions about our present and future. I define gambling as anything we do that involves a high degree of risk and uncertainty but is intended to bring a return. Gambling destroys human life value because it replaces certainty with uncertainty. It replaces deliberate value creation with the unprincipled "get-something-for-nothing" attitude. It replaces faith in principles with hope for luck.

Any time we want something for nothing we're not focused on how we can create value for and serve others. We're only in it for the short run, and for no one and nothing beyond ourselves. Gambling prevents us from serving people. The road to true wealth is honest value creation. If we're gambling, we're either not creating value or we don't know how we're creating value, and if we aren't focused on how we are creating value, we won't prosper. Some gamblers actually do make a lot of money, but they quickly consume it, and it consumes them. They don't value it because they didn't create value to receive it.

That which we obtain too cheaply we esteem too lightly.

—Thomas Paine

Love and service are the essence of living Soul Purpose. Gambling is at complete odds with both of these—by definition, it avoids the pursuit of serving others. It's all about what's in it for the person gambling, and no thought at all is given to what can be done to make another person's life better. For gamblers, money and material things are their primary concerns. They place more value in things than in people. When they see people, they see dollar signs, and are constantly scheming of ways that they can get money from people without creating value. As we stated earlier, *producers love people and use money; consumers love money and use people.*

Replacing High Risk with Wise Investing

If we behave like wise investors, prudent investments and prosperity will follow. Never accept the propaganda that you must be willing to stomach high risks in order to achieve high returns. The truth is exactly the opposite—the better you can manage your risks, the higher your returns will be. There is, in fact, a direct relationship between risk and reward, but that relationship is what banks and other financial institutions practice themselves, *not* what they want the public to believe. They teach the propaganda in order to transfer their risk to end consumers—the more risks consumers take on, the fewer the banks must take. It may be a brilliant strategy on their part, but it's a crippling mistake on our part to believe it. If we want to prosper, we must learn how to reduce our risks and simultaneously raise our returns. We do this by recognizing that we as individuals are our most important assets, and by making the time and effort to increase our human life value through education.

To overcome the myth that to enjoy high returns we must take high risks, we must become wise investors, which requires

> Understanding the relationship between risk and reward

> Investing, not gambling with, our assets

> Recognizing that no investment is inherently risky or secure; only people's approaches to investing are risky or secure

> Identifying sound value propositions

> Realizing that you and your Soul Purpose are your best investment

> Educating yourself and building knowledge to lessen your risk and improve your returns

> Having zero tolerance for losses that result in larger opportunity costs

> Investing to extend your Soul Purpose

> Mitigating risk by thinking and acting like a financial institution

For more information and examples, go to killingsacredcows.com

Risk and Reward

The truth about the relationship between risk and reward is precisely the opposite of what the myth would have us believe. Our rewards are tied directly to how well we *reduce* risk, because we're decreasing our potential losses. The most lucrative investments are the least risky, and conversely, the worst-performing investments are those with the highest risk.

What the myth in question proclaims is that, in order to increase our chance of winning, we must increase our chance of losing. Let's try applying this approach in other contexts. Does it increase your chance of convincing someone to marry you if you start doing everything you can to make her not want to be with you? Does it increase your chance of winning a marathon if you never train and eat junk food every day? Does it increase your chance of making your business succeed if you don't maintain and develop it properly? By never consulting a map and driving blindfolded, do you increase the likelihood of driving safely from San Francisco to New York?

If it's so clear how ridiculous these examples are, then why is this myth overlooked in the financial world? Why do we continue to believe that it makes any sense to increase our chance of winning by increasing our chance of losing? If we want to succeed financially, we must do everything possible to increase our chance of winning. Just as it makes sense to take the time and effort to create a lasting marriage, so too does it make sense to take the time to create optimum conditions for success in the financial world. Any time we increase our chance of winning we also decrease our chance of loss; in other words, we decrease our risk.

For example, if you're starting a business, here are a few questions and factors to consider to decrease your risk. How much do you know about the industry? What evidence do you have that there is actual demand for your product or service? How soon can you start generating revenues? Do you have enough experience to succeed? If not, are there ways for you to gain that experience, possibly by working for another company for a time? How much money does the business need to start? Do you have that amount in cash, or will you need to borrow it? If you borrow money, will that require you to give up a portion of control of the company? Are there seminars, books, or other outlets for you to deepen your knowledge of your business, and of business in general? Are there ways to collateralize your investment, or in other words, will you be buying hard assets that could be sold if the business is struggling? Are there partners you could team up with who could add needed knowledge and experience?

In short, the point is that in order to increase our chance of healthy rewards, we must do everything in our power to decrease our risk, or chance of loss.

Gamblers vs. Investors

I'm always amazed at whom the financial media labels an "investor." To *Money* magazine and similar publications, an investor is anyone who has money placed in the stock market. But for most of these so-called investors, money decisions amount to gambling. Too many people are throwing money into mutual funds and 401(k)s and patting themselves on the back that they've entered the ranks of the prestigious "investors." What they fail to realize is that they've been duped to taking on all the risk for their financial institutions.

The financial institutions, meanwhile, have wisely and deliberately transferred their risk to "investors." If you have $1 million in mutual funds, and lose $200,000, the mutual fund company is still going to get paid through their fund fees; they get paid by getting you to invest and taking a percentage of everything you invest, regardless of how their fund performs. They get paid a percentage of assets under management, so it is in their best interest to make their funds increase, but in a losing scenario the investors have everything to lose, while the institutions are still making money. In

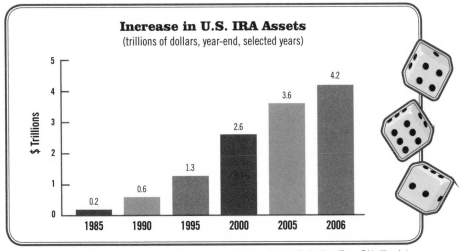

Increase in U.S. IRA Assets
(trillions of dollars, year-end, selected years)

Source: http://www.icifactbook.org/fb_sec7.html#market

other words, they figure out ways to profit regardless of circumstance and transfer the risk of loss to individual investors.

Incidentally, this is why financial institutions love 401(k)s so much: they get both individual investor money and government money, because money is contributed to 401(k)s on a pretax basis, meaning they have more assets under management than on funds with posttax contributions. In fact, such financial institutions have little concern over rising tax rates because the money they control and earn returns from is protected from tax rates until withdrawal. This is one reason why they have such a vested interest in convincing you to keep your money in your 401(k) for as long as possible.

Just placing money in the stock market does not automatically make people investors. In fact, the majority of Americans who have money in the stock market—mostly through 401(k)s and mutual funds—have no idea what their money is doing, no idea what kinds of returns to expect, little or no way of mitigating their risk, no way to control the returns of their "asset," a poor exit strategy (meaning that they don't know how they are going to eventually utilize their "investment" productively), no idea of how they are creating value in the world, and a mindset based on accumulation rather than utilization. Yet the financial pundits continue to refer to these people as "investors"—and the "investors" continue to feel good because they're doing what everyone else is doing and don't have to think much about it. They are not investors, they are gamblers.

Gambling for most of us doesn't come in the form of lottery tickets, slot machines, and roulette tables. Gambling usually comes in the form of following hot stock tips, jumping into soaring mutual funds, lending money to family or friends for unsubstantiated business ventures that promise high returns, or a spectacular real estate property or development. Gamblers are often driven by fear and greed. They jump into markets at their peak because of greed, then when the markets drop they jump out because of fear. They chase markets rather than *creating* markets.

We are gambling, not investing, unless we know exactly how we're creating value for others, how we can manage the growth and disposition of our investments, and how we can mitigate our risks to near zero. I define investors as those who possess the ability to contribute to and create favorable

THE MYTHS IN REALITY:
How Risky Is It for You?

My friend and client Nate learned how to mitigate his risk the hard way. Nate is an investor, with experience in everything from real estate to precious resources to intellectual property. However, the first time he got involved with development real estate, there were many aspects that he didn't understand, and he didn't fully utilize the expertise and knowledge of others to mitigate his risk. He put half a million dollars into a land development, but failed to properly use trust deeds, which allow investors to collateralize and place liens on properties. He trusted his partners, but wasn't doing everything possible to reduce the risks. When the investment failed, he lost every bit of his money and had no recourse to gain it back.

However, Nate quickly learned from that experience, studied trust deeds in detail and met with title companies to learn more. A couple of years later, he placed another half million into a land development that also eventually failed. But this time he was able to use his newfound knowledge to mitigate his risk. Although the development failed, he was able to regain all of his principal with a small profit because his firm had utilized appropriate trust deeds.

conditions to get healthy returns on their investments, mitigate their risk, have an exit strategy that allows them to profit under almost any circumstance, and practice the theories of utilization and velocity as opposed to accumulation. How many Americans with a 401(k) meet those criteria?

True investors don't invest in anything that they don't know how to make productive. Because they know how they're creating value with every one of their investments, they also know how they're going to make a profit, and so there's little risk involved. For example, I have very little knowledge of the oil business, and so I would never purchase a stock or otherwise invest in an oil company, unless I mitigated my risk by increasing my knowledge. Without knowing the mechanics of the business, I won't be able to do proper due diligence. I might be able to read a business plan, but won't have the experience to judge if something is amiss. On the other hand, a person with intimate knowledge of the oil business might be able to take a flawed business plan and/or company and apply her knowledge and expertise to fix the problems and make the company and investment profitable.

Generally speaking, we're not a nation of investors; we're a nation of gamblers led to believe by those with vested interests that we're investors. Not only do relatively few of us feel certain about our ability to control the outcomes of our investment decisions, but even those who feel certain are often deceived and experience rude awakenings.

Investments vs. Investors

One of the most important things to learn about investing is that *there are no inherently risky investments; there are only risky investors.* This is a critical point that cannot be stressed enough. No investments are inherently risky; it is people who make them safe or risky. It is people who make investments productive or not. Just as money and material things have no intrinsic value, neither do investments. Contrary to what the financial and accounting industries tell us, our real assets are not our material things; they are our own skills and abilities and our relationships with people. No house or mutual fund has ever paid anyone a dime. The only money you ever receive comes from other people. The value is not in the mutual funds; it is in people. People are behind every investment; understand the people and you understand the investment. For example, a corporation isn't an organic, self-sustaining entity; it's an institution comprised of people. The integrity, productivity, and effectiveness of the individuals, or lack thereof, determine whether or not it's a good company to invest in. Enron is a great example of a company that appeared to be doing well, but which certain people within virtually ruined.

Another aspect of this key point is that any investment may be either risky or secure depending upon the investor. What is risky to one person could be the safest investment in the world to another. Any time someone asks me questions such as, "Is real estate risky?" or "Isn't it risky to quit your job to start a business?" my answer is always "It depends." These things certainly can be risky—to some people—but they can also be very wise and safe for others.

I have friends who have done very well in real estate, and others who have lost big with real estate. The difference is that those who do well have more knowledge, they write better contracts, they know how to manage the properties, and they mitigate their risk by doing thorough due diligence on the people who use their properties. In addition, those who I've seen thrive with real estate happen to love working with real estate; it's in their Soul Purpose. The others have very little knowledge of real estate (most of the time they get into it only because they think it will make them a lot of money), they write poor contracts that open them to great risk, they manage their properties poorly, and often these properties are damaged by renters the owners never checked out properly. The risk or lack thereof isn't in the real estate; it's in the people who invest in it.

Understanding this concept helps us to develop what Robert Kiyosaki calls "financial intelligence," or the ability to train the mind to see investments that the eye cannot see.

Peter Drucker, one of the most influential and widely read modern thinkers, shares a story in his book *Innovation and Entrepreneurship* that drives the point home:

> A year or two ago I attended a university symposium on entrepreneurship at which a number of psychologists spoke. Although their papers disagreed on everything else, they all talked of an "entrepreneurial personality," which was characterized by a "propensity for risk-taking."

financial intelligence:
The ability to train the mind to see investments that the eye cannot see. Investing well is a product of knowledge, not of luck, of understanding what principles are operating behind the investment, and then creating ways to apply the principles in a productive manner.

A well-known and successful innovator and entrepreneur . . . was then asked to comment. He said: "I find myself baffled by your papers. I think I know as many successful innovators and entrepreneurs as anyone, beginning with myself. I have never come across an 'entrepreneurial personality.' The successful ones I know all have, however, one thing—and only one thing—in common: they are *not* 'risk-takers.' They try to define the risks they have to take and to minimize them as much as possible. Otherwise none of us could have succeeded."

Drucker adds, "The innovators I know are successful to the extent to which they define risks and confine them" (139). Social myths like those perpetuated by the psychologists in Drucker's story cause us to think that it's risky to invest in what we can personally control, as ironic as that sounds. But it's not risky to live Soul Purpose. When we truly understand the field we apply ourselves in, we know what risks we need to prepare for and how

Questions to Consider When Investing

> What are the underlying economic principles at play?

> Who is accountable if the investment goes into default?

> What is the value proposition of the investment?

> Is the investment a one-time-only opportunity, or does it offer ongoing systems and possibilities for wealth creation?

> Other than rate of return, for what reasons would you commit money to this investment?

> Does this investment create personal confidence or fear?

> Does the investment support, utilize, or contribute to your Soul Purpose?

Are you ready to invest? For information, go to killingsacredcows.com

to protect ourselves against them (and I will explain more about how we can protect ourselves from risk further on). Staying captive to destructive myths is perhaps the highest risk of all, and breaking through them is one of the safest things we can do.

So, name any single investment and pass it through the test. Are blue chip stocks risky? How about mutual funds? Are small company stocks risky? Is commercial real estate risky? Is hard money lending risky? The real question is, "Risky for whom?" The answer is always that it depends on the person engaging in the investment, and not on the investment in and of itself. If you know nothing about the process, then it's risky for *you*.

Value Proposition

One of the most important and effective ways to mitigate risk and identify a good investment is to understand the value proposition of any investment opportunity. Going through the process of identifying the value proposition of an investment is what I call the "Value Creation Evaluation." The value proposition is simply the identification of how one is creating value for others. Whenever you're approached with an investment opportunity, the very first question you should ask is, "What is the value proposition?" A value proposition should come in the form of a very clear and concise statement that explains how value is being created for whom and how it will be sustained.

All investment decisions ultimately come down to people, and there must be a basis of trust between investors. At times it may be difficult to intimately know the person with whom you are investing. Producers develop a healthy sense of discernment in their relationships with people. If a person cannot tell you quickly and clearly how, exactly, she is creating value with her idea, she may be hiding something. This is important; since all value comes down to people, even a good idea can fail because the wrong people are attached to it.

> . . . good deeds can be shortly stated, but where wrong is done a wealth of language is needed to veil its deformity.
> —**Thucydides, in *History of the Peloponnesian War***

You must understand the complexities of any investment in order to mitigate your risk, but the value proposition must be simple, clear, and easy to understand. It must make sense.

A perfect example of a lack of a good value proposition is a company called 12 Daily Pro, which recently collapsed. The company was promising returns of 12 percent daily, and many people were jumping on the bandwagon because of the high returns alone, without understanding the value proposition. 12 Daily Pro was an auto-surfing company, which is a way to make money by viewing websites that advertisers pay to be put in a rotation. You join a program, give the company money, and then view a certain number of ads (websites) per day. The problem with 12 Daily Pro was that it created a "revolutionary" way to go about this: a person could give the company money, and then do nothing but click on a program that would cycle through the ads; the person didn't even have to look at the ads. The individual subscribers were able to click a button, enabling the automatic ad cycle, walk away from their computer, and make a lot of money.

Where is the value proposition in that? How does that create value in the economy? Companies were paying 12 Daily Pro to advertise for them, but the subscribers weren't even viewing their ads! The company failed because it was not creating true value for others, and many people lost money because they failed to explore and recognize this fact.

Your primary concern with any investment—even more important than the potential returns—is the value proposition. If you know exactly how you are creating value in the marketplace, your chances of failure are significantly reduced. If you do good market research and know that people will value what you're doing, then you have an excellent chance of success, depending, of course, upon your skill in implementation. An example of a solid value proposition would be to identify a location where there is a high demand for apartment complexes, and then set out to build them. The exact value proposition would be something like, "Our town has a critical demand for apartment housing, as evidenced by . . . (insert market research). I am creating value for others by providing affordable housing."

Invest in Yourself

There's one critical litmus test to perform on yourself whenever you are wondering what to invest in. The answer is always—without exception—to invest in yourself. If your human life value were developed enough and if developing it was your first priority, you would never need to ask what to invest in, because your path would be clear. The best investment you can ever make is to increase your human life value, or your ability to utilize your knowledge and abilities to create value in the world. Turn inward for personal improvement and value will flow outward to those around you.

What this means is that you are your best investment. Not your 401(k), not your Roth IRA, not your mutual fund, not your house or your rental properties—YOU. If you want to mitigate your risk and enjoy high returns, then start doing everything you can to invest in yourself. Read books, go to school to gain new knowledge and learn new skills, attend educational seminars frequently, associate with people that you can learn from, take action and learn from your mistakes. Create a daily routine to increase your knowledge every day (visit killingsacredcows.com/action today for some powerful tools to help you achieve this). Experience new things. Find a mentor or pay an expert to shadow you and critique your habits and techniques. Whatever you do, always remember that the gap between your ears is the single most important place on which to focus your time and effort. Your 401(k) isn't going to make you rich—only you can do that. Diversification and dollar cost averaging can't decrease your risk automatically; you have to have the knowledge to make any strategy effective and productive.

The problem with viewing anything other than yourself as your best investment is that it's fundamentally based on the fallacy that material things have intrinsic value, and it presupposes a dependence upon external products and investments. Producers aren't dependent upon investments; they create investments. They are not subject to markets; they create markets.

Recall this every time you hear or read in a magazine that such-and-such is the best investment, whether it be real estate, a Roth IRA, or anything other than yourself. Don't buy into it. Realize that you are your best investment, and that your knowledge is far more important than the nature of any deal you enter into.

Increase Knowledge to Decrease Risk

The way to mitigate risk with any venture is through increasing knowledge and applying universal principles. Investing well is a product of knowledge, not of luck. Donald Trump and Robert Kiyosaki have become so wealthy because they know—through education and experience—how to make virtually any real estate deal work. They're not out there taking a lot of risks and crossing their fingers. They are certain that they can make a profit in any market, whether down or up, because of their knowledge. The more they learn, the less risk they are exposed to, and the less risk they face, the more money they make. This is true for any investor. The first step is to find what principles are operating behind the investment, and then create ways to apply the principles in a productive manner.

To illustrate this further, let's explore the Warren Buffett philosophy of investing. In his book *Warren Buffett Wealth,* Robert P. Miles explains Buffett's philosophy in detail. He writes that Warren's entire philosophy can be reduced to two rules: (1) Don't lose capital, (2) Don't forget rule number one. Buffett says that active investors should perform three activities every day: read, research, and think. The investment standards that Buffett adheres to are the following:

> Know what you own.

> Research before you buy.

> Own a business, not a stock.

> Make a total of only twenty lifetime investments.

> Make one decision to own a stock and be a long-term owner. (Buffett is speaking of something entirely different than the "long-haul" accumulation approach; he's teaching you to hold on to a stock because you've done proper research and you know it will increase in value. He's not talking about holding on and riding out downturns in the market because of fear of loss.)

The point is that Warren Buffett, the most successful stock market investor in history, never gambles. He never takes high risks. He mitigates his risk by investing in himself with knowledge and education. He doesn't follow the crowd or get caught up in "hot" trends.

Opportunity Costs

We are often told that the younger we are, the higher risks we can afford to take, because we have time to make up for any losses we experience. The advice is to "wait it out" any time we experience losses to our portfolio, because, say the so-called financial gurus, "the stock market has averaged 11 percent since 1926," or as I like to say, since 2000 B.C. (as if either of those dates have any real meaning to individual investors). The message is, don't think, don't do anything to manage your returns or mitigate your risks; just sit tight and wait for the long-term averages to settle the score. It sounds more like a strategy for staying alive when you're lost in the woods than a sound method to make money.

. . . research shows that stocks have been incredibly generous to the people who have bought them, returning an average of 11 percent a year—including both dividends and price increases—since 1926.
—James Glassman and Kevin Hassett

The fact is that the more money you lose when you're young (or at any time, for that matter), the more you expose yourself to opportunity costs. Opportunity costs are the often-unseen costs beyond an initial loss. For example, if a person has $10,000 in a mutual fund, and that mutual fund drops and leaves them with only $9,000, what we see is that they lost $1,000. What we might not see is what that $1,000 *could have been*, had it been more appropriately invested. Therefore, the younger a person is, the more chance he has of increasing his lost opportunity costs through poor investment decisions.

Lost opportunity costs are critical to take into account, whether a person is young or old. A loss is a loss, regardless of age, and every loss takes us further away from realizing our full potential and living Soul Purpose. What we must realize is that *every* decision we make in life involves opportunity costs—every decision, without exception, means sacrificing the potential benefits of the paths we don't take. Therefore, the goal isn't to eliminate opportunity costs; it's to recognize them, take them into account, and by so doing maximize the effectiveness and efficiency of each of our decisions.

If we allow ourselves to fall prey to the concept that in the long-term our returns will average out, we're allowing untold and unanalyzed opportunity costs to affect the course of our lives. The bottom line about averages is that they are completely useless in making investment decisions, particularly because they don't take lost opportunity costs into account. To individual investors it doesn't matter what the stock market has averaged for seventy-five years or more; the only thing that matters is how well their particular investments perform in the present. To say that the stock market has averaged 11 percent growth per year since 1929 does not automatically translate into similar returns on present investments, contrary to what retirement planners routinely imply.

Your returns are a product of you, not a product of averages. Anyone who relies heavily upon averages is subject to stagnation and loss. You can manage the production of an investment with minimal risk. But the more risk we take on, the more we expose ourselves to lost opportunity costs, and these are often so profound that they make all the difference between wealth and mediocrity.

Mitigating Risk

The most important way to overcome the myth of risk is to learn how to reduce your risk to near zero in any investment opportunity. This is accomplished through education, understanding your abilities and how to produce value with them, and aligning with principle instead of being driven by technique and strategy alone.

I've spent a lot of time discussing financial institutions, and I want to be clear that my intentions have not been to be overly critical of them. In fact, I believe that everyone must learn to think and act like a financial institution in order to prosper like one. I point out where financial institutions have vested interest, not so that we can condemn and reject them, but rather, so we can learn from them. I am not necessarily telling anyone to replace them; I just want us to understand why they succeed so that we can be educated and learn from them.

Banks, insurance companies, and other highly profitable financial institutions do everything in their power to reduce their risks to near zero. They do this by transferring their risk to people and companies who are willing to assume the risk. Insurance companies may be taking on risk that is transferred to them, but they do it in a way that pools resources and therefore mitigates risk.

Financial institutions examine, scrutinize, and analyze every investment decision they make to ascertain that they will profit. They never blindly throw money at opportunities and just hope that, because it's risky, they might make a lot of money. They know exactly *how* they're going to make money, and usually they know within a very close range *how much* money they will make.

Consider this for a moment: when was the last time you applied for a mortgage loan? Based on the process you went through, did the bank strike you as a high risk taker? How many ways and means did they use to mitigate their risk of loss? Some ways that banks mitigate risks when offering loans include the following:

> Check your credit

> Secure their investments with collateral

> Require a down payment

> Determine the interest rate

> Determine the payment

> Determine the time period for each investment

> Impose prepayment penalties

> Verify your work history and income

> Cover all of their investments with insurance (and interestingly enough, make you buy it)

> Have an exit strategy that allows them to be profitable, or to at least return their initial capital, in almost any scenario imaginable

> Transfer their risks to the borrower in any way possible

The funny thing is that all of this is minor compared to what they're really after. What they really want to know—beyond how they can make money in the property value world—is if your human life value is a worthy and profitable investment for them. They want to know you as a person, and to know how likely you are to pay them based on your capability and reputation. Think about it: Do they give loans to great properties, or to people with good credit scores?

Now consider this: How many owners of mutual fund shares utilize any of these risk management tools? When a person loses some or all of her money in a mutual fund, what is backing that loss in the form of collateral? In other words, if a bank lends money on a home and the homeowner defaults on his loan, the bank forecloses and resells the home—the home was their collateral. What collateral exists in typical stock market "investing"? How many so-called investors can control the interest rate, payment, down payment, and time period that affect their investments? Few, if any at all. How can this even remotely be classified as investing? The main selling point of mutual funds is that within each fund there are winners and losers (an outright admission that neither the investors nor the fund managers understand the risks associated), and so there is supposedly risk management through diversification. But this is another way of telling the "investor" that she doesn't have to think; she can just throw money in and good things will happen. This is clearly a philosophy for the ignorant.

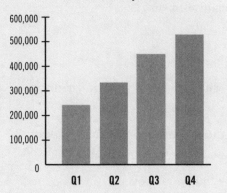

Breaking the Rules

In 2007 we witnessed firsthand what happens when banks don't follow their own rules. Lending institutions decreased their lending standards, only to have a large percentage of those high-risk loans default, driving many institutions out of business.

U.S. Household Properties with Foreclosure Activity (2007)

Source: RealtyTrac Press Releases of "U.S. Foreclosure Market Report"

The sad irony about this myth is that the institutions that want us to believe it teach it as a way to reduce their own risk; the more risk we take, the less risk they have. At its root, this myth is a way for knowledgeable people to transfer their risk. When it comes to risk, we have just two options: we can either retain it or transfer it. By falling prey to the myth that we're discussing in this chapter, we both retain our risk as well as take on even *more* risk that is transferred to us by financial institutions. Those who transfer risks enjoy high and consistent returns; those who retain them suffer from extreme fluctuations and ultimately lose money and opportunities. There is an entire industry that specializes in transferring risk, and this is insurance. This will be discussed in greater detail in the next chapter.

* * *

We destroy our human life value, limit our potential, and keep ourselves away from living Soul Purpose if we believe and practice the myth that high risks translate into high returns. It aids us in avoiding responsibility for our investment decisions; it fills our lives with unnecessary fear and worry that prevent us from thinking productively; it ignores the fact that the individual investor, not the particular product, is the factor that determines the outcome of investments; it leads us to gambling and away from actual investing; it guides us towards following the crowd and suffering from the herd mentality; and it prevents us from seeing lost opportunity costs. To the extent that we educate ourselves to take control over returns and mitigate risks, we will prosper. The lower our risks, the higher our rewards, and the more sustainable our long-term investments.

MYTH 7:

{ **Self-Insurance** }

The cheapest insurance is self-insurance.

—From *The Boglehead's Guide to Investing*
by Larimore, Lindauer, LeBoeuf, and Bogle

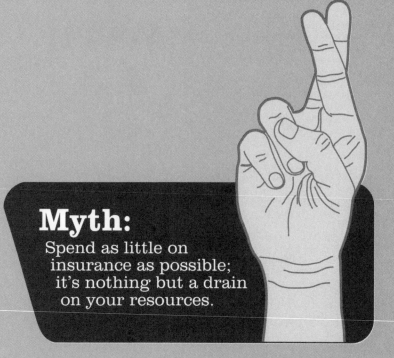

Myth:
Spend as little on
insurance as possible;
it's nothing but a drain
on your resources.

Reality:
Get the best
insurance you can.
It decreases your risk (when
understood) and increases
your productivity.

I n our current financial environment, we are taught that insurance is a necessary evil at best, and that the smartest route is to get minimum coverage with the lowest possible premium payments. The underlying goal is to accumulate enough assets to be "self-insured"—to have enough money in the bank to cover every eventuality that insurance would protect us from. Once we achieve this wonderful state, we can eliminate any insurance that we aren't required to carry by law and save the expense of premiums.

The fact is that there's no such thing as self-insurance; either you have insurance or you don't. You either have a way to transfer your risk of loss, or you retain that risk. Simply having a lot of money in no way protects you from the loss of that money. In fact, the more money and assets a person has, the more important insurance becomes to protect him from the risk of loss. Self-insurance is really *no* insurance and the unnecessary assumption of risk.

The best way to be financially free and to feel confident in utilizing our assets productively is to reduce the risk of losing those assets, including our own knowledge and abilities—our human life value. By transferring risk to those more efficiently equipped to manage it (insurance companies), we protect ourselves from unforeseen losses and release the fear that we might not have accumulated enough assets to cover the losses we might face. Proper insurance coverage can dramatically improve our ability to think abundantly and therefore be creative and productive. Ultimately, we are our greatest assets, and we had better protect ourselves fully.

The Destructive Nature of Self-Insurance

The myth of self-insurance is destructive to our human life value because it is based on price, ignoring the value insurance offers and the cost of not having it. The costs of not insuring assets go beyond simple loss—they include intangible effects such as the confidence, freedom, and peace of mind we lose when we assume all risk. The self-insurance theory is based on protecting income and material assets, as opposed to human life value. It teaches people to retain rather than transfer risk that could hamper their potential.

Most people either hate insurance or love it. If a person hates it, it is usually because she views it as nothing but a necessary expense. Those who love insurance understand how important it is to transfer risk; incidentally, the wealthy tend to fall into this category more so than any other group. But even the people who fall into the first group don't really hate insurance—they just hate paying for it. Many people view insurance as a necessary evil at best, and they fail to see the benefits that it provides. Under the myth of self-insurance, the focus is only on the price of insurance. Those who base decisions on price alone fall prey to anyone who is able to provide goods and services cheaper, with less quality, and with more risk. (This concept will be discussed more in chapter 9.)

 There is scarcely anything in the world that some man cannot make a little worse, and sell a little more cheaply. The person who buys on price alone is this man's lawful prey. —Attributed to **John Ruskin**

Those who teach that we should get as little insurance as possible in order to save money on premiums don't understand the relationship between risk and return. They don't understand the economic value of certainty. They don't know why it's so critical that we transfer as much risk from ourselves as possible, and that the more we do so, the more we prosper. Buying the minimum amount of insurance at the cheapest price does nothing but retain a lot of risk for the individual that could be transferred away with the proper type and amount of coverage.

The philosophy ignores critical unseen factors in our decisions regarding wealth. It is based on an ignorance of the fact that we are our own single most important investments, and the individual person must be protected above all other considerations, including income and material assets. It is our human life value that we must protect and that is in greatest danger of being lost when we don't adequately insure ourselves.

Believing that insurance is a necessary evil at best and operating with the philosophy that we should work toward being self-insured severely limits our capacity to produce and to live up to our potential by making us subject to fear, doubt, and worry. When we retain risk we're hesitant to act and to produce because we're not certain what the result will be. Hesitation means decreased productivity, and decreased productivity means that we're kept from living up to our full potential. *Every moment you spend worrying about loss is a moment that you are not thinking productively, and you can never recapture those lost moments.*

I've heard some say that they have no fear of loss, even though they have no insurance, but this is naïveté plain and simple, not abundance. It's a counterfeit of faith-based abundance because it completely ignores risk, rather than managing it. When we utilize insurance properly, we can have true peace of mind, actually protected from negative circumstances. We must never confuse peace of mind with laziness and naïveté—true peace of mind comes from applied knowledge, which requires effort and stewardship. The less worry we have in our lives, the more productive we will be, and insurance is one excellent way to legitimately eliminate worry.

15%
of motorists
are uninsured.

According to the 2006 study on uninsured motorists conducted by the nonprofit Insurance Research Council (IRC), the estimated percentage of these drivers is increasing overall. According to the study, the magnitude of the uninsured motorists' problem varies widely from state to state. In some states such as Mississippi, Alabama, and California, 25 percent or more of drivers are uninsured. The national average percentage of uninsured motorists is around 15 percent.

Replacing Self-Insurance
with Risk Transference

In my financial services practice I have a core philosophy regarding insurance: buy as much of it as possible, and get the best coverage available. To me, that's the only responsible answer to the question of how much insurance a person should have. What I'm really saying is that people should transfer as much risk as possible away from themselves. The less risk a person is exposed to, the more wealth she can create.

Producers love insurance because they focus less on the price of premiums and more on the cost of not being properly protected. They ensure that their human life value is viable and productive in any situation that they can control, whether they are sick, disabled, or dead. They are able to see the intangible benefits of insurance beyond the tangible premiums and paid claims. By ridding themselves of fear of loss, they ensure that they maintain a productive mindset. And producers act as good stewards of their responsibilities. They understand that the first step of being a wise steward is ensuring that their current stewardships are protected before they concern themselves with acquiring more.

When we understand what insurance can provide, we want the best, most durable, most certain policy that money can buy. We know that there is never a time when we will want to do without insurance. We realize that self-insurance is a waste of human life value because insurance companies are so much more efficient at managing risk than we are as individuals.

We overcome the destructive myth of the benefits of self-insurance by realizing the following:

> Being self-insured requires allowing vast resources to sit stagnant.

> The best way to reduce our insurance expenses is to get as much insurance as possible.

> Insurance coverage must be designed to protect human life value, not just property value.

> Insurance coverage increases our financial freedom and productivity, regardless of our age or financial situation.

> The more assets a person has, the more insurance he should have.

As I'll demonstrate throughout the rest of the chapter, more or better insurance is preferable to less insurance in terms of transferring risk and improving our chances of financial freedom and productivity.

Self-Insurance Equals Stagnant Assets

If a person is going to be truly "self-insured," she must keep on hand a cash amount at least equal to all of her other assets. Of course, what this means is that she's not insured, because she has no way of indemnifying the loss of the cash should she use it to cover other losses.

Let's suppose a person has a house with a market value of $1 million, and also has $1 million in a bank account. She thinks that she is "self-insured," at least for the value of her house. But what's more expensive—two thousand dollars per year for a homeowner's insurance policy, or not being able to use that $1 million in cash, because it must be available to indemnify the possible loss of her home?

Insurance companies work by pooling risk, and therefore reducing the cost of indemnifying risk for individual policy holders. They figure out the probability of any given disaster and charge a bit more per year to protect against it than the likelihood of it occurring in that year. Since they have many, diverse customers, there is an extremely small chance that all the disasters they insure against will occur in any given time frame, thus they don't need to keep the full value of each policy they sell on hand any more than banks need to keep the balances of all savings

Be careful to read all policies closely. Disability policies in particular have many elements that affect the payout dramatically: adjustments for inflation, coverage if you can't work in your chosen profession versus if you can't work at all, changes in the benefits over time, the percentage of your previous income that it pays, etc.

indemnify:

1. To compensate for damage or loss sustained, expense incurred, etc.

2. To guard or secure against anticipated loss; give security against future damage or liability.

—Source: *Random House Unabridged Dictionary* 2006

accounts in the vault at once. The scale of their operation means that the same million dollars will cover the possible loss of several houses of that caliber without the owners tying up their resources or the company losing money. Everyone comes out ahead, whether anything happens to the house or not.

Are you better at providing insurance than the insurance companies? Can you provide equal benefits at a comparable price? If so, then you should become an insurance company for more clients than just yourself. But if you cannot provide insurance as efficiently as an insurance company, then economically it is much more productive to use professionals.

Insurance gives us a permission slip to utilize all of our other assets. It unlocks the productive potential of our assets because, when insured properly, we are free to utilize them without fear of loss. We have but two choices when it comes to risk—retain it or transfer as much of it as possible. When people advocate self-insurance, what they are in effect saying is that people should retain their risk. No matter how many assets a person has, retained risk is retained risk, and it provides no option to replace lost value and production.

Think of it this way: for every ten dollars of insurance you buy, what does it cost for the insurance coverage? Less than ten dollars, right? But what about self-insurance? If you're self-insured, it always costs more than ten dollars because you don't have any way to replace the money you will use to cover losses, and you must reject any opportunity to use that money in more productive ways than as "self-insurance."

If I own a 6,000-square-foot home and I also have $5 million in assets but no insurance coverage, if my home burns down I may be able to use my assets to replace the home. But what replaces the money I use to rebuild? Nothing—I simply no longer have the assets I had before. This is why self-insurance is so completely ridiculous—it only means NO insurance. A person either has a way to replace lost production, or he doesn't. Having a lot of money to replace things does nothing to transfer your risk. It may give you a better ability to rebound from disasters than most people have, but it can never fully replace what is lost. Only the transference of risk through insurance coverage can do that.

Prosperity is not a do-it-yourself game. We all have different abilities and different Soul Purposes. Unless your Soul Purpose is to be an insurance company, why waste time, energy, and worry thinking of ways to be self-insured—especially when that is impossible anyway? How can you turn protection into production? Proper protection gives you the ability to focus on things that actually matter in your life because of the certainty that it provides. When understood correctly, the better your protection, the greater your productive capability and the lower your real cost of insuring yourself against potential losses.

Understanding the power and principles of using insurance to manage risk comes before trying to figure out what type and what amount one should secure. But some types to investigate include car, homeowner's, renter's, long-term disability, medical, life, and liability (beyond auto).

The Best Way to Reduce Insurance Expenses

Producers understand that the best way to reduce their insurance expense is to buy as much of it as possible, because it saves them money in the macro sense, over the course of their lives. Those who retain risk in the name of reducing expenses inevitably and ironically end up paying much more than the wise producers who transfer their risk.

Consider the following example. Two families live on the same street. Their homes, ages, income, and assets are all the same. The only difference is that Family A has their home paid off and carries no homeowner's insurance, and Family B has a mortgage and carries homeowner's insurance. Both homes burn down at the same time. Family B indemnified the loss through insurance and so their assets are unaffected, while Family A is using assets out of their own pocket to replace the damage and likely must take out another mortgage in order to rebuild their home. The financial freedom and productivity of Family A has been reduced dramatically. Even though they paid less in premiums, in the long run, Family A paid far more than Family B because they retained, rather than transferred, their risk.

This example compared having insurance to not having insurance. But what about the expense associated with different levels of the same type of insurance? For instance, a common debate regarding life insurance within the financial services industry is between the strategy of buying term life insurance to save money on premiums, money that supposedly is invested in other productive pursuits, and the strategy of buying permanent life insurance (sometimes called whole life insurance). Term insurance is precisely what the name implies—life insurance that provides a death benefit for a certain period of time. Permanent life insurance policies are designed to provide coverage for the duration of a person's lifetime, not a specified term only. They carry a cash value that accrues with premiums paid, and provide many benefits that a policyholder has access to while he is living, such as tax protection and waiver of premium riders/disability protection, among others. Unlike permanent life insurance, term carries no cash value within the policy and has no tangible living benefits.

Many financial strategists teach BTID: Buy Term (insurance) and Invest the Difference (in premium prices) because the premiums on term insurance are much cheaper than permanent policy premiums, at least in the early years. For example, a thirty-year-old male could get a $1 million term death benefit for thirty years for $750 per year ($63/month), if not less. That same person might pay as much as $9,000 per year ($750/month) with a permanent policy.

Many of you may be thinking, "There's no way I'd pay that kind of money just for life insurance." But the actual cost of term and permanent life insurance isn't quite that simple. One major problem with term is that it's based on the assumption that coverage will be dropped after the term expires. In fact, insurance companies pay benefits on only about 1 percent of term life insurance policies. The assumption that the policyholder will drop coverage is based on the idea that a person's assets will build over time; their income after retirement will decrease (requiring less protection); and their responsibilities to others (family) will decrease, so the need for life insurance is diminished. Like other financial myths, though, these assumptions don't take a variety of other factors into account, factors that we'll address throughout the rest of this chapter. For now, let's assume the opposite: our original buyer decides to continue coverage for his entire life.

The cost of term insurance rises dramatically over time, whereas the cost of insurance within a permanent policy remains the same—or even decreases in some cases—over a person's lifetime. The thirty-year-old who buys the term policy will find that, after the term expires, the same company's rates can be more than ten times the original premium. Term policies become prohibitively expensive over a person's lifetime.

For example, with one company I viewed, a thirty-year-old male who buys a convertible, thirty-year term policy with a death benefit of $1 million and an annual premium of $1,320 will find that the premium increases to $46,490 when the term expires. By age 74, this person has paid $767,930 in premiums for his $1 million death benefit, and by age 84 he has paid $2.78 million for his $1 million death benefit.

During the retirement years, people will find that with term insurance their premium payments exceed the death benefit, which nullifies the purpose of carrying the coverage. When a person looks beyond the cost in the early years of term policies, they find that term is actually the most expensive insurance on the market when considered over a person's entire lifetime. Even if only the cost of the insurance during the term of coverage is examined, term life only pays out if one dies.

If a person buys a thirty-year term policy for $750/year and then drops it after the term, they will have spent $22,500 on premiums, which is money lost that can never be recovered. Not only are the premium dollars lost, but so is what that $22,500 *could have been* had it been invested instead—the lost opportunity costs. Worse than this, the lost opportunity cost also includes the amount of the death benefit that is lost (remember that only 1 percent of term life policies are ever paid out), and the fact that the person may not be able to qualify for insurance coverage again when the current term runs out, which is incalculable.

We get what we pay for, and term insurance is cheap in early years for a reason—it provides very little value, and the value that it does provide is almost guaranteed to go away before it is even used. For people who truly don't have the money to buy permanent life insurance, term is better than remaining uninsured, but it's a shortsighted and ultimately unproductive alternative.

Permanent life insurance, on the other hand, has a higher price in the short term because it offers much greater value in the long-term. The common response to this is that through a term policy a person can save money and create more assets by taking the money that he would have spent on a permanent policy and investing it in things that have higher rates of return than a person can find inside of a permanent policy. The internal rate of return in a permanent policy is the interest rate on the cash value that is guaranteed by the life insurance company, a cash value that builds as premiums are paid, in addition to any dividends the company may pay. The guaranteed interest rate in a permanent life insurance policy, for example, might be up to about 5 percent. So, says the term life camp, why not take all of that premium money and put it into real estate or a mutual fund and earn 10–12 percent instead?

What this camp ignores is that permanent life insurance policies, aside from offering guaranteed death benefits, also provide living benefits beyond the internal rate of return, which gives them infinite value over term policies, which have no living benefits. These living benefits include

> Tax protection (the cash value grows tax-deferred, and in some cases tax-free with some strategies),

> Waiver of premium riders/disability protection (if a person is disabled throughout the term of a policy, this rider will pay for the policy so the policyholder doesn't have to continue making premium payments during her period of disability),

> Liability protection (in most states, if a policyholder is sued, plaintiffs cannot access life insurance cash value),

> The ability to utilize the cash value (cash values can be accessed through policy loans or dividend withdrawals and used to make other investments),

> And the freedom to leverage assets without worrying about lost principal (if I have $1 million in assets, $1 million in death benefit, and $1 million in cash value, I can spend down my assets, keep my cash value, and keep my death benefit without adverse affects to my retirement years or my heirs).

Permanent policies also provide the economic value of certainty; you can be certain that permanent policies will be there to protect your human life value the day you die.

The BTID advocates base every assumption and every comparison on a person leaving their cash value inside the permanent policy. They gloss over the fact that the cash value is available to the policyholder to be used for things outside of the policy, whereas no premiums on term policies are available for use. For example, suppose I have $30,000 in the cash value of my life insurance policy. I find a real estate property that I can purchase for $150,000 and sell immediately for $175,000, but it requires a $20,000 down payment. I can assess my life insurance cash value through a policy loan, buy and sell the property, and pay back the loan to my life insurance policy.

Basing insurance decisions on premiums and the internal rate of return is a classic case of price versus cost and value. Most planners and policyholders see the price of permanent insurance and ignore the cost of not mitigating their risk and creating as much certainty in their lives as possible. Permanent life insurance may not give a person the highest internal rate of return, but its certainty and its other living benefits give a person the ability to be infinitely more productive in all other areas of life.

Life insurance must not be regarded as an expense to be grudgingly borne. To the thoughtful policyholder its creative aspects, by way of personal initiative and productiveness, much more than counterbalance the cost involved.

—**Solomon Huebner** in *Economics of Life Insurance*

A useful analogy is to consider complimentary information given out by a company. The internal rate of return for the information is 100 percent negative, because the information is given out freely. But it's easy to see how ridiculous it would be to base the decision of distributing company information solely on its internal rate of return, because the incalculable external rate of return—the added branding effects and goodwill afforded to the company—more than justifies the lost return internally. To only consider what the information costs on a monthly basis is to completely ignore all of the benefits that the information provides. Such is the case with life insurance.

A person who understands the purpose of insurance wants the best policy that money can buy, one that provides the most certainty by transferring as much risk away from the individual as possible. The strategy of BTID is fundamentally built upon the misguided belief that insurance is a necessary evil, and that we should find the cheapest method of insurance possible. But producers base their decisions on macroeconomic cost, not microeconomic price. They want a policy that provides them with the most benefits in a holistic sense, beyond mere internal rate of return alone. They want a policy that will make them more effective with the creation and utilization of every other asset inside their plan, which can only be achieved through living benefits provided by permanent policies.

Human Life Value Protection

People produce value, and any time they become sick, disabled, or die, their ability to produce is limited or can even stop completely. Producers don't insure houses and cars because the houses and cars have value; they insure their human life value as it relates to their ability to produce value with material things. And through the proper use of insurance we can ensure that we can continue producing value even in the event that the worst case scenario comes true.

The point of protecting property value is to ensure that we can utilize our human life value as completely and effectively as possible. It's so we can live life focusing on and planning for production instead of recovery from property value losses. Even though some insurance appears to protect property

The Advantage of Disability Insurance

Financial implications for a disability are typically more disastrous than those for a premature death. When someone dies, their expenses go with them, but for the disabled the expenses typically increase.

Meanwhile, Social Security disability is one of the most difficult benefits to qualify for. "You have to be completely disabled for at least a year, with no hope of recovery," Steve Crawford, Guardian Disability, said. "Even when you meet those requirements, you're unlikely to receive more than $2,000 a month." When you're using your human life value to produce the maximum amount of value you can, disability is the hardest blow next to death—unless you mitigate your risk to protect yourself.

Source: money.cnn.com/2002/03/25/pf/insurance/q_disability/index.htm

value, ultimately the purpose of all insurance is (or should be) to protect our human life value and our ability to create value.

Misguided retirement planners also teach that the purpose of insurance is to replace income; therefore, everyone should buy term insurance, and then drop it as soon as their income stops and they retire. But just because a person retires doesn't mean that she ceases to have human life value. A person either wants insurance or she doesn't, or in other words, she either wants to transfer her risk of loss or she doesn't. If she wants insurance, it doesn't make any sense that there would come a time when she wouldn't want it. It only makes sense when we think that insurance is to protect income and property values, as opposed to human life value.

When we understand the true power of insurance, we realize that there should never be a time in our lives when we would have a reason to drop insurance coverage. Insurance does much more than replace our income to our spouse and children if we die; it provides a way for us to create a legacy of our lives and ensure that we can continue creating value in the world, even if we are sick, disabled, or dead.

When we experience the epiphany that the purpose of securing insurance is to protect our human life value and not our possessions, we realize that there will never be a time when we will not have human life value. So we will never engage in strategies that are designed to drop our coverage at a later date. We will want the best, most certain, most valuable, and most durable insurance coverage that money can buy.

Not only is proper insurance protection an excellent way to increase our prosperity, but it's also a way to fulfill our responsibilities as wise stewards. Ignoring insurance protection is not only unwise as relates to our wealth, but it's also irresponsible. What is the difference between a man who abandons his family in the middle of the night and a man who dies without life insurance protection? Does the family not experience the same economic impact in both scenarios?

Producers understand that not having proper insurance coverage is irresponsible at the least, and immoral at the worst. We have been given stewardship over our human life value, our families, our material possessions, and all of the people that we have the ability to impact. Utilizing insurance properly is one of the most important ways that we can fulfill, protect, and increase the value we deliver to others in any possible case. A person who purposely does not use insurance protection is an unwise steward at best.

Do you want your family to live in the same, better, or worse conditions if you die, are sued, or become disabled? Have you ever known a widow or widower who felt like she was overpaid by insurance when she lost her spouse? It is

Disability vs. Life Insurance

Despite advancements in medical technology, disability rates have climbed due to the increased numbers of survivors who suffer poor health.

* **48%** of mortgage foreclosures are caused by disability

* **3%** of mortgage foreclosures are caused by death

Source: Disability Insurance Resource Center, 2008

* Men have a **43%** chance of becoming seriously disabled during their working years

* Women have a **54%** chance of becoming seriously disabled during their working years

Source: *Why Disability* by National Underwriter

* At age 42, it is **4 times** more likely that you will become seriously disabled than that you will die during your working years.

Source: *Why Disability* by National Underwriter

only through insurance that we can ensure that our stewardships will be taken care of if we lose any level of ability to provide for them. If you have no other reason, love insurance because you love your family, and you want to ensure that they are always provided for despite any catastrophe.

As we explained in the last chapter, *you* are your best investment. If you want to protect your investments, or provide a way to indemnify them in the case of loss, then why would you ever consider not protecting your most critical investment, and your only true asset? Why are you concerned about insuring your home, but not the source of your home's value?

Understanding that its purpose is to protect human life value rather than things external to people (such as houses, cars, boats, etc.) sheds an entirely different light on insurance. We begin to see the profound nature of our responsibilities, and with that deeper understanding comes increased productivity. When we begin to get a sense of our stewardship and responsibility to produce, we then start thinking of how we can continue producing in the worst possible scenarios.

Insurance Supports Freedom and Productivity

Let's assume for a moment that you live your entire life paying the maximum amount of insurance premiums; you never experience any loss (your eventual death set aside for the moment); and therefore your insurance never pays a claim. How can insurance create value in your life, if you never file a claim? If nothing happens to trigger a payout, are all of your paid premiums just dollars lost?

Many people focus on low deductibles when purchasing insurance, but then only file claims that are well above their deductible and don't file claims that are smaller because they are trying to keep their premiums low. If you aren't going to file claims below or at the lower deductible, save yourself some money and get a higher deductible.

The consumer mindset prevents most people from seeing that ultimately any insurance coverage is paradigm insurance. How much peace of mind can you have when you drive a car with no insurance? When you know you are at great risk with no protection, will not fear of loss be a constant companion, that prevents you from thinking productively? If you cancel your home insurance and are constantly worried about losing your home, you're taking time away from thinking about the things that really matter.

Insurance goes so much deeper than people in the Consumer Condition realize. It is not just dollars lost if you pay into a policy and never receive money through a claim; it is a way for you to free your mind, stay in the proper paradigm, and to minimize the fear of loss.

Certain types of insurance may be used to leverage into other investments, but what most people fail to consider is that insurance allows us to invest even if we never use the actual insurance as a specific investment tool.

For example, if a person owns a $1 million home and has no homeowner's insurance, and he also has $1 million cash, where can he invest his cash in such a way as to keep his home protected? According to most people's perceptions, the safest place to put it is in a bank account, because otherwise he will constantly have the fear of loss. Nobody who understands risk will expose principal to loss without the proper protection. So this person may be saving $2,000 per year on the price of insurance premiums, but at what cost? If he simply had insurance, he could invest without the fear of lost principal constantly haunting him. Assuming he could get just 10 percent per year on that money in an investment vehicle other than a bank account, he's losing $98,000 per year in potential cash flow.

Because consumers think that dollars and material things have power, they love to deal with tangibles that they can touch, smell, taste, and see. But producers understand the deeper intangibles underlying all material things. Can we really place a value on an investment that helps us to stay in the proper paradigm and increases our ability to produce?

Any worthwhile investment should help to keep you in abundance, and lower returns are acceptable if the particular investment keeps your mind in abundance. In other words, it is your personal productivity that is the highest return you can ever receive. Remember, too, the principle of using the same investment to serve several different purposes. If your investment

What Should I Insure?

The following questions can be used to perform a comprehensive assessment of risks you face in life, and how those risks can be effectively mitigated through the purchase of appropriate insurance products. First, identify a specific risk (such as the risk of a car accident, a debilitating disease, a natural disaster, or death), and then answer each of the questions for that risk. If you do not know the answer to specific questions, visit killingsacredcows.com for further information on insurance protection.

1. If you retain this risk, how will that impact you?

2. Is there ever a time you would not want to transfer this risk?

3. Why do you have insurance against this risk?

4. If you do not insure against this risk, what impact does that have on your peace of mind?

5. Does this risk threaten your property value, or your human life value? Might it threaten both? How would insuring against this risk protect your property value, human life value, or both?

6. Is the amount of insurance you need the same as the amount you want?

7. In the event that you need to make a claim, is the coverage you've chosen going to accomplish the purpose of owning the insurance in the first place?

8. If you knew the event you're insuring against would occur tomorrow, how much insurance would you get today?

9. If you experienced this event, would you want your family to live the same lifestyle, a better lifestyle, or a worse lifestyle economically?

10. Do you know how much insurance a company would extend to you to cover this risk? If there were no costs to the insurance, how much would you acquire?

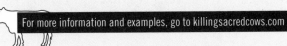
For more information and examples, go to killingsacredcows.com

in an insurance policy keeps you thinking productively, indemnifies you against loss, and provides a return on your investment, you have increased the productivity of your assets. Consumers ignore the macroeconomic picture, of which insurance is a key component, by reducing insurance to chase a perceived microeconomic rate of return. They may have one piece of their financial puzzle functioning well, but at the expense of their big-picture prosperity.

My colleague, Les McGuire, once wrote an article titled "The Economic Value of Certainty," in which he explores the importance of transferring risk to our ability to be financially free and productive:

> Many at-risk products or investments, such as Variable Universal Life, mutual funds, IRAs or 401(k)s, may work out great in hindsight, but people will not feel safe making significant, bold choices in other areas of their lives based on the expected performance of these assets because there is little certainty ahead of time. They will be in a cautious, wait-and-see mode through most of their lives . . .
>
> The real economic value of [permanent life insurance] is not in the rate of return on the cash value, nor in the ability to borrow at low rates, nor in the estate created for charity or heirs upon death, nor in the tax treatment of the policy. Rather it lies within the world of economic possibility that opens up to the insured during his own lifetime because of the certainty he now has because of the contract guarantees and the resulting choices he can now make in other areas of life without fear, worry, or doubt. The insured quite literally becomes the beneficiary of his own life insurance policy during his own lifetime, perhaps many times over. How do you quantify the economic value of that freedom, or in other words, the macro-economic rate of return on a [permanent life insurance] policy? I believe it is impossible.

Transferring risk opens up possibilities that are unavailable to us when we retain them. When we create certainty in our lives, we act much differently than we do when we're operating in a risky environment. Certainty dramatically increases our productivity.

THE MYTHS IN REALITY:
Windows to a New Life

My coauthor, Stephen Palmer, was able to propel himself from an employee into the world of entrepreneurship because he was able to create certainty through research and action. At age twenty-seven, Stephen was tired of being an employee, but he needed the certainty of income to provide for his family. He was in college and worried that starting a business was risky, and that it would jeopardize his school pursuits and family responsibilities. But when his brother started cleaning windows on the side and making great money doing it, Stephen saw an opportunity.

He started working with his brother, and they quickly found that there was a ready demand for their services. Although his brother quit soon after, Stephen kept at it, and soon was making more money cleaning windows than he was at his regular job. He found that he could literally go out any day of the week—without any previous jobs scheduled—and make several hundred dollars just by knocking on doors and offering his services.

Because he had certainty, a sure knowledge that he could replace the income from his job with no risk at all, he quit his job and became an entrepreneur. The shift from employee to business owner soon revealed to Stephen some things about himself that he never knew before. He discovered that he had a gift for creating and implementing systems. He discovered a love for entrepreneurship. He cherished the newfound control he had over his life and his finances. Stephen didn't necessarily love window cleaning, but he loved the process of creating something that could outlast and grow beyond his individual efforts. He developed systems, wrote an operations manual, and less than two years later he was able to sell the business for a healthy profit and move on to bigger and better things.

Stephen has been an entrepreneur ever since, and his entire life and perspective on himself and life changed fundamentally and dramatically. He awakened to a whole new world of possibility and unleashed massive amounts of potential that previously had lain dormant. He thought differently and viewed and interacted with the world with more confidence, courage, and hope. If he hadn't capitalized on the opportunity, it's unlikely that we would have ever met and been able to team up on this book.

All of this happened because Stephen was able to create certainty where uncertainty, doubt, and worry existed. Through research, action, and persistence, he realized that it really wasn't risky to quit his job to pursue something that actually made him more money and with more certainty than he had ever had before.

Many people focus on which doctors are available under their medical insurance while ignoring the lifetime maximum benefit of the insurance. This should be a primary consideration, because if your lifetime max is low, it can be eliminated by a single catastrophic event, and then you would be unprotected.

The more certainty we can create in our lives, the more likely we will be to produce and to take on projects that we otherwise wouldn't even consider. Conversely, the less certainty in our lives, the more fear—and the more fear, the less productivity.

One critical way to remove fear and to increase certainty in our life is to transfer our risks through the proper use of insurance.

More Assets = More Demand/ Opportunity for Protection

The myth of self-insurance is based on the false idea that we can (and should) drop our insurance coverage as soon as we have "enough" assets and accumulated money. The question I have is, how much in accumulated assets is considered enough: $1 million? $5 million? What is it that determines *enough*? What if I accumulate $5 million, drop all insurance coverage, then get diagnosed with a terminal illness and spend my entire fortune on treatment? Would I think that I had enough then? Insurance protection should be designed to take care of the worst-case scenario.

The fact is that the more assets a person creates, the more they should want to have insurance to protect them. The idea that there will come a time in your life when you will not need insurance is a crippling fallacy that is diametrically opposed to the creed of producers: to produce value in any given situation. To return to the life insurance example, with a term policy, the time when you can use insurance the most—because you have the highest risk of potential lost production—is precisely the time when you will lose your insurance coverage.

The more assets people have, the more ability they have to produce, and the more ability they have to produce, the more insurance coverage it is better to have, because the more they are exposed to financial loss. The truth is exactly opposite to what is taught in the financial industry. Let me repeat: The more assets you have, the more insurance you should have because the more risk you have of lost production.

If I live in a 1,500-square-foot home and it burns down, it represents a significant loss of human life value in the form of thought, energy, and labor. Yet if I own a 6,000-square-foot home and it burns down, that loss is quadrupled. We can either provide a way to indemnify or replace our loss by transferring our risk, or we can retain our risk.

Contrary to the theory of self-insurance, the more assets a person has, the more there is to protect with insurance. To quote Les McGuire again, "Producers are committed to creating maximum value in all situations, regardless of circumstance, and they manage their risk to near zero. Consumers think that risk means losing money; producers know that risk refers to lost production, whether created in the past or yet to be created in the future. Producers reduce both risks to near zero." The most important way that producers mitigate the risk of lost production is through insurance, properly understood and wisely utilized.

* * *

Any person who is a producer, loves life, and understands freedom should do everything in her power to leave a legacy and to ensure that she can produce value in any given situation, whether she is sick, disabled, or dead. The proper use of insurance helps producers mitigate the risks of life to their productivity to near zero. They understand that production without protection is irresponsible at the best and destructive at the worst. Producers ensure that no matter what happens, they will find ways to produce value from the situation, and because of this, producers love insurance.

MYTH 8:

{ **Avoid Debt Like the Plague** }

The concept of debt is not difficult to understand. You need something, you borrow it and you're in debt to the lender. When you give it back you're out of debt.

—From www.ihatedebt.com

Myth:
Debt is bad,
dangerous,
and scary.
Keep out of it.

Reality:
Understand the
difference between
debt and liabilities
and wisely incur
and leverage the
right liabilities
to increase your
prosperity.

We're taught by financial pundits to avoid debt like the plague, and on the surface, I agree that debt should be avoided. The problem with this pronouncement is the common perception of debt. Most of us don't understand debt in the true accounting sense, instead relying on the common usage of the word: anything that is owed to somebody else. But if we don't understand exactly what debt is, how can we avoid it effectively?

To create a foundation for this chapter, let me first explain a critical point. Debt is not the same thing as having liabilities. A liability is something that is an expense in our life, including many of the things we think of as debts, such as mortgages, car loans, small-business loans, and so on. The only time we are in debt, in the true accounting sense, is when our liabilities are greater than our assets, those things that provide income or potential cash flow in our lives.

If we perceive debt to mean having liabilities, and we hate, fear, and want to avoid debt, how can we function financially? How is it really possible to eliminate liabilities from our lives and be productive? I argue that it is not, and this is where the concept of avoiding debt goes awry. We *do* want to avoid true debt (having more liabilities than assets), but we *don't* want to avoid incurring liabilities (owing something to someone else) that can be beneficial to our productivity, value creation, and prosperity. In fact, in many instances, the way to increase our prosperity and wealth is to increase—not decrease—our liabilities.

The name of the game of wealth is not to focus on ridding our lives of as many liabilities as possible. Rather, it's to identify which liabilities are consumptive (take more value from our lives than they put into it) and which are productive (provide more value to our lives than they take from it), and then focus on increasing our productive liabilities. By definition, a productive liability always creates a corresponding asset—an asset that we never would have had access to had we not incurred the liability. The converse is also true— every asset comes with a corresponding liability, at least in some form.

In this chapter we will challenge the prevailing perception of debt and replace it with a more accurate definition, exploring the relationships between assets and liabilities and debt and equity. We will talk about why false perceptions of debt are destructive to human life value. Furthermore, we will explain why productive liabilities lead to greater assets. When we understand exactly what debt is, we'll understand why and how it can be avoided and how our current perceptions lead us down the wrong financial path.

The Destructive Nature of Avoiding Liabilities

The fallacious advice to avoid all liabilities (what most people commonly and mistakenly refer to as "keep out of debt") destroys our human life value, limits our potential, and keeps us from living our Soul Purpose because it is fundamentally based on fear and scarcity. Its destructive dilemmas fill us with guilt and paralysis. And it prevents us from creating true and long-lasting wealth by causing us to focus more on expenses than on cash flow.

The financial industry teaches that a large part of financial security comes from having all of your material resources paid off. Paying something off may or may not be a good strategy, but we must consciously identify what our reasons are for wanting to pay things off. From my experience, most people desire a complete payoff because of fear of loss, not as part of a comprehensive and principle-based strategy. An example of this is the goal of paying off a mortgage as quickly as possible. Many people pursue that goal because they believe it will bring economic security. But does having no mortgage really translate into more security? Are there more productive things you could do with your current home equity that would, in fact, give you more security than simply paying it off? I'm not necessarily saying that you shouldn't pay off your home; I'm simply making the point that we make a lot of financial blunders when we fail to explore our reasons and our options.

In large part, it is the attitude of hoarding that originates with the accumulation theory of wealth that dictates our emotions regarding debt and liabilities. It is fear and a desire for security that gave us the myth that all forms of borrowing, all liabilities, should be avoided. Most people are in fear mode when it comes to the subject of debt and liabilities because they're afraid to lose their accumulated material wealth, primarily because they focused so much of their time and energy on accumulating it and they have little protection from loss. It took so much effort to achieve that wealth because they're living according to the accumulation theory, rather than the utilization and velocity theory. They have a hard time accepting that there are principle-based and productive forms of incurring and maintaining liabilities because their fear overrides their logic.

It is fear that tells us that we can derive security from paying all of our liabilities off. We believe that when we have liabilities, somebody or something else is in control of or could even take possession of our material resources. Suppose a person has a sizeable real estate portfolio, and his number-one goal is to pay off every real estate liability that he has. If he does that, has this really given him more true security, or has it just given him a greater *feeling* of security? Just because he paid off the liabilities, does this make the properties any more productive? Does it truly maximize, macroeconomically, his cash flow? Does it maximize his human life value? And, most important does it allow him to live his

40%
of credit card users paid their balance in full each month in 2006.

Source: Federal Reserve Bank of Philadelphia

Fear is not the only thing that drives misconceptions about debt and liabilities; contradictory advice also adds to our confusion.

Soul Purpose? Aside from the "security" of no longer owing the money, what has paying off these liabilities gained him?

Principle-based, productive borrowing is one of the most critical concepts to grasp if we want to prosper. If we let our knee-jerk emotional reactions take precedence over our interests, we will reject this concept, effectively limiting our ability to produce. Any time we concentrate on fear and scarcity we are, by default, limiting our potential.

Fear is not the only emotion that drives our misconceptions of debt and liabilities. I believe that we're emotionally torn in many different directions based on the variety of advice that we hear. One person tells us that all borrowing is inherently wrong and should be avoided like the plague; we hear from another that some debt is good; our childish greed tells us that it's okay to buy items for personal consumption now and pay later; and our ignorant fear tells us to accumulate, hoard, save, and cut as many expenses as possible.

Because of the stronghold that myths have over our minds and emotions, we often feel guilty for taking part in any form of lending or borrowing (even if it's for productive use and is not technically debt), and our financial decisions are paralyzed by our inner conflicts. In the absence of clear knowledge, we vacillate back and forth between the most forcefully promoted opinions, only to resort to the common, "safe" path of saving and accumulating investments in products that we know hardly anything about. Those who are really dedicated to living debt-free, but who operate under a limited definition of debt as liabilities, see borrowing money as a necessary evil to use for big purchases like homes and cars. But each time they go into debt, it eats at their conscience, because they feel that they've sacrificed principle to pragmatism. The debt is like a monkey on their back that constantly tells them, "You can't be safe or free until you don't owe anything to anyone. When this 'debt' is taken care of, then you can enjoy life." In other words, false definitions of debt hold us captive and in many cases prevent us from enjoying the present moment.

One of the main reasons that we're so afraid of debt is because we're afraid of expenses. We're not trying to escape from the *concept* of debt so much as we're trying to avoid the expenses that "debts" incur. Think about it. Suppose a person came to you and told you that they would lend you $1 million, but that the loan terms were no-interest, and that you never had to make a payment during your lifetime. Would you be afraid of this, and try to avoid it like the plague? Granted, there may be a few people who would, but I think that most people would jump at the chance. Again, they're not so much concerned with the money borrowed as they're concerned with what is entailed in paying it off, or what will happen if they can't. (As a side note, in a scenario like this I would just structure my life insurance to pay it off at my death, which gives the fear of liabilities even more context.)

The focus on expenses expands beyond why we avoid debt to how we go about eliminating liabilities. The common advice we hear on how to get out of debt is a complete model of scarcity that tells us to focus on reducing expenses more than increasing production, if it even considers that option at all. The myths that abound about money make us feel guilty for wanting to ever spend money for any reason. For many, the frustration leads to repeating cycles of "binging and purging": We spend a lot of money and rack up credit card debt, then feel guilty about it and confine ourselves to strict budgets. That lasts for a while until we can't stand it anymore and then we go on a spending spree again.

Nationally syndicated talk-show host and financial pundit Dave Ramsey says, "Getting out of debt takes getting mad. It takes the willingness to live off rice and beans for a while. It takes getting a second or third job and selling stuff. If you really want to get out of debt, this is what you will do. It's called 'getting mad.'" But reducing your expenses is limited, while increasing your production is unlimited! Why do so few people succeed with the formula proposed by Dave Ramsey? Because nobody wants to live on rice and beans and sell everything! More important, this is a technique-based approach that doesn't last because the people using it rarely change themselves; they never address the root cause of why they're in debt and what causes them to consume more than they produce.

When we understand how truly easy it is to be productive and make money, we'll realize what a ridiculous concept it is to live in guilt-ridden and anger-filled scarcity in order to get rid of something that may make us more productive. I'm completely with financial pundits when they are teaching people to stop borrowing for personal consumption. Yet it's frustrating to me that the misperceptions in their teachings are crippling our ability to really create value in the world.

 I haven't heard of anybody who wants to stop living on account of the cost.

—Kim Hubbard

If people can understand the true nature of liabilities, they will be able to overcome the guilt, fear, and paralysis that surround their money decisions. They will be able to break through the scarcity thinking of eliminating all liabilities; they will start to learn how to use liabilities productively to become truly debt free, and therefore begin to prosper more rapidly than they ever before thought possible. Once they overcome the internal battles this myth causes, they can enjoy much more production and prosperity.

Replacing Debt with Productive Liabilities

While it's true that true debt should be avoided, it is a complete fallacy that all forms of borrowing, all forms of liabilities, are debt in the business sense. Believing this myth is a recipe for financial mediocrity at best. Instead, we should work to understand how liabilities affect our financial status and potential and how owing somebody money may improve our productive potential, not limit it.

To overcome the myth we must understand

> The true definition of debt, including the difference between unhealthy debt and liabilities;

> That liabilities are an inherent part of life;

> The differences between productive, consumptive, and destructive liabilities;

> Why we must focus on increasing our liabilities to increase our wealth and prosperity; and

> How to use our human life value balance sheet to improve our property value balance sheet.

What Is Debt?

In common usage, debt is usually defined as any borrowed money or material resource. This definition of debt creates real problems when combined with the common teaching that we should avoid debt like the plague because we assume that all forms of borrowing are bad. If we don't know the correct definition of debt according to business economics, we may be avoiding the very thing that is the most essential to our financial health.

Debt is *not* any form of borrowing. Debt is simply having liabilities of greater value than our assets. Liabilities are anything that incur an expense in our lives, now or in the future. They may or may not result in true debt, but they always create an expense, monetarily or otherwise. Some common examples of liabilities include mortgages, car loans, small-business loans, and credit cards.

An asset on a balance sheet is anything that results in or can easily be converted to cash flow. Many of our material resources are considered assets, and they are usually listed at their fair market value. So the market values of your home and your car, the current cash value of your life insurance policy (if it isn't term), and the current value of your investment accounts are all financial assets.

The opposite of debt in accounting is equity, or having greater assets than liabilities. You can analyze your current financial status by preparing a balance sheet. The purpose of a balance sheet is to itemize assets and liabilities and determine if you have either an overall equity position or an overall debt position.

Let's consider two examples to clarify. Shown here are balance sheets for Jane and Bill: Jane has a home with a market value of $150,000, a mortgage of $50,000, a car with a market value of $15,000, a car loan of $20,000, a rental property with a market value of $100,000, and a mortgage of $90,000. To determine if she has equity or debt and what that number is, we subtract her total liabilities ($160,000) from her total assets ($265,000) and arrive at a positive $105,000 ($265,000 – $160,000). How much debt does Jane have? Zero, right? And how much equity does she have? $105,000.

JANE'S BALANCE SHEET			
Assets		**Liabilities**	
Home	$150,000	Mortgage (home)	$50,000
Car	$15,000	Car loan	$20,000
Rental home	$100,000	Mortgage (rental home)	$90,000
Total assets	*$265,000*	*Total liabilities*	*$160,000*
Equity $105,000			

Bill has a home with a market value of $200,000 and a car worth $8,000. His mortgage is $205,000 and his car loan is $12,000. If we subtract his total liabilities ($217,000) from his total assets ($208,000), we end up with a negative $9,000, or $9,000 in debt.

BILL'S BALANCE SHEET			
Assets		**Liabilities**	
Home	$200,000	Mortgage (home)	$205,000
Car	$8,000	Car loan	$12,000
Total assets	*$208,000*	*Total liabilities*	*$217,000*
Debt –$9,000			

To create your own balance sheet, go to killingsacredcows.com

Because I've stressed the importance of cash flow, let's continue to explore Jane's financial status. Let's assume that Jane makes $3,500 a month from her job; her rental property brings in $1,100 a month; her home mortgage payment is $500; her car loan payment is $425; and her rental mortgage payment is $850. Her income statement is shown here.

Obviously, most people's finances are much more complicated than this, but we're keeping it simple just to illustrate the concepts. According to this,

JANE'S INCOME STATEMENT	
Income	
Salary	$3,500
Rental income	$1,100
Total income	*$4,600*
Expenses	
Mortgage payment (home)	$500
Car loan payment	$425
Mortgage payment (rental)	$850
Total expenses	*$1, 775*

Jane's gross income is $4,600, and her net (after expenses) income is $2,825. So to summarize our example, Jane has $105,000 of equity and a net monthly income of $2,825. She has no debt because she has more assets than liabilities, and she has a positive cash flow because her income exceeds her expenses. Her liabilities are two mortgage payments and a car loan payment.

Remember, the proper definition of debt is having more liabilities than assets, and the definition of a liability is something that incurs an expense. The important thing is to be able to produce more than you consume on the balance. If your productivity exceeds your consumption at all times, then liabilities are generally not a problem. The more productive liabilities (like Jane's rental property, which incurs expenses but also creates income) we have, the more assets we have, and the more assets we have, the more opportunity we have for greater cash flow. As long as you are defining debt as having more liabilities than assets, it really *is* good advice to stay out of debt as much as possible. But that's a very different thing from never borrowing money at all.

Liabilities Are a Part of Life

In reality, it's impossible to ever take on an asset without also incurring some form of a liability, which is why it's completely ridiculous to focus most of your time and energy with your finances on getting rid of liabilities. When people begin to understand the intimate relationship between assets and liabilities, they stop worrying so much about liabilities and focus instead on the corresponding asset that any liability brings into their life. They realize that no asset ever comes without a liability, and that the only way to get rid of liabilities is to also get rid of assets. It may be productive to restructure, cultivate, and ensure the efficiency of liabilities, but it's impossible to ever get rid of all of them.

Even the relationships that you have with other people and the actions you take create both liabilities *and* assets. Consider a business owner; all of his employees are both an asset *and* a liability. The value and revenues they bring to his business are the assets, and their pay is the liability. *The critical thing to realize is that he cannot have access to the asset without also taking on the liability. And the only way for him to get rid of the liability is to also get rid of the asset.* If the business owner thought that the road to wealth was to get rid of as many liabilities as possible, then he would immediately fire all of his employees and get rid of his biggest liabilities (and in the process, also get rid of his biggest assets). For the business owner (and anyone else for that matter), it's having the liabilities that makes the benefits of the assets possible.

There are the obvious liabilities we face in order to build assets—those that show up on a balance sheet—and there are the less obvious liabilities, such as the responsibilities we incur when we manage certain assets. For instance, if I buy a rental home, on the balance sheet, the asset is the home, and the liability is the mortgage. But there are also the hidden liabilities of time, money, and effort I have to spend on the home in order to maintain it as a productive asset. It's most useful to classify liabilities by their overall effect on our prosperity and the assets they introduce into our lives, not solely by a number on a balance sheet.

Productive, Consumptive, and Destructive Liabilities

We're often taught to get rid of as many liabilities as possible so that we can "save" money. It is true that liabilities usually translate into expenses on our income statements. However, those liabilities also often translate into assets, income, or both. The key is to examine closely the types of liabilities we incur.

There are three types of liabilities: productive, consumptive, and destructive. Productive liabilities are any liabilities that are attached to a corresponding asset that provides an increase in our immediate or possible positive cash flow, even in the long-term. Real estate is an excellent and simple example of this. If by incurring a liability in the form of a mortgage payment a person is able to control an asset that pays them more than the liability, this is productive and desirable. If a person decides to go back to school to earn a degree and can turn that degree into a new career that allows her to live her Soul Purpose, increase her human life value, and increase her income, then the student loans she takes out are likely productive liabilities.

This does not mean that incurring liabilities is necessarily a step to financial freedom. Use liabilities wisely and productively and remember that what makes an asset productive or not is you—how you decide to utilize the asset and how you apply your human life value to it.

Using liabilities wisely and productively means never borrowing money for personal consumption (consumptive liabilities). In other words, don't take out a second mortgage to buy a boat, unless, that is, you know how to turn the boat into production that increases your cash flow. Consumptive liabilities are any liabilities that do not produce a subsequent positive cash flow. They are liabilities that incur an expense *only*, without a corresponding income from the acquired asset. They take more money out of our pockets than they put in. For example, if I buy a sofa using a credit card, the credit card balance is the liability and the sofa is the asset. If the sofa does not put more money than the credit card payment into my pocket, it is a consumptive liability.

However, it must also be understood that some consumptive liabilities indirectly contribute to my ability to produce. For example, although having a car directly takes more money out of my pocket than it puts in, it also increases my ability to create income; it enhances my productivity indirectly. Cell phones and computers used for business purposes can also be good examples, depending on how they're used. Even still, a good rule of thumb is never to borrow money to purchase things that don't directly increase cash flow.

In incurring liabilities—spending—as in many other things, we must learn to think and act like financial institutions. Financial institutions don't borrow to consume; they only borrow to produce.

Finally, we must discern between consumption and outright destruction. Consumptive liabilities are examples of personal consumption that may not increase our income, but that often have an indirect positive effect on our ability to produce. For instance, if we buy a new sofa, we may enjoy that sofa and the comfort in brings to our home for years, improving our happiness and potentially making us more productive. Likewise, though a car does not generally contribute to our cash flow, it makes our lives easier and more productive through fast and reliable transportation. Destructive liabilities are things that do nothing but detract from our ability to produce and damage our human life value. For example, if I use heroin, that is a liability that has nothing but a destructive effect, both on my human life value and on the value I could potentially create for the people around me. Destructive liabilities also include activities like gambling, pornography, addictions, and engaging in criminal and destructive behavior.

Now that we understand that there are different types of liabilities we can incur, we can explore a few general rules to follow concerning liabilities.

1. *Never have destructive liabilities.* Get rid of anything in your life that destroys your human life value and your ability to produce.

2. *Choose your consumption wisely. Never incur consumptive liabilities that exceed your assets and therefore put you into debt.* For example, a trip to Hawaii may be consumptive, but if it doesn't put you into debt and it indirectly increases your ability to produce by giving you much-needed rest and relaxation, then you can feel great about it. (A word of caution: Be very careful never to use this rule as justification to be overly and irresponsibly consumptive. It's very easy to slip

Productive Liabilities

Result in present or future increase in cash flow (rental property, student loans, small-business loans)

into the habit of justifying purely consumptive purchases with the thought that it will increase your productivity.) This gets complex when people use this idea to consume more than is reasonable, or in such ways that lead them closer to being in debt. For example, if people use this rule as justification to eat out at a five-star restaurant every night and they don't currently have the cash flow to support such a habit, then they're abusing this rule.

3. *Never borrow to consume.* A good way to make sure you stick to rule 2 is to pay cash for everything that does not directly produce for you. For example, if my only use for a big-screen TV is to put it in my home and use it only for me and my family, this is consumption; I should not put it on credit. On the other hand, if I own a home theater installation business, it may be productive for me to put a big-screen TV on credit to place in my showroom. If by doing so I increase my income greater than the liability of the TV, then this is an acceptable use of credit.

4. *Focus on increasing productive liabilities, or the liabilities that come with a greater corresponding asset.* If my cash flow created by incurring the liability is greater than the liability, then this is a productive use of liabilities.

Consumptive Liabilities
Cost more than any increase in cash flow, but may contribute indirectly to productivity (sofa, car, nice shoes)

Destructive Liabilities
Do not increase cash flow and destroy human life value (drugs, excessive junk food)

Incur Liabilities to Increase Productivity

Every single asset comes with an accompanying liability. The way to become wealthy is to simply create more assets than liabilities. When we realize this, we lose our fear of liabilities and learn how to deal with them to increase our human life value and our prosperity. We begin to focus on increasing our productive liabilities instead of trying to eliminate all expenses.

This was a lesson that I learned early on in my married life. When my fiancée (now my wife) and I were discussing marriage, she said that she was looking forward to living in a house and making it our home. At the time, I was so entrenched in the scarcity and poverty paradigm (because I believed in the myths) that I told her no. I wanted to live in an apartment so we would have the lowest payments possible and accumulate as much money as possible. My focus was on reducing expenses and getting rid of as many liabilities as possible. I wasn't concentrating on enjoying my life or creating joy for myself and my wife. What's so ironic about this is that I actually owned fourteen real estate properties at the time, yet I was unwilling to utilize any of them for my own family.

Shortly after I was married, I had a conversation with a great mentor who helped to set me straight. I was able to take a long hard look at my life and the way I was thinking. I started to ask myself, "What am I waiting for?" I realized that I was crippling myself with the thought of "someday." I immediately called my wife to tell her about my changed mindset, and shortly thereafter we moved into a nice home within our means.

Furthermore, soon after we bought our home my business exploded—not because I bought a house, but because of the change in mindset that led to my buying a house. I was more confident, and this confidence brought me more and bigger clients. I met and networked with more influential people. I learned new strategies and gained new tools and resources that previously were unavailable to me because of my limited mindset. And ultimately, my cash flow increased.

This is not to say that everyone should go out and buy houses, cars, or anything else just to be productively oriented. I'm saying that your mindset makes all the difference between poverty and mediocrity or wealth and prosperity. My own life is proof of the fact that when we switch from ridding ourselves of liabilities to focusing instead on productivity and employing resources to bringing joy to ourselves and others, our entire outlook and results change dramatically for the better.

The way to become wealthy is not to spend our lives in scarcity, decreasing our expenses as much as possible. The true path is to focus on productivity and increasing cash flow instead. One important way to maximize productivity and cash flow is to get as many productive liabilities as we can be responsible stewards over. Focus on having more assets than liabilities and more income than expenses. The best way to do this is to incur liabilities that make it possible for us to purchase or control assets. This could include using loans such as mortgages for investment real estate, education or small-business loans, business lines of credit, or collateralized loans. Or it could even mean borrowing other, nonmonetary tools and resources to increase our productivity.

When our liabilities bring in more money than they take away from us, and when our assets exceed our liabilities, we need not worry about debt. A liability is simply the price we pay to have an asset; the asset, upon being utilized, provides the cash flow. The goal is to bring in more income with the asset than the liability takes out in expenses. We can borrow without going into debt. As long as when we borrow (and therefore add a liability to our balance sheet) we also create an asset on our balance sheet, we will always stay out of debt. This is what financial institutions do.

How we use liabilities productively has little to do with ownership, so the common goal of paying off mortgages and other liabilities as quickly as possible becomes rather pointless as a general strategy. Producers aren't so much concerned with ownership as they are with productivity. They are just as happy being able to control an asset in a way that is productive as they are if that asset were in their name. An example of this is lease options in the real estate world. To a producer, there's no significant difference between controlling a property in a productive way under a lease option contract and having the title in their name. In either scenario the goal is productivity, not ownership. Producers don't require ownership to produce, and they understand that they will always have, if nothing else, the liability of responsibility.

Lives based on having are less free than lives based either on doing or on being. —**William James**

What determines whether or not producers pay a liability off is the consideration of what will be the most productive decision and action in any given scenario. If by paying something off they can be more productive, or in other words create more value for other people, they'll pay it off. Of course, to make this decision they will consider every factor involved, so that it's a macro, not a micro, decision. If, on the other hand, they can create more value in the world by carrying a productive liability, they won't hesitate to do so. Now, did I say that they go into debt? Absolutely not—they may use liabilities productively, but they stay out of debt (their assets remain greater than their liabilities).

Learning to think like a producer or a wise steward rather than a consumer is a significant step toward understanding how liabilities can be used

How Producers Get Out of Debt

Many people reading this may understand the concept of how to get out of debt, according to the proper definition, but still want practical advice.

Numerous strategies exist to help people get out of debt, such as paying off the highest-interest accounts first, using home equity lines of credit, and so on. The problem is that without a fundamental change in consciousness, none of these strategies will work long-term; producers, therefore, concern themselves with solving the root causes of debt, rather than hacking at the byproducts of debt (interest and bondage) with nothing but techniques. They'll employ the techniques as appropriate, but only as a function of a certain mindset and root principles. In other words, the standard approach focuses on the tool as opposed to the person using the tool. In contrast, producers identify what went wrong with themselves and their finances before creating strategies and using techniques and products.

The first thing to do when addressing a debt problem is find out what caused it initially. In what areas of your life are you consuming more than you're producing? Why? Are you valuing things over people in certain areas (i.e., your desire for a new car and/or clothes outweighs the responsibility you feel for your family)? If so, why? Were you seeking consolation in material things and borrowing to enjoy them? If so, what could replace those feelings you thought you were receiving from the material things? Was your debt caused by gambling, or using credit to put money into things that weren't in alignment with your Soul Purpose—perhaps things you thought would make you a lot of money—but you weren't able productively. The goal becomes to make the best use of every resource you have access to because you understand that you are responsible for your productivity, or lack thereof.

If we want to prosper, we must focus less on reducing or eliminating expenses and more on increasing our productivity. The strategy of reducing expenses is built upon a foundation of scarcity. Seeing the world and our finances through eyes of abundance and productivity helps us to see how liabilities can, in fact, be used to increase our productivity, cash flow, and wealth.

Let's reconsider the example we used earlier of Jane's balance sheet. If you recall, Jane had a rental property that she could sell for $100,000. She also had a mortgage liability of $90,000, leaving her with zero debt and $10,000

to mitigate your risk? When you made purchases that led to debt, how did you justify them, and why?

Once you've identified the root cause, the next step is to learn the lessons and never repeat the mistakes. This is facilitated by even further questions. What have you learned from being in debt? If you could go back and change anything that led you into debt, what would it be? Are you blaming others for your situation? If so, how can you take responsibility?

With the root cause identified, and the lessons learned, producers can then move forward to create a practical plan for getting out of debt, which may include a number of strategies, products, and/or techniques. Perhaps this section is disappointing to some who were looking for the techniques, but I can't emphasize enough the importance of digging deeper to deal with the root causes first.

I've learned this lesson the hard way myself. The times I've found myself in debt were when I was living in the Consumer Condition. I was gambling in investments that weren't aligned with my purpose, but I thought they would make a lot of money. I didn't mitigate my risk, and when the investment failed, I found myself in debt. What worked for me was not clever techniques, but, rather, learning and applying the lessons.

Getting out of debt requires a fundamental shift in outlook and behavior. It takes a person changing who he is, then what he does flows from that change. If you're struggling with debt, focus on increasing your knowledge, improving your mindset, and developing your character, and the practical solutions to your debt problem will naturally follow.

in equity for that property. Furthermore, her payment on the liability was $850, and the rent brought in $1,100 per month, for a positive cash flow of $250. (Yes, there are many other financial considerations involved with rental properties, but this is just a brief, simplified example.) The common advice would be for Jane to work as hard as possible, probably by limiting her expenses, to eliminate her monthly payment of $850, proposing that by paying off the home she can increase her monthly cash flow.

From a standpoint of scarcity, this is true. But from a standpoint of productivity, Jane must consider every aspect of the equation—both what is seen and what is unseen—in order to make the determination of what is most productive for her. To pay off the mortgage would require $90,000 cash— $90,000 of her own money out of her own pocket. Right now she controls the property with little of her own money. The productivity equation requires that she consider if there are other things she can do with $90,000 cash that could possibly create more income than $850 a month. For example, suppose she had access to $90,000, and instead of paying off one mortgage, she used it on down payments for seven other real estate properties, each increasing her monthly cash flow by $200. That's a total cash flow increase of $1,400, which is obviously greater than the $1,100 cash flow she would have by simply paying off her mortgage.

Of course, there are many factors involved in such a decision, but right now the point is to consider the *possibility*. It all depends on her human life value and her understanding of how to invest, because this is only one strategy, and the effectiveness of a strategy depends upon how each person deals with her stewardships. The point is to say that we radically open up our outlook on life, and subsequently increase our wealth, if our focus is on finding how to be as productive as possible as opposed to cutting as many expenses as possible. This is especially true when we realize the productive capability of the assets that have liabilities attached. When we understand that there are ways to borrow that do not translate into debt, we can break through the scarcity of that false thinking and set out on a liberated and liberating path to financial freedom through the wise and productive management of lending and liabilities.

Again, it is ridiculous to believe that we should strive to get rid of all of the liabilities in our life. Liabilities in and of themselves are value neutral—they can be either productive, consumptive, or destructive depending on how we use them. What's productive for one person may be consumptive for another, and vice versa. It is our knowledge and financial intelligence that determines their productivity or lack thereof.

Human Life Value Balance Sheet

To round out the discussion of liabilities and productivity, let's explore the concept of the human life value balance sheet, or the HLV balance sheet. I've discussed numerous times the principle that people have intrinsic value and material things do not. When we really grasp this principle, we begin to see balance sheets through different eyes, with a much greater depth of understanding. Because human life value is the source of all property value, our property value balance sheet is but one piece of this bigger, more comprehensive puzzle.

The common usage of and inordinate focus on property value balance sheets has, in large part, contributed to the myth that material things have intrinsic value. Consumers think that the worst form of loss is the loss of material resources. Producers understand that material things have no intrinsic value, and that people are the only true assets. For instance, when you have a rental home in your portfolio, most people view the home as the asset and your renters as the liability. From the perspective of the producer and the HLV balance sheet, the truth is the exact opposite. The rental home can't write you a check. The only money you have or can ever get comes from other people. Your renters are the primary assets, not the rental property. Producers understand this truth. Therefore, to them, the loss of material things is not the issue. Rather, producers are more concerned about lost production.

The human life value balance sheet is the accounting tool to measure your productivity as a person. A person's HLV assets include such things as knowledge; integrity; character; relationships; an ability to teach, persuade, or lead other people; faith; humility; confidence; the ability to serve; mental and emotional intelligence; wisdom; education; responsibility; dependability; trustworthiness; self-discipline; courage; respect for and from others; conviction; the ability to create, transfer, and sustain vision; adaptability; sense of humor; mental, emotional, physical, and spiritual health; and relationships. A person's HLV liabilities include deficiencies of knowledge, wisdom, or intelligence; lack of character and integrity; pride; fear; lack of discipline; inability to manage thoughts or emotions; limiting rigidity and inflexibility; lack of confidence; and the like.

A generic human life value balance sheet looks like this:

HLV Assets	HLV Liabilities
Knowledge	Ignorance
Wisdom	Näiveté
Productive relationships	Destructive relationships
Integrity	Dishonesty
Faith	Fear
Humility	Pride
Energy	Lethargy
Discipline	Laziness
Physical health	Sickness
Courage	Cowardice
Talents or Skills	Lack of ability

Just as we want more assets than liabilities on our property value balance sheets, so too do we want to have more HLV assets than liabilities. In fact, our HLV balance sheet is far more important than our property value balance sheet because it is what determines the health and productivity of our property value. Human life value is the source of and the reason that any property value exists or has utility.

With our property value balance sheet, we learned that we need not fear liabilities; we only need to recognize them and manage them for productivity. The same holds true for the HLV balance sheet. The goal is not so much to eliminate our HLV liabilities as it is to make them as productive as possible. For example, the fact alone that we have liabilities provides impetus and motivation for us to add to our HLV assets. Or, we may choose to hire people who are strong where we are weak, rather than trying to focus on our weaknesses.

It must also be stressed that the rule about destructive liabilities is as true for our property value balance sheet as it is for our HLV balance sheet.

We must always strive to rid ourselves of purely destructive HLV liabilities such as addictions and character flaws. Deficiencies in *character* should always be eliminated; deficiencies in *ability* can be managed with the help of other people or systems.

It's especially important to understand the HLV balance sheet when it comes to our relationships with others. All people have their own HLV balance sheets. To the extent that their HLV assets exceed their HLV liabilities, they have the ability to produce value *for* others. Conversely, to the extent that their HLV liabilities exceed their HLV assets, they will tend to consume value *from* others. Every relationship that we have with other people, even with our dearest friends, incurs both a liability and an asset. The time and effort spent strengthening and deepening your relationships are liabilities in the sense that they take time away from what you could have done instead. Yet the relationship itself is also an asset. The only way we could eliminate every liability from our lives would be to eliminate every person in our lives.

Our ability to be prosperous, wealthy, and debt-free depends on our HLV balance sheet. It is a person's human life value that determines what their property value assets are worth, because it is HLV that determines if those assets will be put to productive use or not. The property value balance sheet can be very misleading if it's taken out of context, because it is nothing but the reflection of our HLV—the greater our HLV, the greater our income, assets, and wealth. The way to overcome debt is through the utilization of our human life value, not techniques that are temporary Band-Aids that don't solve the fundamental problem of why we are in debt in the first place. Examine your human life value balance sheet and find ways that you can increase your productivity, instead of "getting mad and living on rice and beans."

* * *

Ultimately, the only way to stay out of debt is to create more value in the world than we consume, or in other words, to serve more than we are served. This is done by thinking beyond our relatively petty financial concerns to identify and fulfill the wants of others. The net effect of the common advice we hear on debt is the exact opposite of this; the entire focus is on reducing expenses and living in scarcity, rather than on production. But our human life value is the root of our prosperity; we are our own greatest assets. Our material resources and money are the fruits of prosperity, not the root. The stronger our roots, the wider our branches grow, and the more abundant is our fruit.

MYTH 9:

{ **A Penny Saved Is a Penny Earned** }

What is a cynic? A man who knows the price
of everything and the value of nothing.

—Oscar Wilde

Myth:

Price is what matters more than anything else—don't spend your money if you can avoid it. Except, of course, if you find a good deal!

Reality:

Price is a small concern relative to value. Focus primarily on value, and you will make and save more money in the long run.

F or the most part, price has become our most important consideration when it comes to making financial decisions. Most of us sacrifice what we really want because of our view of and relationship with money. What determines how we make purchasing decisions is if we can "afford" something or not; we often don't consider any factors other than price, at least initially. We're so focused on price that it controls us; it prevents us from focusing on ourselves and controlling our own ability to choose what we actually want, regardless of price. Some people buy things they don't want because they "got a deal," others don't buy what they need and can afford because it's "too expensive."

Price certainly is and should be *one* factor in our financial decisions—just not the main basis for our buying decisions. Instead of focusing on the price of items, the overriding factor of all of our financial decisions should be value. By value I mean quality and utility. When we're considering any purchase, before we ask "How much does it cost?" our thought process should be, "Is this what I really want?" "Does this item do everything that I want it to do?" "Is it the best quality?" "How long will it last?" and other such questions. After we've determined that we've found the value that we're looking for, then and only then should we consider price. Price alone should *never* be the reason why we do or do not buy something.

In this chapter, we'll talk about the difference between price and value, and how focusing on value can change our entire financial outlook. We'll explain why the myth of price over value is so destructive, and we'll explore the relationship between each dollar that we spend and the world that we live in. And we'll examine how to use our financial decisions to create our ideal life and our ideal world.

The Destructive Nature of Price over Value

Excessively magnifying the role of price in our financial decisions limits our potential and destroys our human life value because it dictates our decisions, pulls our focus away from productivity, allows us to sacrifice quality, makes us vacillate between being a saver and a spender (which are two sides of the same consumer coin), and limits the quality of our lives and world.

When we fall prey to the myth in question, price begins to strongly influence our choices and ends by dictating our every financial move. Under the influence of this paradigm, we don't go on dream vacations because they cost too much money—as opposed to creating enough value to pay for our dreams. Or, if we go on a vacation, we can't fully enjoy ourselves because we're so worried about what we're spending. We eat at restaurants that we normally wouldn't even go to, but we go because we have a coupon for a free meal. We don't buy things that we really want and that could actually increase our productivity until they go on sale. We save dimes to lose dollars.

I know a person who makes a six-figure income and is worth $10 million. He wanted to buy a flat-screen TV, so he spent eight months researching on the Internet to find the absolute best deal. When he finally made the purchase, the decision was based primarily on price. He ended up saving five hundred dollars, yet at the cost of literally hours over the course of eight months—despite the fact that he makes more than five hundred dollars per hour. What value could he have created in the world in the time he spent trying to save a few hundred dollars? How much lost productivity does that single incident represent?

The price phenomenon makes us do things that we otherwise wouldn't do. Our national fetish for getting "good deals" overrides our reason and allows our emotions to control our decisions. Consider this: On November 30, 2003, in Orange City, Florida, a woman was trampled and knocked unconscious by a mob of people rushing into a store to take advantage of a sale on DVD players. Only her sister, a store employee, and a few shoppers tried to help her up.

The price sensation leads to such puzzling mysteries as people "saving" money by shopping. We'll spend five hundred dollars and then come home and talk about how much money we saved. There's five hundred dollars less in our checking account (or five hundred more on a credit card, as the case may be), and we think we've saved money. How does this happen? Yes, I understand that people use this logic when they buy things on sale that they normally would have bought anyway, such as groceries or other essentials. But we also use this logic to fill our homes and lives with unnecessary stuff because we got "good deals." Some people even ask, "How could you *not* buy it when it was so inexpensive?" Right? Ironically, we're so concerned about "saving" money that we spend much more money and receive much less value than we could have if we'd considered other factors.

A cheap price is a shortcut to being cheated.
—**Chinese proverb**

We let prices make our decisions for us, rather than making conscious choices about the things that we want. We're not buying because we've determined what we *really* want through calm introspection and logical thought processes—we've fallen prey to the emotional price mania and, in the process, have forgotten considerations much more important than price. I've even heard stories of people going to big day-after-Thanksgiving sales and putting their arms out and swiping entire shelves

According to the Federal Reserve Bank, **40%** of American families spend more than they earn.

clear without regard to what they were putting in their shopping carts.

The natural result of buying the cheapest products and services with little or no regard to value or utility is stagnation and mediocrity. It leads us further from living our Soul Purpose because we aren't focused on value. In chapter 7 I included a quote from John Ruskin that is worth looking at again. He said, "There is scarcely anything in the world that some man cannot make a little worse, and sell a little more cheaply. The person who buys on price alone is this man's lawful prey." When we ignore value and base our decisions on price, we allow ourselves to be preyed upon by mediocre products and services. Living within our means is important, but too often I see people limiting their productivity through confining budgets; their primary focus is on not spending too much, as opposed to creating more value and increasing their productivity. Rarely do people who hold to strict budgets think about ways to increase the *size* of their budgets.

In *Rich Dad, Poor Dad* Robert Kiyosaki teaches that the poor say things like, "I can't afford it," while the rich replace that confining thought with, "*How* can I afford this?" When all of our financial decisions are fundamentally based on price, we prevent ourselves from considering all possibilities. If we come across something that we want, but we don't currently have the money to pay for it, that's the end of our mental processes. It's tyranny of the mind, and the saddest part about it is that we do it to ourselves. As long as we're focused on price alone we're never able to dream, envision, create, and find solutions.

Approximately

14%

of Americans use half or more of their available credit, and this group carries an average of 6.6 credit cards.

Source: Center for Media Research

For more information and examples, go to killingsacredcows.com

We paint our lives, our abilities, and our potential into little boxes that are completely based on our current level of income, and there we stay. Rarely do we consider that we control the size of our income "box," and because of that, we don't have to be slaves to price. We don't have to spend our lives buying the lowest-quality goods and services because "we can't afford it." We can choose to afford anything we want to afford. We can have anything and everything we want, if we can just be creative and maximize our productivity.

One thing that I consistently observe is the dichotomy between savers and spenders. It's obvious to most people that the spenders are überconsumers who make many consumptive purchases on credit and routinely go on shopping binges. What's not so obvious is that savers are also consumers; they're the opposite side of the same coin. When I talk about savers, I'm not referring to those who make wise and judicious preparations for the future. I'm talking about those people subject to the myths of the accumulation theory who hoard and accumulate out of fear, and avoid all expenses, regardless of value.

One August a few years ago, I was talking to the guy sitting next to me on a flight from Los Angeles to visit his father-in-law. I asked him if he was excited about his trip, and he said that he looked forward to seeing family, yet he lamented that though his father-in-law lived in a multimillion dollar home, he wouldn't even turn on the air conditioner in August because he was so concerned about saving money. Furthermore, the man related that although his father-in-law had a nice car, he was going to pick him up from the airport in an old beater car that had no air conditioning, again because his overriding concern was to save money.

His father-in-law isn't alone. I have another friend who lives in Las Vegas and makes a six-figure income, but he refuses to turn on the air conditioner during the summer so that he can cut his expenses and save money.

Savers and spenders both make the majority of their financial decisions based on price. Spenders gloat about all of the "good deals" that they constantly find; savers are smug about *not* buying things. Where spenders get excited about the items they found for cheap, savers derive a sense of fulfillment by not making purchases that, in reality, they probably should have made. Spenders are reckless and foolhardy with their spending; savers are stingy and have limited productivity. Both of them ignore value; the spenders buy lots of low-quality items, and savers don't buy much of anything, even when there are valuable things that would make them infinitely more productive if they could convince themselves to part with the cash.

Neither spenders nor savers focus on productivity—the spender is a profligate waster of productivity, while the saver is too busy conserving productivity (which is also a form of waste, since unused productivity can't be regained). Spenders exceed their current productivity, while savers suffer from considerable amounts of unused and unutilized potential. Neither of these types is primarily focused on how they can create value in the world, and neither of them fully understand stewardship; spenders consume value and savers hoard and limit value.

We have become conditioned to allowing prices to dictate the quality of our lives, rather than taking responsibility to create our ideal lives. Utilizing money is one critical way that we create our world. We vote with our money; every dollar we spend is a vote for the kind of world that we want to live in. Many people fail to see the significance of their individual actions. They think that their monetary "voting" won't really make a difference in the world. But it is precisely this kind of thinking that perpetuates cheap, low-quality goods and services. Of course, one person doesn't determine the entire marketplace, but if most individuals buy into the collective myth, their collective decisions tell the market that poor quality is acceptable. Through conscious choice, we can become empowered to choose quality, value, and utility over price.

Replacing Price with Value

Think back to the discussion about what money really is and where it comes from. It is evidence of value creation, no more, no less. The people who create real value are those who are inspired and who inspire others, who are able to think as if money was not an issue, who don't allow fear of loss to rule their lives, who are willing to speak of great things and then make them happen; in short, the producers. Producers consider many factors in their financial decisions, but prioritize value and the creation of value above all.

We can become producers and overcome the myth that price is (or should be) the most important consideration in our financial decisions by learning to do the following:

> Break out of the price trap and focus on productivity.

> Recognize opportunity costs in our financial decisions.

> Prioritize value and utility over price.

> Understand the difference between price and terms and focus on directing and determining terms.

> Use our purchasing decisions to create our ideal world.

Focus on Productivity

Price is a deceptive measure that artificially limits our choices. As artificial as it may be, however, it still has an immense and tangible impact on our lives. To break out of the price trap requires a greater level of conscious awareness and increased personal responsibility.

The best way to get outside of the price box is to learn how to spark our value-producing abilities with questions that bring our focus to productivity. As Kiyosaki has explained well, closed statements such as "I can't afford it" turn our creativity off; open-ended questions such as, "How can I afford it?" turn on our creative juices, help us to arrive at innovative solutions, and open up limitless possibilities. Generally speaking, questions that begin with "how" are more helpful than questions that begin with "why." For example, a "why" question would be, "Why can't I afford this?" In contrast, a "how" question would be, "How can I create more value in the world that will help me to afford the things that I want?" The "how" question helps us to turn inward and take responsibility. With such questions we start with the premise that options do actually exist for us to afford our wants, and we just have to find them.

The human mind is incredibly powerful, yet it must be consistently trained and guided if we are to truly tap its limitless capacity. An excellent way to facilitate this mental discipline is to consistently ask ourselves the right questions. Our brains are designed to answer the questions we pose to them. The types of questions we ask determine the answers we receive. By learning to consistently ask the right questions we can access power we never knew we had.

Price is (or should be) a relatively petty concern when it comes to making financial decisions. It should be *one* factor, but it should *never* be the most important factor. We, individual people, must learn to make decisions based on what we want, rather than what we think our current income limits us to. We don't have to be subject to prices. We set the intrinsic valuation that determines our perspective of anything external to us, including and especially the price of any product or service. We decide what anything is worth to us, and we don't have to accept any price, any lack of quality, or any deficiency of value.

The bottom line is that if we are able to break through the destructive price myth, we can stop spending and saving, and instead start utilizing and velocitizing. Our focus will turn toward productivity, and as we improve our ability to produce, we will stop simply consuming and start maximizing our previously unused potential.

Recognize Opportunity Costs

When we understand the potential of our human life value we spend our time focusing on how to fully develop it and how to increase our productivity, rather than making bulk purchases to save a few dollars, buying things we wouldn't normally just because there's a bargain to be had, or avoiding paying others for services we believe we can do ourselves, but don't enjoy, in order to save money.

Both savers and spenders fall prey to the "Costco" mentality, or the habit of buying things in bulk that they don't really use. The spenders are excited about all of the stuff they buy, while the savers are excited about all of the money they "saved" because they bought in bulk quantities. Let me clarify that I'm not preaching against Costco or other bulk stores; there are many productive uses of such stores and concepts. The problem is that many false myths are perpetuated by our inability to differentiate between price and cost, price and value, and saving and utilization.

 Join a wholesale superstore such as Costco or Sam's Club . . . do your grocery shopping on double coupon days.

—**Richard Paul Evans**

For example, suppose I can buy one pound of mixed nuts at a regular grocery store for $3.50, but at Costco I find a five-pound container of the same nuts for $10, or $2 per pound. The price-focused see that I've saved money on the per-pound price of the nuts. What they don't see is the fact that I now have five pounds of nuts that will remain in my freezer or pantry for months before they are used, if they are ever used at all. It's very probable that the nuts will become rancid before my family uses them all. The large container of nuts has become an unutilized resource that just sits in the form of potential without creating any value whatsoever.

In addition to the money I may lose by not utilizing all of the product I've purchased, there are additional opportunity costs inherent in the purchase. What *could I have done* with that money had I bought the smaller container (with less unused potential) and paid the higher per-pound price? I would have had $6.50 with which to make other, more immediately useful purchases. When we focus on productivity and utilization, as opposed to saving or spending, we begin to think differently. You may be saying that $6.50 is hardly anything to be excited about, but I've just given one example. When we add up all of the unnecessary "bargain" purchases we make in our lives, the lost opportunity costs become quite substantial for many people.

A bargain is something you cannot use at a price you cannot resist.
—Franklin P. Jones

Along these same lines, coupon clipping can also lead to much lost opportunity cost. Spenders will use coupons for things that they wouldn't normally buy, when they just can't pass up the good deal. And savers waste time poring through coupons—time that could have spent much more productively. To use a standard cliché, they are penny wise and pound foolish. They might spend a half hour clipping coupons that will save them $5. They see the $5 savings; what is not seen is what they could have done in that time that would have been more productive, like discovering ways to live their Soul Purpose. Assuming that by using their greater abilities they could have earned $20/hour (a low amount to be sure, but we'll use it for the sake of argument), they actually lost $5 instead of saving $5.

Another way we lose money through opportunity cost is by focusing on price is the "do-it-yourself" attitude that makes people automatically avoid or reject things that come with a price. Books, magazines, and financial pundits teach people to get their own stock trading account in order to save money, although in the process, they automatically reject the value that a stock market expert could have brought into their lives. They spend much time researching stock picks rather than focusing on Soul Purpose, when it would actually make them more money to pay someone whose ability—and full-time job—was to choose good investments.

> There is only one difference between a bad economist and a good one: The bad economist confines himself to the visible effect; the good economist takes into account both the effect that can be seen and those effects that must be foreseen.
>
> —Frédéric Bastiat

Consumers, particularly savers, think that they save money by mowing their own lawns. I pay $150 per month to have someone take care of my lawn. The price I pay is obvious. What isn't so obvious is what it would actually cost me if I chose to do it myself. I would immediately have to pay a few hundred dollars to get all of the equipment, and attached to those dollars are opportunity costs of what they could have been had I invested instead in something that is a more productive use of my abilities. Once I have the equipment, I must count the time it takes me to take care of my lawn and calculate what I could actually earn if I spent those hours using my greatest abilities instead. When I consider all of the factors, it becomes clear that it would be incredibly foolish for me to mow my own lawn for the sake of saving money.

Although I'm capable of doing it, I personally don't get energy from mowing my lawn. What if I were mowing my lawn instead of writing this book? It might only take half an hour a week to mow my lawn, but that adds up quickly over the years. Which activity is more productive for me? Which is of higher value to the world? Mowing my lawn would also take time away from my family, and that is too high a cost for me.

Now, it may be a joy for you to work on your landscape or in your garden, in which case it makes sense for you to do it yourself. This example is not meant to discredit those endeavors. But there's more to seemingly simple choices like this than it first appears.

The concept of the division of labor as originally taught by the eighteenth-century economist Adam Smith sheds further light on the do-it-yourself philosophy. In his classic book *The Wealth of Nations* he wrote, "The greatest improvement in the productive powers of labor, and the greater part of the skill, dexterity, and judgment with which it is any where directed, or applied, seem to have been the effects of the division of labor." Through the division of labor, we as a society or as individuals can exponentially increase our economic efficiency and productivity. Not only are we able to produce more products and services, but this concept also allows each of us to specialize in our Soul Purpose and draw from the Soul Purposes of others. Where I am weak, others are strong, and I can pay them to compensate for my weaknesses, and vice versa. I may not enjoy mowing my lawn, but there are people who can't get enough of lawn mowing. I can pay them to mow my lawn, freeing up my time, which in turn allows me to focus on the things that I actually enjoy and am good at. We all enjoy things that others can't fathom as ever being enjoyable. Just because we don't want to do something doesn't mean that there aren't people out there who do.

If it truly is part of your Soul Purpose, and if it really does bring you joy, then by all means mow your own lawn. But if it's not, stop thinking that you save money by doing it yourself because it's simply not true. The opportunity costs you aren't considering are substantial enough to outweigh any immediate reduction in expenses.

Prioritize Value over Price

The most important thing to consider with all of our purchases should be value, with the corollary of productivity. Before we ever ask, "How much does it cost?" we should ask more important questions like, "Will this help me to increase my productivity?" "Is this item of a high enough quality to meet my wants?"

The more we focus on value and quality, the more productive we can be. For example, I know people who refuse to get medical attention for critical ailments because they're so concerned about the price of going to the doctor. (See chapter 7 to remind yourself why producers love insurance.) But what they're ignoring is the effect on their productivity when they don't take care of themselves. If they were to focus instead on optimizing and maximizing their health, it would translate into exponentially greater productivity, and as a byproduct, more cash flow for them. They might spend more money initially, but it would come back to them multiplied. When we focus on price and ignore value, we starve our goose that lays the golden eggs in an effort to cut our expenses. A better approach is to do whatever is necessary to take the best care of our "goose," which, of course, happens to be us.

Let's look at another example. I may be considering two cars and deciding which one to purchase. One is priced at $1,000, and the other at $10,000. If price is my only consideration, I'll drive away with the $1,000 car. But what if that particular car has 250,000 miles on it, and after driving it for a short while the transmission goes out, and later the engine needs to be replaced? Furthermore, what if the gas mileage is five miles per gallon because it's running so inefficiently? All this detracts from the value of the car, and that's without even considering the stress, worry, and lost production that the purchase incurred because of all the hours that the car is in the shop and I'm not able to use it. The price of the car was $1,000, but what was the cost? What has it done to my human life value? When you consider all factors—both immediate and future—it's probable that the car cost me much more than I would have spent had I just bought the $10,000 car instead. The $10,000 car had much more *value* than the other car, and the value is much more important than the price in this case.

Price is a micro piece of a macro puzzle. Our financial decisions should be based on the macro picture, through a holistic process that considers every aspect of our financial puzzle. Inordinately focusing on price is like trying to put together the entire puzzle with one middle piece. To get the full picture, every piece must be included.

I recently had a revealing experience that showed me how prevalent the price myth really is. I was looking for some running shoes because my current shoes weren't ideal for my purposes. I went into the store and immediately told the salesman that I wanted the best shoe they had, and that price was not a concern at all. Even though I made that clear from the beginning, the salesman still showed me ten pairs of shoes before he brought out the highest-priced pair. This last pair was the best and felt the best on my feet,

Questions to Help You Prioritize Value

Would I buy it if it weren't on sale?

How can I be more productive with this resource?

How does it benefit me?

Will I enjoy it once or many times?

Why do I value this purchase?

Is the product of high quality and value?

Does it increase my human life value?

but because they cost a hundred dollars more than any of the other shoes the salesman was hesitant to bring them to me. The shoes took five years to design, they offered amazing support for my feet, they were extremely light and comfortable, and they were just what I was looking for. Because of my exercise regimen, the comfort of my feet is so important to me that I value being pain free and being able to work out longer much more than I value the additional hundred dollars. But even after I made it clear that price was not an issue, the salesman couldn't get over the myth in his own mind.

Price should always come after *value* has been considered. I'm not saying that we should live expensive lifestyles for the sake of lavish living—I'm talking about value and productivity. It's a given that if we're comparing two items with equal value we should choose the less expensive item. Stinginess and greed are equally destructive to human life value, but there are no universal guidelines for what prices represent the best value for an individual. To again use the example of cars, in order to maximize productivity a person might need to spend more than $10,000 on a car, but to spend more than $30,000 might not do anything to positively impact their productivity. For some, a $200,000 car might be the most productive given their circumstances and purposes.

Value is closely aligned to, if not synonymous with, productivity. When we're comparing items to purchase, one might be cheaper than the other, but when the more expensive one has more value, it could make us more productive, and the obvious choice should be the higher value. It might cost me more money immediately, but in the macro view it will actually bring more money into my life. I can buy a cheap machine to meet minimum requirements, but if I spend twice as much for a computer with twice the capability, how much does that affect my productivity? It influences my ability to produce, a fact that most people don't stop to consider. The cheaper computer might be much slower, and that fact alone could decrease my productivity. I could have accomplished more with the better computer.

Another important consideration when we're weighing value is other people who supply us with products and services and their applied human life value. When we are inordinately caught up in the mindset that price is the most important consideration in our purchases, we may forego products and services that we value highly because we still feel the need to get them at a lower price. Why do we want to discount the value that other people are bringing into our lives, especially if we see tremendous value where the price of their product or service currently stands?

We should want to see other people succeed every bit as much as we want to succeed ourselves. When we're living abundantly we're focused on the value that people bring into our lives, not the prices of their products and services. Although price is still one consideration, our goal is to compensate them for the value that we are receiving, according to our perception, rather than to win at their expense by getting them to lower the price as much as possible.

Price is what is usually seen, but to make wise financial decisions requires that we look beyond the seen to identify the unseen, and often more important, factors. We do this by focusing primarily on value. If we think as economists rather than as consumers, our wealth will increase even though it may appear on the surface that all we're doing is spending more money than we normally would. A focus on value, as opposed to price, makes us more productive, helps us to view the world through completely different eyes, and dramatically increases the quality of our life, and subsequently, the quality of the world at large.

Understanding Terms vs. Price

Another consideration that affects value is the concept of terms in reference to the subject of borrowing and lending. When terms are controlled properly, they can render the actual price of an item virtually irrelevant.

One of the ways that I've seen this concept taught in seminars is for the speaker to ask the audience, "How many of you would pay more than a hundred dollars for a hundred-dollar bill?" Without much reflection, most people say that they wouldn't. The irony, of course, is that we do this every day of our lives by purchasing on credit. There are times when it is more productive for us to pay interest on something for the privilege of being able to purchase it immediately. For example, if I can make $20,000 on a real estate property by borrowing $100,000 and paying back $110,000, it is worth it to me to pay more than $100,000 to have access to $100,000. Banks do this every day. For example, banks buy your money for, say, 3 percent more than you gave them, then turn around and lend that same money to another person for 7 percent. They're willing to pay more than a hundred dollars for a hundred-dollar bill, as long as what they do with the money exceeds the value of what they paid for it.

What's interesting about this concept is that we deal in the world of terms all the time, yet most people are still unaware of the powerful affect terms can have on price. Let me offer an example. In real estate, most people only consider the price of a home in making their purchasing decision. But there are many terms that they are ignoring in the process, things like payments, interest rates, the length of the term, down payments, and other factors. Suppose you find a home with a price of $250,000. You do some research and find that you can get a 7-percent interest rate on a thirty-year loan from a bank, with a payment of about $1,700 a month. With your current budget, you've only allotted yourself $1,400 a month for a house payment. At this point, most people stop thinking about it and move on to a cheaper home. But suppose you develop a relationship with the owner of the home, and she tells you that she only owes $100,000, and her payment is only $800 a month. Furthermore, she is willing to work with you on the terms by entering into a lease/option agreement. After some negotiation, she agrees to a $5,000 down payment, a lease payment of $1,300 a month, and a lease term of two years.

You're happy because you've just gained control of an asset that would typically cost you about $1,700 a month for $400 less than that, and you don't even need to get approved for a loan immediately. She's happy because she has a positive cash flow of $500 per month. If this sounds atypical or unrealistic, I can assure you that these types of arrangements happen all the time with people who have learned to utilize their human life value and look deeper than price.

Others might say that they can't control the terms of real estate transactions, and that they are subject to whatever banks will give them. Consider this: you control every term of every economic transaction you're involved in, assuming no deception and/or fraud or deception take place. You control them by agreeing to them! It's your responsibility and your privilege to choose if you accept the terms you're offered or not. With a healthy dose of responsibility and just a little creativity, limitless options abound for you to control the terms in such a way that renders the price of an item virtually irrelevant.

Terms to consider in any financial arrangement may include, but are certainly not limited to, down payment, interest rate, monthly payment, time period before payback, and the ability to transfer risk. If we can control the terms and make them favorable to our particular situation, price becomes negligible. Price is still one factor in the whole package (and usually the factor easiest to see), but its importance depends a great deal on how the terms are arranged.

Creating an Ideal World

Every dollar we spend is a vote for the kind of world in which we want to live, and in which we want our children and grandchildren to live. Producers only produce what someone will buy, and if we cease to buy certain things, such as low-quality products, no one will have an incentive to produce them.

To the extent that we focus on price at the expense of value, we create a market for mediocrity and poor quality, which spreads into every other aspect of life. A society whose primary concern is price is a society that emphasizes pragmatism over principle. It's a society that will come to sacrifice integrity to money. It's a society that cuts corners to save money, and by so doing creates more problems and destruction than can ever be solved by "saving" money. A price-focused society is one that collapses over the long run because of all the destructive short-term, price-based decisions.

We can tell our values by looking at our checkbook stubs. —**Gloria Steinem**

Of course, a society is nothing but the aggregate of individual people. Individuals who ignore value and magnify price are people who never live to their full potential because they live in self-constructed, limiting mental boxes. They are people who fail to calculate the aspect of "what is not seen" into their financial decisions, and hence become unconsciously enslaved to "what is seen." By failing to see the difference between price and cost they severely limit their potential (financial and otherwise) and never find and live their Soul Purpose. They fall prey to the "do-it-yourself" fallacy that keeps them busy with activities outside of their greater ability in order to save money. But there is no reason that they can't change, or that you have to be one of them. You can be an example for others to follow, a force that helps to release the stranglehold that the myths have on our minds—in other words, you can kill the sacred cows in your life and pave the way for others to follow.

My vision of an ideal world is one where every person is developing and living his Soul Purpose in the service of others. As we all do what we were born to do and thereby serve each other, we eliminate so much wasted time and opportunity. I know that the more I focus on my strengths and pay for others to compensate for my weaknesses, the more I contribute in a small yet significant way to my vision of the ideal. Conversely, if I ignore my strengths and try to do everything myself, that takes me that much further away from the ideal.

There is a direct relationship between our spending and the quality of our lives, both individually and collectively. Every dollar we spend is an invitation to whatever we spend it on to be a part of our lives; it is tangible evidence of what we consider valuable. Every time we buy a mediocre product we send the message that we want to live in a mediocre world. When we purchase high-quality products, we send the message that quality and value are more important to us than price alone. I want to repeat this concept because it is so critical: *Every dollar you spend is a vote for the kind of world in which you want to live.* Take time to create a vision of your ideal, and once it's created, contribute to its creation by becoming highly conscious of your spending. If we do or do not buy something as individuals we may not change how that particular item is produced and sold, but if we all learn to live the philosophy of value we can release ourselves from the grip of the price myth. Contribute to the creation of an ideal world by reflecting your ideal through every one of your purchasing decisions.

* * *

The idea that price should be the most important consideration in our financial decisions is a destructive myth that limits our potential and keeps us away from our Soul Purpose. Furthermore, when we fall prey to it we keep other people away from their Soul Purposes; when we are overly concerned about price we adopt the do-it-yourself mentality that shuts off the option of leveraging other people's abilities in our lives. It sacrifices quality and value on the altar of stagnation and mediocrity; it prevents us from seeing infinite possibilities; it leads to damaging forms of saving and spending; and if taken too far, it dictates our decisions and the quality of our lives. We can overcome the myth by tapping into our human life value and thinking outside of the limitations of price; focusing more on value than on price; recognizing and utilizing the difference between price and terms; and using our purchasing decisions to create the ideal world in which we want to live.

DEFEATING THE MYTHS:
The Formula

The despotism of custom is everywhere

standing up to human advancement.

—John Stuart Mill

Although we've spent a lot of time picking apart specific myths, the purpose of this book is not to identify each and every financial myth that exists. The purpose is to get us to stop and think about the advice we hear instead of quietly internalizing it. It's to get us to analyze things more deeply than we normally would; to train our minds to see the secondary, or the unseen, consequences of the decisions we make; and to pose the questions that will help us achieve our ideal lives—beyond the power of the myths.

To accomplish this, I've identified and exposed some of the myths that I've observed to be the most limiting and destructive. The risk, of course, is that some may view this as an exhaustive list detailing all money myths, and fail to recognize others that arise in their lives. I want it to be clearly understood that there are many more myths and social agreements that must be identified and overcome in different areas of our lives. My purpose has been to show how much misinformation exists about wealth and prosperity so that we can become educated about our approach to finances.

The first step to overcoming myths, obviously, is to become aware that they exist, and then to identify them as myths. After we've recognized them for what they are, it's relatively simple to overcome them. The purpose of this chapter is to provide a duplicable formula that can be used to raise our awareness of how to deal with any financial teaching that we encounter. The formula will help you test the validity and veracity of anything that you hear from the media, friends and family, financial institutions, and retirement planners that has an impact on your prosperity and the quality of your life. It consists of six key elements:

1. Have a clear definition of your interests, and analyze how what you're being told aligns with your interests.
2. Determine whether following the teaching will help or hinder your efforts to find and live your Soul Purpose.
3. Ask the right questions, and educate yourself to make sure you know which questions to ask.
4. Understand the value proposition behind what you're being told (particularly with investment advice) and act accordingly.
5. Apply the concept in other areas of life to see if it holds true.
6. Commit to a lifelong process of education.

Know Your Interests

Suppose you are a sailor, but you have no final destination in mind. How could you guide your ship unless you know where you want to go? If you don't know where you want to go, how can you determine if someone is steering you in the wrong direction (or the right direction, for that matter)? It may sound silly that I even have to point out such a simple, self-evident truth, yet the sad fact is that most people don't really know what they want. We must question the basic assumptions of any teaching or proposition to see if they are in line with our purposes and interests before we take action.

Most people have poorly defined goals and lack a vision of what they want their lives to look like. For instance, most have bought into the myth of retirement without questioning it, as if retirement is an incontrovertible law of the universe. What is retirement? What does that even mean? Does it mean, as much of the advice for preparing for it seems to indicate, becoming economically dead? What kind of ideal is that to shoot for? It's such a strange concept, and yet almost the entire financial services industry makes retirement the Holy Grail, the purpose for and ultimate end of all financial planning. Consider this: If a person is living Soul Purpose, why would she ever want to stop doing whatever it is that she does? But even if a person really did want to "retire" in the traditional sense of the word, the question of what that means remains. If a person's ultimate ambition is to retire—without having a clear vision of his "retirement"—he's like the poorly prepared sailor saying that he wants to sail to someplace nice.

The way to determine whether a proposal is in your best interests is to know what you want and determine if it will get you closer to that desire. Until you know what it is, exactly, that you want out of life, you're unprepared to discern between fact and fiction, truth and myth regarding your financial state. How do you know what types of insurance or investments you want until you know what purposes you're aiming to accomplish? How do you know if a retirement planner has your best interests in mind if you don't even know what those are yourself?

If we don't have a clear vision of what we want our lives to be about we can be easily swayed by any financial proposal, especially if the numbers look good. For example, suppose you don't know what your ideal career is, and you're given an opportunity to make a high income doing something that you don't really love. Most people will take the position because of the money, without considering the holistic picture of how it will affect them long-term. Five years later they may be making good money, but their health, relationships, and outlooks are dramatically suffering. Was the money worth it? Was the money the best thing to base the decision on?

Of course not, yet we do this all the time. We make financial decisions that look good on paper because we haven't thought about what our true interests are. Instead of actually pursuing our best interests, we merely chase high rates of return or live by clichés fed to us all our lives. We don't live by design; we live by default, and that is a life where unconscious exploitation is the rule. Like sheep, we graze in stifling pastures surrounded by sacred cows instead of breaking through the limiting fences built with myths to create freedom in our lives.

What do you really want right now? Five years from now? Ten years? Twenty? How do you envision your ideal life and your ideal self? What principles, strategies, products, and companies are best positioned to help you achieve your goals and your vision? You can never know if any financial proposition will get you to where you want to go if you don't know where you want to go. Of course, it's impossible to predict where you'll be in any number of years, what you'll be doing, and why, and if your goals will have changed years from now, but you can at least start today with a vision of your current ideal. The idea is to maximize production today, in the present moment, by working toward a vision of the ideal, not to plan and wait for that ideal to magically arrive twenty years from now. What are you waiting for? Why not live like you really want to today instead of buying into the financial myths that tell you that your dreams are only possible tomorrow, or in thirty years?

 Immortality will come to such as are fit for it, and he who would be a great soul in the future must be a great soul now. —**Ralph Waldo Emerson**

People who don't know what is in their best interests are people who, unthinkingly and by default, sacrifice their interests to whoever happens to come along and give them a strong proposition. If we don't know what our interests are, we are easily exploited and taken advantage of in the interests of other people or institutions.

I believe that this is a major reason why so many people buy into the fallacy of waiting for retirement and living with the accumulation theory. They don't know what they really want, so they let custom formed by social agreements and vested interests dictate what they want. It's like having a $200,000 car in our driveway but not knowing how to drive it, and so we just hand it over to someone who comes along with a proposal for using it. Actually, it's much worse than this, because our human life value is infinitely more valuable than any car. Metaphorically speaking, who do you want to steer? Do you want to play by the rules of the myths, or rules of your own making where you control the results? Do you really want to play by rules such as "high risk equals high returns"? Is that how you drive your car?

We're handing away our human life value on a silver platter because we don't know what to do with it. This is the destructive power of myths, and this is what I'm dedicated to overcoming. Sometimes it seems easier to hope the myths are true and resign ourselves to them rather than to think and become educated. This is a destructive course to take, however, because it's easier in the moment but it sets us up for long-term failure. People don't usually notice the failure until they feel it's too late; then they're so exhausted from the thought that they have to do the same thing all over again to succeed that they perpetuate the scarcity and live according to the myths.

When it's over and you've lost, you can't just start this life over again from the beginning. This is your shot to make it happen, and to make it happen in a big way. You can guarantee success by aligning with principle, but it takes a dedication to education, a willingness to act, and the courage to break through the stronghold of the myths and not follow the crowd. It takes a consistent effort to choose faith in principles over the fear of how you might look to others. It takes the ability to see past your present actions and thoughts to envision the end results and to ask yourself if it's worth it to do what everyone else is doing, even though it's not working. What will be the story of your life? What are you writing in the pages of your life today? Do you even know what you want to write and how you want your life to read?

Simply knowing what your best interests are is an excellent step toward developing the ability to see through any myth that you encounter. It is in your self-interest—and the interest of the world at large—that you learn how to see through the myths so you can be more productive and engage in developing your full potential. You can't produce at your highest levels until you know what your highest potential is. And you can never learn what your highest potential is if you allow other people and institutions with vested interests to tell you what your ideal *should* be. You are the only one qualified to determine if a proposal aligns with your best interest and your highest capability to produce and create value. Knowing what is in your best interest is a monumental step toward overcoming destructive myths and performing at your highest level.

Soul Purpose

The ultimate end of every one of our decisions—financial and otherwise—should be to get us closer to finding and living our Soul Purpose. Our Soul Purpose is the reason that we were born. It is the thing that brings us the most joy and creates the most value for others. It is the development of our full potential. It is what causes us to reach far beyond the mediocrity of social agreements. *It is what gets us beyond a "normal" life to live extraordinarily.*

If it's possible that there is something like this for you, would you ever want to retire? Does living life in scarcity for thirty years to accumulate money in financial products appeal to the greatness within you? If you were truly being the best person that you could be, would you ever depend upon Social Security or corporate benefits for your financial freedom? If people live in scarcity during the accumulation phase of their financial lives, then during retirement they will live in a mental prison of worry—worrying about interest rates, taxes, inflation, and anything else that threatens to make them run out of money. Is this the kind of life that we really want to live?

Financial decisions become relatively easy when we hold them up to the test of how they affect the discovery and fulfillment of our Soul Purpose. Are you working in your current occupation because it maximizes your productive capability, or because it pays well and has good benefits? If it's the latter, you are severely limiting your ability to produce and taking yourself further away from your Soul Purpose. Are you "investing" in mutual funds, CDs, and 401(k)s because you really think that they're the best thing for you and create the most value in the world, or do you do it because you're doing what everyone else does? Are you afraid to break through social agreements to do what you really love because of how you think you'll appear to others?

We buy into myths when we don't see any better choice. One of the most critical keys to breaking through myths is to make your purpose bigger than you appear to be at that particular moment. It's accomplished through dreaming and envisioning your best self. And pursuing your Soul Purpose is the key to greater dreams and higher thoughts.

 Nurture great thoughts, for you will never go higher than your thoughts.
—Benjamin Disraeli

I believe that every person trapped inside the destructive power of myths has an innate sense that he or she is capable of much more than this state allows. Everyone stuck in a dead-end job, everyone afraid to leave a bad situation for fear of losing benefits, everyone dependent upon the government or a corporation, everyone who watches their 401(k) and realizes that it's not going to do for them what they thought they were promised, all of these people know deep down that something is wrong with what we're being taught. We all know that there's something better out there than what we're taught to pursue. We're afraid to try something different, but also, we don't even know what else to look for.

Soul Purpose is what to look for, and, once found, it will give you the desire, courage, and strength to break through the fear caused by lies and mistruths. Here are some questions to ask yourself that will aid in the discovery of your Soul Purpose:

> If money were of no concern, what would you spend your time doing?

> What would be so exciting that you would want to jump out of bed early each morning to get to it?

> What strengths, abilities, skills, or advantages do you feel you bring to the table that could be utilized to create maximum value in the marketplace?

> In what areas do you have superior skill and extreme passion?

> What things could you do all day long, without thought of fatigue, or what could you do that would *create* energy?

> What do you do that brings compliments?

> What do you believe in and consistently talk about?

> What causes are worthy of your life?

> What activities offer you the most fulfillment?

> If you were doing exactly what you wanted, what would that be?

> What are your priorities?

> What are your values?

> What opportunities or circumstances do you currently have that may be helpful in creating value for others?

> What people do you know who have tremendous success, knowledge, and ability? What do they do? How do they think? What can you learn from them?

It is my firm belief that any person who is honest about asking and answering these questions will significantly change some things about how he thinks and what he does.

I would argue that it's incredibly selfish to allow ourselves to be blown about by the wind of mediocrity because we're not grounded in and aligned with the principle of Soul Purpose. Following Soul Purpose doesn't mean that everything we do should be based on our selfish desires. Rather, we must know exactly how we're best suited for creating value in the world, and then do everything in our power to be as productive as possible. We should never feel guilty about following our Soul Purpose.

When we have precise visions of what our lives are about, and a clear sense of our Soul Purpose, we can see through any proposal that is not aligned with our principles and our purposes. When we have an overwhelming sense of purpose we don't get sidetracked by fallacies and myths. We don't get swept up emotionally in chasing high returns, or fall prey to the fear of "playing it safe," or become consumed with concern of what other people think of us. Both greed and fear are largely eliminated when we're doing what we absolutely love to do. Understanding the power of Soul Purpose is one of the best ways to cultivate judgment regarding financial advice.

Ask the Right Questions

As we discussed in chapter 9, the more productive questions we ask, the more productive answers we receive. It seems like such a simple technique—and it truly is—but I can't stress enough how effective this small step can be. We can't let its powerful effect be overshadowed by its simplicity.

The following are some possible questions to ask yourself when you're considering a teaching, an axiom, or an investment proposition:

1. Why is this being taught? What is the background that led to the development of the teaching?

2. Who benefits if this lesson, axiom, saying, myth, or investment is trusted and believed in? Who has a vested interest in seeing that it is perpetuated?

3. After identifying where the interest lies, then ask: What is the interest of this person or institution?

4. Is this teaching truly in alignment with my best interests? If so, how? If not, how?

5. Does the approach on offer utilize my human life value? What do I have to provide other than my money? Will this increase my human life value?

6. Is this proposition productive today, or does it merely represent a hope in the future? Does it create value immediately or does it get stored as potential?

7. What level of management do I have with this proposition? What level of management do other people, institutions, and market factors have?

8. What are the opportunity costs of this approach? What are the secondary and tertiary effects?

9. Am I educated enough to make this decision? What education am I lacking and how can I get it?

Questions are infinitely superior to answers.   —**Dan Sullivan**

Of course, this list is not meant to be exhaustive and comprehensive; it's meant to provide a basic framework of how to go about asking productive questions. These are suggestions, but you should be able to come up with many more on your own. The trick to asking good questions is to make them open ended, and to ask them in such a way that our minds are open to considering every possibility. It's also a good idea to seek out mentors, or people that you consider producers, to help you to ask the right questions, especially when you know you may not have the education you need to make a sound decision.

Value Proposition

A value proposition is simply the identification of how value is created for others through specific actions, investments, business proposals, etc. A good value proposition comes in the form of a very clear and concise statement that explains how value is being created and how it will be sustained. The value proposition must be simple and easy to understand, and it must make good economic sense—that is, the receiver must truly value what's offered, and the giver must be able to provide it efficiently.

Looking for and identifying the value proposition (or lack thereof) of any teaching that you come across is a powerful way to find out if it is truth or fiction. If you are unable to see how value is being created, the chances are high that you're dealing with a myth.

One excellent way to analyze opportunities and mitigate risk is to ask and answer the following five questions:

1. Is this in alignment with my passion and values?
2. Will it increase and/or utilize my human life value?
3. How will it benefit others?
4. How will it benefit me?
5. Is it based on sound economic principles?

So many people buy into hype and fallacies (such as high risk equals high returns) that when they're given financial proposals they unhesitatingly jump onto the bandwagon because they're chasing high returns. Why do we do this? Why do we even get involved in any investment? Is it just for the returns? What happens when we lose money? Do we learn a valuable lesson or do we continue making the same mistakes? What most people fail to realize is that high returns follow solid value propositions. If the focus is on the value proposition instead of the returns, mistruths and deceptions become easily apparent.

For example, if a stockbroker insists that you have to invest in a particular stock, you can stop and carefully analyze the proposition to identify whether or not it's a wise decision for you. The broker might be appealing to your fear of loss and say that you absolutely have to buy it now or the opportunity will be lost, or she might rave about how high the returns are expected to be, or she might appeal to authority or popularity by showing you all of the other people who are getting involved. But if you can't clearly identify the value proposition you are violating the principles of human life value to get involved. Take the proposition through the five questions without falling prey to the pressure and the unfounded hope of high returns. Unless you know exactly how you are creating value for others you should never be involved in any investment.

Of course, I understand that this means recognizing an additional level of responsibility, but we cannot have freedom—financial or otherwise—without responsibility. Are you willing to do what it takes?

> Never doubt that a small group of thoughtful, committed citizens can change the world; indeed, it's the only thing that ever has. —**Margaret Mead**

Identify the value proposition of any investment in order to determine if it's a myth or if it's legitimate. We expose myths quickly when we approach them this way, and they lose the power over our minds that they might otherwise have.

Test for Universal Application

If something is clearly wrong and ridiculous in one context, the chances are good that it will be ridiculous in other contexts as well. Ironically, most people act in their financial lives in ways that they never would in any other area of their lives An excellent way to test if a financial teaching is a myth or not is to apply it to any other area of your life and see if it holds true.

For example, if you're taught that high risk equals high returns, apply that to parenting. Would you throw your two-year-old son into a pool and then just walk away because you want him to learn to swim? How logical does that sound? If it's so clear to us how ludicrous that would be, then why do we buy into the financial myth that we should take high risks and that just because we do so we will be successful?

What about the concept of deferral? How wise is it to defer changing the oil in your car, or to defer putting gas in it because you're too busy driving?

How well does deferral work in that scenario? We don't defer eating until we die, do we? If the concept of deferral is ridiculous in these examples, it's equally ridiculous with our finances. Deferring our chance to enjoy our money is just as destructive as deferring our responsibilities. It just doesn't work and we know it, so why do we buy into deferral when it comes to money?

Suppose some people say that they want you to go into a business partnership with them. Their proposal is that they want you to give them as much of your money as possible on a systematic basis, that you will have no control over how the business is run, that you won't know what the business is doing, that there are no guarantees about what your return will end up being, and that in thirty years they will give you whatever your money is worth at the time. Furthermore, the agreement states that you'll be penalized if you withdraw any of your money from the partnership before a specified age. Would you enter into that business partnership? You would be absolutely crazy to do it, right? What's ironic about this is that I've just described a 401(k). Nobody in their right mind would enter into the business arrangement I just described, yet so many people blindly throw money into a 401(k) because everyone else is doing it.

Would any of us parent the way that we deal with 401(k)s? Imagine raising children by just feeding them systematically, choosing a day care to have almost full control over them, and not thinking much about how they're performing until they're fully raised and it's too late to do anything about it if things have turned out badly. Of course it wouldn't work very well.

What if we were to apply the dogma that reducing expenses is the road to wealth to a real estate property? We start by buying a rundown rental house (we pay cash for it so we won't have to pay interest on a loan), and then we never put a dime of improvements into it because we're so concerned about cutting expenses. As a result we attract undesirable renters who destroy the place even further, which actually increases our expenses in the long run. We could have increased our expenses in the short-term to fix the place up and attract better renters, but that went against common advice.

If it's true that cutting expenses and getting rid of all liabilities is smart, why don't we sell our cars and ride bikes to work? Why don't we get rid of

Is your 401(k) serving you? Go to www.401khoax.com

our telephones and Internet connections (even though they may drastically increase our productivity)? Why don't we live off cheap, unhealthy food instead of spending the time, energy, and money to live as healthily as possible?

When we start applying myth-based financial advice to other areas in our lives, the fallacies become readily apparent. Most people wouldn't deal with anything else in their lives the way that they deal with their finances. But the myths are powerful and encourage us to act irrationally and illogically. We can break through them more easily if we try to apply the teachings to other areas in our lives to see if they hold true.

Lifelong Education

One crippling societal myth is that education should cover a short period in our lives, and that after we're in a career we don't need to worry about it again. I see too many people who get out of college and then for the rest of their lives rarely, if ever, read a book. These same people, when presented with something that challenges their beliefs, discard it by saying, "Why haven't I heard of this before?"

Real knowledge is to know the extent of one's ignorance. —**Confucius**

One of the best ways to cultivate the ability to see through myths, recognize them for what they are, and then break through them is to constantly increase our knowledge. The more we know, the more context we have. The more complete our knowledge is, the better informed are our decisions. For example, the more an entrepreneur knows about historical cycles, her market, her product or service, her customers, and how to run her business, the less risk she is exposed to and the more profitable she can be. Ignorance is perhaps the highest risk of all. Always be aware of how little you really know, and never stop doing everything in your power to increase the depth and breadth of your education.

... since, in comparison with what a man knows, those things of which he is ignorant are infinite, and beyond comparison greater and more beautiful, he is out of his mind who extols himself in regard to his own knowledge . . . Let no man, therefore, boast of his wisdom.

—Roger Bacon

I have made available on my website (killingsacredcows.com) a list of downloads, books, CDs, and DVDs that I know are excellent educational resources for anyone wanting to increase his productivity and live his Soul Purpose. It's critical that we continue striving to increase our knowledge and improve our education. Educational products are one excellent way to do this. I recommend that people read a book a month at the very least. For educational products dealing with concepts and philosophy similar to what you have read in this book, visit killingsacredcows.com, find the available books, and begin building your library and increasing your knowledge and prosperity.

I recommend that you pursue as much as possible your higher education and attend every educational seminar that you can. Industry events that relate to your Soul Purpose can be a good resource, and now much information is available over the Internet, including university classes and seminars with experts. Another excellent possibility is developing a relationship with a mentor who can guide you through difficult choices and aid your development. My company also offers extensive educational programs, the details of which you can find in the back of this book. The more effort and interest you apply to increasing your knowledge and understanding, the easier it will be for you to tell truth from falsehood. Overcoming myths, reducing risk, and increasing productivity are largely a product of education.

If a man empties his purse into his head, no man can take it away from him. An investment in knowledge always pays the best interest.

—Benjamin Franklin

Defeating the Myths

Many, if not most, people are held captive in their financial lives by destructive myths. These myths have become so ingrained into our social consciousness that they are extremely difficult to identify and overcome. Furthermore, powerful institutions have a vested interest in ensuring that they are perpetuated. When we begin to analyze financial myths and trace them back to their roots, we find that there is actually very little truth to them. They are sacred cows that, upon scrutiny, prove to be false illusions that distort our thoughts and decisions about money and prosperity.

The great enemy of the truth is very often not the lie—deliberate, contrived and dishonest—but the myth—persistent, persuasive and unrealistic.

—John F. Kennedy

. . . if we do not set to work with all the desperation due a matter of life or death, the truth will be nothing more in fact than whatever the greatest number thinks, and the good whatever the greatest number does.

—Jacques Lusseyran

Greatness is in the very nature of human beings, but that greatness is more often than not overshadowed by mediocrity and fear. Much of our mediocrity and negative emotions originate in false and limiting social agreements, many of them dealing with finances. Our greatness can only emerge when we develop the courage to break through these financial myths and become free.

As long as money is our primary concern in the world—the first thing we think of when we awake in the morning and the last thing we think of when we go to bed at night—we will never become who we were born to become. The less we think about the fruits of prosperity (money) and the more we think about the roots of prosperity (human life value), the more capable we are of unleashing our potential.

The ideal world where everyone develops his or her own particular talents in prosperity will never be realized as long as we are in financial bondage, both because of our personal choices and because of social myths concerning finances. The way out of financial bondage is easier and closer to home than it may seem at times. The power to kill the sacred cows of social myths is within us, and the power to become financially free is through our personal choice to be responsible, not in some amazing financial product or hot stock tip.

 The real voyage of discovery consists not in seeking new lands but seeing with new eyes. —**Marcel Proust**

We can and we must overcome the destructive myths that limit our potential if we want to be free as individuals, as a nation, and as a world. My main purpose is to get people thinking more deeply and to raise the level of financial awareness in order to see through lies and fallacies. It's to discern truth from falsehood so that more of us can avoid the inevitable pitfalls that come from living myths. It's to help more people have more power, more happiness, and more purposeful lives. The more clarity we can achieve, and the less we are subject to myths, the more productive, valuable, and happy we can become.

I invite you to question and analyze the typical teachings about finances and see if they bring you closer to or take you further away from being all that you have the power to be. My experience has been that most of the financial ideas that people buy into limit their potential. I invite you to test the formula found in this chapter for seeing through and defeating financial myths. In short, I invite you to kill the sacred cows of money and prosperity that may be limiting your potential and begin the satisfying and worthy journey of financial freedom and Soul Purpose.

Acknowledgments

To my friend and brother, Les McGuire—your legacy lives on through the writing of this book. Our time spent on retreats, driving together, philosophizing on airplanes, and in events and study groups has been invaluable to this work. Thank you for recognizing and increasing my human life value.

To my spiritual guide, partner, and brother, Steve D'Annunzio—my creative juices flow when we are together. Thanks for being a light that uplifts mankind. I love you, man.

To my coauthor, Stephen Palmer—it is a rare instance to find someone with the skills to articulate these principles on paper whose life is consistent with the teachings. You were confronted with the truth and were able to break through the myths that you thought were core to your beliefs. Now you are a personal friend whose intellectual honesty was crucial to bringing about this work.

To my parents—you did an amazing job raising me, living your lives, and instilling values and compassion in me. You did an even more amazing job at transforming your lives when confronted with the myths uncovered in this book (and actually taking advice from your son).

To my wife, Carrie—thank you for teaching me what I have not been able to learn on my own. You are an example of beauty, and of being able to see the value in all of humanity.

To my son Breck—you are a beacon of joy. I love dancing, running, throwing, and playing with you. Most precious of all though are your kisses. (I know this will be embarrassing when you are older, but I just love ya.)

To my son Roman—thanks for sleeping through the night, it really helps in doing a project like this. I love your noises, your smiles, and your spirit of love and abundance.

To the team at Greenleaf—thanks for your dedication, energy, and commitment to this project.

To Michael Drew—thanks for helping me reach more people.

To Brandon Allen—thanks for your commitment and passion behind this project.

There are so many people who have influenced my life and this book. The following are just a few: Kim Butler, Todd Langford, Dan Sullivan, Babs Smith, Ray Hooper, Mike Isom, Rick Koerber, Dorian Drage, Dee Randall, Greg Blackbourn, James and Katie Eaquinto, Earl and Karla Gunderson, Randy and Margaret Van Ness, Derick Van Ness, Garrett White, Tom Fry, Dr. Paul Jenkins, Robert Castilogne and all the trainers at LEAP Systems, Ron Zeller, Dean Carl Templin, Steve Harrop, Joe Baker, Andrew Howell, Greg Barrick, Darron Miller, Blair Arnell, Matt Randall, Dan Roether, Chau Lai Kibildis, Phil Manning, Jason Byrne, Anthony Petersen, everyone associated with the Freedom FastTrack and Producer Power Hour, my Sigma Chi Kappa Iota Fraternity Brothers, family, friends, and many others—thank you for your relationships and value you bring to me.

The 401(k) Hoax

The 401(k) is the ultimate sacred cow of personal finance. It is the supreme representation of the marketing genius employed by financial institutions to get you to hand
over and lock up your money. If you haven't yet noticed, I'm out to kill this sacred
cow. Too often, Soul Purpose remains undiscovered and unrealized because individuals lock up resources in financial vehicles, which remain unutilized and untapped.
Such accumulation is undermining to your success. My goal is to help you unleash
your hidden financial potential and unlock the genius of your Soul Purpose.

To achieve this, I have issued a public challenge called "The 401(k) Hoax"
(401khoax.com, see details below). Not only do I firmly believe that the 401(k) and
its accompanying mindset are destructive to most individuals, but I am also willing to
put my money where my mouth is. For a select few, I'm willing to offer my personal
time and assistance. So if you have a qualified plan—a 401(k), IRA, TSA, 403(b), 457,
Keogh, SEP IRAs, etc.—visit 401khoax.com today to learn more about how you can
escape the trap.

The point of the 401(k) Hoax program is to show you that, contrary to what is
taught in the accumulation theory, your greatest asset is you. Through education, systems, and mentoring you can increase your knowledge and become empowered financially and aligned with your Soul Purpose.

Are you up to the challenge? If I'm wrong, you have nothing to lose but limitations. And if I'm right, you can rapidly accelerate the journey to your ideal life.

Consider the following questions to determine if the 401(k) Hoax program is
right for you:

- How much cash flow do you receive from your qualified retirement plan and
  how much liquidity does it offer?

- Will your plan allow you to retire guaranteed, or only if the market cooperates with your projections?

- How much control do you have over market factors?

- Is your employer match really resulting in a guaranteed 100 percent rate of return? Are you absolutely sure? (Hint: It's not.)

- How much do you know about your plan and the funds it is invested in?

- Are you investing with full knowledge, or gambling with hope?

- If you don't like paying taxes today, why would you want to pay them in the future? Is tax deferral really the benefit it's made out to be? (Hint: It's not.)

- Do you have a solid exit strategy?

- Do you trust the government to not change the rules?

- Are you practicing direct stewardship of your retirement funds, or are you depending primarily on institutions and other individuals and crossing your fingers?

- Do you want to learn about far better ways of investing than qualified retirement plans?

- Are you ready to discover your ideal life and align your investments with the best version of yourself?

How Can You Kill This Sacred Cow and Increase Your Wealth?

If you have money in a 401(k) or other qualified plan, this is an opportunity for you to go to 401khoax.com to find out how the challenge works. You may apply at 401khoax.com and you will find the necessary criteria for approval. Be aware that this challenge is absolutely not for those who are unwilling to take personal responsibility for their finances, who are looking for quick fixes and easy returns, or who are looking for a place to put their money without understanding or controlling the investment.

I will work personally with all 401(k) Hoax participants, a privilege reserved for very few clients. There is a specific process for entering the challenge that is found at 401khoax.com with proper disclosures, rules, and disclaimers.

I'm challenging you directly and personally to take control of your financial future. I defy you to find any person or institution who cares more about your prosperity and has more control of and responsibility for your financial well-being than you do. You are the ultimate determinant of the quality of your life—but I'm willing to be a mentor in helping you choose the right path. I'm willing to put my own financial resources on the line to prove to you that you can do a far better job at managing and growing your wealth than money sitting inside of a 401(k) or qualified plan.

Take the challenge by applying to the 401(k) Hoax. You're worth it, your dreams are waiting. Visit 401khoax.com today for more details.

Why is the 401(k) the Ultimate Sacred Cow?

You may be wondering why I give so much attention to 401(k)s. When the evidence is plainly presented, it becomes overwhelmingly clear that putting money into 401(k)s and similar qualified plans is not investing at all—it is one of the riskiest gambles for most individuals. I emphasize the 401(k) Hoax for the following reasons:

- **Limited opportunity for cash flow.** 401(k)s do not provide immediate cash flow, which means that you cannot benefit from them through velocity and utilization. The theory is that letting the money sit allows it to compound, but for most people this really means that it stagnates. Most people will not choose to utilize these funds even when a particularly compelling opportunity arises that will make them far more than the 401(k) would, even accounting for the penalties. This means that numerous legitimate opportunities are passed by as people compliantly stay "in it for the long haul."

- **Lack of liquidity.** The money is tied up with penalties attached for early withdrawal. Although there are a few technicalities that allow penalty-free withdrawals, the restrictions are so numerous that very few know how to navigate them.

- **Market dependency.** The performance of the funds is dependent upon market factors that most individuals do not have the knowledge nor the ability to understand or mitigate. This means that your retirement plans are based on unknowable projections, making for a dangerous and uncertain planning environment. Uncertainty causes fear, and fear leads to mistakes, worry, scarcity, and ultimately lost hopes and dreams. Do you want to live your ideal life only if the market cooperates?

- **The match myth.** "Take the match—it's a guaranteed 100 percent return before you even get started in the market!" You've heard that before, right? The problem is that it's a complete myth—were it true most 401(k) savers could end up with literally billions of dollars at retirement (see chapter 3). What is the true impact on the bottom line to you? When do you utilize the match? To answer these questions and prove this is a myth for yourself, use the calculator found on the 401khoax.com to calculate your real returns in matching scenario.

- **Lack of knowledge.** How much do you really know about your 401(k)? Do you know what happens to the money? Do you know what funds you're invested in? Do you know the companies that your funds invest in? Have you seen financials for these companies and do you know their key executives? Do you know the fund manager by name, her history, her investment philosophy, her performance? How can you expect to gain a return from something you know so little about? How can you create real, tangible value in the world in the 401(k) scenario? And how can this be called investing? Without full knowledge of an investment, placing money amounts to little more than gambling, which is the desire to get something for nothing. The "something-for-nothing" attitude—no matter how subconscious—is exceedingly destructive.

- **Administrative fees.** The funds are subject to various administrative fees in addition to expense ratios and 12-b1 fees (for marketing expenses). This is a fact which most people and even many advisors ignore. This means that your returns will be negatively impacted and your projections can be substantially off. To calculate the difference of your retirement plan performance with or without fees, go to 401khoax.com.

- **Underutilization because of tax deferral.** If you don't like paying taxes today, why would you want to pay them any more in the future? In other words, the tax deferral aspect, which is touted as a great boon, is actually a primary factor contributing to qualified plan money being notoriously underutilized. Most retirees let the money sit, even during their retirement years, for fear of triggering tax consequences. If you just have to pay the taxes at a later date, how is there a tax advantage? The reason there is no tax paid is because you have deferred income by never taking constructive receipt of your earning and instead deferring earnings into a qualified plan.

- **Higher tax brackets upon withdrawal.** Closely related to the previous problem, the other issue with taxes is that most advice fails to take into consideration the likelihood of you being in a higher tax bracket during your retirement years than you were previously. Think about it: If you have achieved any measure of success living the accumulation theory, you should actually be in a higher tax bracket at retirement, although most advisors project that you will be in a lower tax bracket. So this means that deferring your taxes results in a far greater tax burden than would otherwise be incurred using different products and strategies than the conventional route. It's a profound irony that people project healthy returns on their qualified plan while also projecting that they will be in a lower tax bracket at retirement.

- **Estate taxes.** 401(k)s are sitting ducks for estate taxes. Much qualified plan money is never utilized by those who actually accumulated it because they hold off so long on withdrawing it for fear of paying taxes, yet when the money is passed on to the next generation, there is not only an income tax that can be triggered, it may be subject to an estate tax that there is no internal provision to avoid either. So, when the money is passed to the next generation, the government is taking a healthy chunk before it passes hands. This begs the question of who the real beneficiary of the program is.

- **No exit strategy.** Getting into a 401(k) seems simple enough. In fact, many companies start employees' 401(k) contributions automatically upon hiring them. They sound great—you're getting a match, tax deferral, and a wide choice of funds relating to your risk tolerance. But how are you going to get out of it? How many people take this into consideration when they start contributions? How many people understand the penalty and tax consequences? Most people don't fully realize the implications until it's too late, and so their qualified plan money sits unutilized. In that case, what is the real rate of return of your money? Once again, in that scenario, who are the real beneficiaries? Not the people who invest, and not their heirs to a large extent—it's the institutions and the government.

- **Subject to government change.** Did you know that your 401(k) does not even technically belong to you? Read the fine print and you will find that it is what's called an "FBO" (For Benefit of). In other words, its held in trust by a custodian on your behalf and subject to a myriad of government regulation and change. It's essentially a tax code. If history proves to be a reliable guide, 401(k) funds are therefore in great jeopardy. In the same way that the government raises and lowers taxes at their whim, it can change the rules and take the money that you so diligently saved

- **Golden handcuffs.** Are you at your current job because it aligns with your passions and purpose, or because of the great benefits? Are you just holding on long enough until your qualified plan funds are fully vested? Are there ways that you could create more wealth and opportunity by living your Soul Purpose, rather than being attached to the deceptive security of a 401(k)?

- **Disinvesting.** Suppose you've retired and want to begin taking interest payments from your qualified plan. You project that you can withdraw 6 percent a year, based on an average return of 8 percent a year. However, what happens to your principal when the funds are volatile and the market experiences down years. Your funds may be receiving an average 8 percent annually, but that means that some years will be lower, some will be higher. If in one year your fund is down 10 percent, you're tapping into your principal to take your interest withdrawal. At that point, you have only two choices: 1) start withdrawing principal, or 2) leave the money alone until your funds are up again.

- **No holistic plan.** I've witnessed on many occasions people whose finances are in shambles and who have much more pressing needs, but still diligently contribute to their 401(k). They've been convinced to do so, of course, because of the match, tax deferral, etc. This is like these people trying to take care of a scraped knee when their wrist is slit. What they really need is a macroeconomic approach to their finances that will help them identify, prioritize, and manage all pieces of their financial puzzle, with all pieces coordinated and working together.

- **Neglect of stewardship.** Ultimately, the most destructive aspect of 401(k)s is that they cause many individuals to abdicate their responsibility, abandon self-reliance, and neglect their stewardship over their own prosperity. People think that if they just throw enough money at the "experts" that somehow, some way, and without their direct involvement they will end up thirty years later with a lot of money. And when things don't turn out that way they think they can blame others—despite the fact that they only have themselves to blame. Fortunately, you don't have to be one of those people.

Is this enough, or should I continue? Believe me, I could continue to give solid reasons why 401(k)s are not the safe harbor many think they are, but hopefully you are beginning to see the point! Qualified plans are promoted on such a wide scale because those promoting them have vested interests—and their interests don't necessarily coincide with yours. Visit 401khoax.com today to learn more about how you can escape the qualified plan trap.

If you currently contribute to a 401(k), stop and think about it for a minute. What is it really doing for you, now and in the future? The desire to save money for retirement is wise and prudent, but after reading the above, do you think it's possible to find other investment philosophies, products, and strategies that would meet your financial objectives much more quickly and safely than a qualified plan?

Are you really comfortable exposing yourself to this much risk? How can you mitigate your risk, increase your returns, and create safe and sustainable investments? How can you create more control and better exit strategies, reduce your tax burden, and increase your cash flow?

If you don't have good answers to these questions, then I urge you to accept my challenge and apply for the 401(k) Hoax. I look forward to helping you discover for yourself how much better your finances can serve you, when you dare to take control of your own money.

Special Offers

For a free glossary of terms used, go to killingsacredcows.com

KillingSacredCows.com

KillingSacredCows.com is an interactive complement to this book. It provides information, tools, and resources to help you understand more deeply the principles and concepts found in the book. As a supplement to the book, this site includes audio files, video, e-books, charts, graphs, Power Point presentations, calculators, financial tests, case studies, and links to more tools for producers. You can learn from actual financial examples and go into more depth on issues you are currently facing in your financial life.

This site will feature a community section where you can watch videocasts or listen to podcasts of people that are participating in the 401k Hoax challenge and watch as they progress and learn from their experience. You can also participate in online forums to discuss the book and financial principles with other readers. For those who want to find out if their 401(k) really saves taxes, or if compound interest is the miracle it is purported to be, the community will feature calculators and videos to demonstrate concepts and expose limitations, so that you can find out for yourself. This calculator is perfect for measuring the true impact of a match on your 401(k) or the impact of expenses on the bottom line of your funds. Use these interactive features to increase your knowledge and destroy the myths that have permeated your life.

You will find a recommended books section, events section, and a place to purchase podcasts to assist with your prosperity journey. These resources are designed to help you keep sacred cows from creeping back into your life. The website offers a wealth of knowledge that will help you continue on a more prosperous financial path.

Another benefit of the site is what I call the Author's Corner. It is a monthly webinar in which I explore chapters of the book in greater detail, provide more context, and try to make it more meaningful and applicable, as well as opening up the sessions for questions and answers.

In addition, there is a special section where I provide various resources to benefit financial advisors. There are tools and systems to bolster their practice, reach more clients, and help with their own educational efforts. If you are in the financial services industry, visit **killingsacredcows.com/advisor**.

Visit **killingsacredcows.com** today to learn more about unleashing and living your Soul Purpose and increasing your wealth, happiness, and success.

Killing Sacred Cows in Action (read more to find out about a complimentary gift for readers)

One of the best and easiest ways to begin to find and live Soul Purpose and go beyond the limitation of myths is through the monthly membership (**killing sacredcows.com/action**). This membership is a support structure, mindset, philosophy, and powerful system to create the most favorable conditions for you to live a life that you love. It's an individualized daily routine consisting of "ten minutes to transformation" in every major track of life including the financial, spiritual, mental, physical, and social realms.

This unique membership includes the support, information, materials, tools, resources, and inspiration necessary to create unprecedented transformation in your life. These include such benefits as the highly-acclaimed Hour of Power events with highly influential guest speakers, Producer Interviews revealing the formulas of well-known producers, inspirational and profound emails, podcasts featuring various members where you can learn what is working for others, a monthly newsletter, incredible books and DVDs exclusive to the membership, and more. These phenomenal and practical benefits arrive on a daily, weekly, monthly, and quarterly basis to help you more fully live and understand your Soul Purpose while experiencing greater joy and abundance in every aspect of your life.

The membership creates a daily system called the Producer Power Hour which integrates the financial, spiritual, mental, physical, and social aspects of your life through practical activities, and becomes an invaluable resource in discovering and living one's Soul Purpose. It's one thing to want to be working toward and maintaining a productive, joyful, and balanced life, but actually doing so is where many of us can become discouraged. Fortunately, the Producer Power Hour system is a simple, motivating, and effective method to help us become more aligned with our own Soul Purpose. It gives you access to the power that you already have within, with enhanced ability to express and live it.

Visit **killingsacredcows.com/action** today to learn more and to sign up for the membership. All readers of this book have access to a complimentary welcome box that includes an Hour of Power DVD, an audio recording of a Producer Interview and 15 minutes to Freedom podcast, a Soul Purpose Advocate newsletter, and more. This will also include two weeks of the membership for FREE: simply go to killingsacredcows.com/action and click on the "sign up" button, fill out your personal information, and pay for shipping and handling.

> "I attribute much of my daily success to my power hours. They bring greater clarity, focus, and production into each day. I am able to rid myself of the scarcity thoughts that hold me back from living the life that I love and accomplish more in less time. Doing your power hour daily allows the rubber to grip the road by accomplishing more with less energy. The only way one can truly be a producer is starting the day as a producer in all five areas of life."—**Chris**

> "I love doing my Producer Power Hour. I am getting so much more done. And best of all, I feel more grateful. That makes every area of my life better."—**Cari**

> "Since listening to the podcasts and producer interviews, and applying the principles in my own life, I am not the same person anymore. My life has been truly transformed beyond recognition, and great things are happening for me, and all those around me. In fact, it has had such a change, I am beginning to get people asking me to speak and teach at business meetings."—**Nicholas D.**

Freedom FastTrack

Freedom FastTrack Programs are advanced, intensive one-year programs available to approved applicants only. These unique programs create extraordinary results in every facet of your life through transformational tools and resources, a wealth of content, personal mentoring, and an effective accountability structure. These programs require a high level of commitment and willingness to progress. Anyone is welcome to apply, but we only accept qualified individuals who are ready for massive transformation.

Participants work with a range of specialized experts who create customized solutions and personalized implementation. We offer five distinct programs corresponding to each major track of life: Financial, Soul Purpose, Mental, Physical, and Social. We encourage applicants to begin with the Financial Track, which cultivates financial interdependence and prosperity. Once people are more financially free, they are better able to embrace the other facets of life. Occasionally, we allow participants to "jump ahead" to different tracks if they have already mastered certain areas.

To find out more about these programs go to **killingsacredcows.com/fasttrack**.
The following is a brief description of each program:

Financial FastTrack provides you with your own personal advisor and board of expert advisors in every area of finance. These experts help you design and implement your ideal financial blueprint. The program begins by identifying your available resources, then coaches you to utilize them to the fullest and create the highest levels of prosperity in the present moment. You will learn how to generate a constant, predictable cash flow from financial resources you already have, but may not recognize or currently underutilize. The process, tools, and resources enable you to live the dreams now that most people save for retirement. Ultimately, the program brings the right education, experts, and opportunities together to turn philosophies and principles into tangible prosperity today. More at **killingsacredcows.com/financial**.

Soul Purpose FastTrack allows an individual to discover, in one year or less, what takes most people a lifetime—if they even find it at all. Personal Mentor Meetings with some of the best prosperity and life mentors in the country will help you unveil the greatest version of you. They act as a catalyst for propelling your greatest future possibility into the now. Inspiring symposiums, workbooks and other curriculum help you discover how to actively live your Soul Purpose every day and naturally enjoy greater abundance and happiness. The program culminates with The Awakened Spirit Retreat, which is an incredible sacred gathering in nature with other participants in the program. At the retreat participants are fed healthy meals prepared by expert chefs, enjoy nature hikes, and are invited to participate in various activities such as yoga, guided meditations, sacred music and drumming, and powerful group discussions. More at **killingsacredcows.com/soulpurpose**.

Mental FastTrack is a powerful program for entrepreneurs and investors. In this FastTrack there are proprietary models and tools to identify legitimate opportunities, analyze potential challenges, and mitigate risk. Through personalized mentoring, this yearlong customized program teaches individuals how to create more space and transform their relationship to time. The skills and tools learned save entrepreneurs years of frustrations in business, while equipping them with the tools to be highly prosperous and successful in every endeavor. Specifically, you have the opportunity to map out that one "impossible" dream you've always had and to make it a reality. You will have the opportunity to work personally with me, listen to other world-class speakers, and network with prosperous individuals at exclusive events. By the end up the process, you can utilize your Soul Purpose to leave a "footprint" of lasting value on the world, and enjoy greater wealth and success. More at **killingsacredcows.com/mental**.

Physical FastTrack is health by design, not default. The program includes instruction from a wide range of wellness experts who effectively educate the individual on how to cultivate and protect their essential wellsprings of productivity: their health and energy. Most people fail to realize their physical goals because they are working against, rather than with, their minds. This health and fitness curriculum goes way beyond diet and exercise. You will learn how to naturally and joyfully stay fit, healthy, and energized by learning how to capitalize on the foods and activities you already intrinsically enjoy. Accountability coaching and personalized training map out a highly effective and customized program that will set you on the path towards living a happier, longer, and more energized life.

Social FastTrack is designed for those who are already highly successful and productive and are now ready to maximize every beneficial relationship in their life and leave a massive imprint on the world. This program teaches advanced skills and concepts that allow individuals to become public or private leaders and dramatically increase their value in the marketplace. The program facilitates the participant in aligning their life with natural motivators. By the end of this program the participant has embarked on living the most powerful, productive, and wonderful life imaginable, and has identified the biggest problem in the world that his or her individual Soul Purpose can make right. Participants of this program leave with the understanding and ability to make a massive contribution and leave an inspiring legacy to the world.

Events

The following are some of the major events and symposiums available to individuals and groups. To find out more about these events visit the website **killingsacredcows.com/events**.

The Big Event is The Freedom FastTrack's annual three-day flagship symposium. Renowned and famous individuals personally teach you the keys of prosperity in every "track" of human life value: financial, Soul Purpose, mental, physical, and social. These high-level mentors help you discover the disciplines, strategies, and techniques to uncover and resolve any obstacle, while increasing your joy, health, and prosperity in life. Attendees mastermind and "rub shoulders" with other prosperous attendees and famous speakers. Call (800) 549-4532 or email events@freedomfastttrack.com and mention Killing Sacred Cows to get a certificate for $2500 off of the price of this three-day event (typically held on a Thursday, Friday, and Saturday).

Curriculum for Wealth symposiums are events designed to illuminate and detail the most critical factors of prosperity and happiness. They offer a solid philosophical foundation for building a life of abundance using proven principles. Participants find these events to be "mini retreats," allowing them to refocus on what's most important in life, to realign, and to better understand true wealth versus conceived wealth. Attendees will have the opportunity to ask questions and participate in exercises that will allow them to break through financial myths and understand and establish true wealth and abundance in life. To find dates or sign up go to **killingsacredcows.com/cfw**.

Soul Purpose Intensive is a multiday symposium that focuses on how to truly live a life of abundance and joy specifically through discovering and living Soul Purpose. Participants are taken on an empowering journey of unlearning, relinquishing, surrendering, and detaching from control issues and old habits that are destructive and counterproductive. This symposium is designed to deepen individual personal power by revealing the spiritual formulas for joy, health, and wealth. To find dates or sign up, go to **killingsacredcows.com/spi.**

Quarterly Quantums are quarterly full-day events, designed specifically for business owners and entrepreneurs, which go through all seven stages of the Mental FastTrack. These events educate participants on how to more fully capitalize on both one's own potential and the potential of his or her team. You will discover how to apply specific tools, strategies, and models to your own business, the same as I consistently apply to my own successful businesses. Due to the advanced nature of the content discussed, participants must get approval to attend this event. For those who are not yet ready for the Mental FastTrack, there is an introduction to the Mental FastTrack called the Idea Optimizer that is done through a teleseminar series over an eight-week period of time. This teleseminar goes through a workbook utilized in the Mental FastTrack with seven distinct sections. If you have ideas and want to make sure you can implement them effectively and profitably, don't miss the Idea Optimizer teleseminar series. Visit **killingsacredcows.com/mft** to find out more.

The Enlightenment is an extraordinary day of transformational discoveries followed by a roundtable session hosted by The Accredited Network. Participants hear from elite professionals who simply can't be hired to come and speak, and who cannot be found at any other venue. These are the caliber of people who "train the trainers." This is a rare and monumental opportunity to learn from the masters of Soul Purpose on how to create the life you want. Visit **killingsacredcows.com/tickets** on the web to reserve two complimentary tickets to this event.

Hour of Power, hosted by Producer Power Hour, is an exciting opportunity to hear from a different elite producer each month. Attendees learn how to live a more fulfilling and abundant life straight from the mouth of those who are actually doing it. Each Hour of Power is followed by a Mastermind session, where participants have the opportunity to network and share valuable insights and ideas. You can also attend the event via videocast by registering at the events section of **killing sacredcows.com/hp.**

Additional Education and Resources

Author's Corner began as the Mission Driven Forum with me and Steve D'Annunzio to coach people in the financial services industry. It has now evolved into the Author's Corner. I spend an hour per chapter on books I have authored to offer more in-depth personal coaching about the principles and ideas covered. Participants get to ask questions after the presentation. To find dates or sign up go to **killingsacredcows.com/ac.**

The Accredited Network is a group of affiliates from all sectors of the financial services industry who have received advanced training in the theory and principles of Soul Purpose. Unlike most financial services, where various experts offer contradictory advice, members of The Accredited Network work together to ensure a seamless, holistic, and integrated financial service experience for their clients. To find out more, visit **killingsacredcows.com/tan.**

Prosperity Paradigm Experience is a 4-DVD set of an incredible full day symposium with Steve D'Annunzio, a teacher who mentors life success coaches all over the country. His radically effective teachings pull people "out of their minds and into their hearts." Steve uses principles of Higher Awareness to inspire others to be far greater versions of themselves than they ever knew to be possible. By combining scientific and spiritual truth, he co-creates inner transformations for people to experience more outer prosperity in their lives. Visit **killingsacredcows.com/prosperity** to order, or for more details.

Expert Advisor Series Videocasts are a series of twelve presentations from experts in the various fields of financial implementation, followed by a thirty-minute Q & A session. This series is hosted by the best advisors in their respective industries. These elite experts share advanced principles from their field of expertise that often even the average industry "expert" doesn't understand. The Expert Advisor Series is like having your own team of highly skilled expert advisors in every financial field brought to your doorstep. Visit **killlingsacredcows.com/expert** for more information.

The Mirror is a multi-DVD presentation that clearly details how to make your physical world mirror your intentions. I host this presentation to teach you how to create breakthroughs that empower you to be who you choose to be, not who you have been in the past. It clearly outlines how to increase and understand your personal stewardship as well as more fully identify, understand, and apply your innate gifts and talents, so that you can live the life you really want. Visit **killingsacredcows. com/mirror** to place an order and for more details.

Soul Purpose Home Tutorial Box Set features me and Steve D'Annunzio addressing the subject of living your Soul Purpose through spiritual disciplines, how to find your Soul Purpose, and how to help others find theirs. This box set offers powerful insights into the spiritual discipline of nonattachment. You will learn about nonattachment vs. apathy, and how to have "preferences" rather than goals. The four steps of nonattachment are covered, which teach you how to stop "leaking" energy, and instead channel that energy powerfully in your life. Visit **killingsacredcows. com/tutorial** to find out more, or to place an order.

Quantum Business Continuum Home Tutorial Box Set features me and renowned life coach Ron Zeller explaining the Quantum Business Continuum. We discuss how to win "impossible games" through the greatest wealth of assets called people. The concepts of being ageless versus aging, teams, integrity, and honor are clearly explained. This box set offers a powerful education on how to generate more productivity through synergy, and how to make ideas become reality. Visit **killingsacredcows.com/qbqtutorial** for more information or to place an order.

Architecture of Abundance, presented by Producer Revolution, contains some of the original, most fundamental radio shows presented on a set of twelve CDs covering topics that lead to living a life of passion, prosperity and purpose. If you are looking for vintage material, these are a "best of series" when I first began doing radio. Visit **killingsacredcows.com/abundance** for more information or to place an order.

Books

Economics of Soul Purpose contains literally lifetimes' worth of wisdom from some of the world's most amazing coaches, entrepreneurs, and leaders. The chapters feature the personal stories of amazingly successful people who share their intimately personal experiences and great wisdom accrued through their lives and Soul Purpose journeys. This book is a highly concentrated dosage of specialized wisdom and inspiration that no one person alone could ever discover entirely in one lifetime. The powerful insights shared inevitably inspire readers toward incredible breakthroughs of their own. Visit **killingsacredcows.com/econ** for more information or to place an order.

The Money Tree: The Roots & Fruits of Poverty & Prosperity is an engaging book that uses easy-to-understand metaphors to explain the fundamental philosophies and practices of a prosperous life. *The Money Tree* contains a detailed model of prosperity showing the fundamental connections between human life value, philosophy, principles, strategies, and results. This model illustrates the natural laws behind the world of finance by using the analogy of a growing tree with all of its various parts, and how each one directly relates to the financial realm. Visit **killingsacred cows.com/money** for more information or to place an order.

Index

A

abundance
  cooperative competition and, 9, 12, 19–22
  definition and characteristics, 4, 22
  human ingenuity and, 15–17
  quality vs. quantity, 18–19
  replacing scarcity with, 11–12
  value exchange, 14–15
  value determinations, 12–14
accumulation
  in 401(k) plans, 44–48
  beliefs about, 27–29, 36–37
  destructive nature of, 29–38, 191
  productivity in the present, 42–48
  utilization as replacement for, 38–39
  value creation, 39–42
Adams, John, 92
adversarial competition, 9, 19–22
Allario, John, 97
Allen, James, 24
Andelin, Anthony, 23–24
Apology (Socrates), 129
asset allocation models, 27–28
assumptions. *See* numbers
average returns, 70–72

B

balance sheets, 195–97, 207–9
bank business practices, 30–31, 51, 133–34,
    159–61, 227
Bastiat, Frédéric, 59
Be-Do-Have order of abundance, 18
Bible, 115

Blitzer, Wolf, 96
Blotnick, Srully, 91
borrowing. *See* debt; liabilities; productive liabilities
Boyce, Roger, 96
Browne, Thomas, 93
Buffett, Warren, xiv, 156–57

C

cash flow, 48–49, 52–56
Castiglione, Robert, 30
Chavis, Ben, 123–24
Clark, Dale, 100–101
commission basis, 6–7, 124
competition, 9, 12, 19–22
compound interest, viii, 45
consumers
  insurance and, 105, 180, 182, 185
  producers vs., 102–8
  wealth views of, 127
consumptive liabilities, 190, 199–201
cooperative competition, 9, 12, 19–22
corporate finance, viii–ix
corporations
  Enron, 96–98, 128, 150
  false security from, vii, xiv, 36–37, 88–92, 150
Corrales, Ben and Heather, 22–23
Costco, 220–21
costs
  opportunity, 157–61, 220–23
  Seen and unSeen, 76–77, 79–80
coupon clipping, 221
Covey, Stephen, xiii
credit card debt, 191

currency value, 14, 116–18, 134. *See Also* money

D
D'Annunzio, Steve, xv
debt. *See Also* liabilities
    beliefs about, 189–90
    definition, 189, 195–97
    human life value balance sheet, 207–9
    mortgages, 190, 199, 202–7
    productive liabilities as replacement for, 194–95
    reducing, 204–5
defeating the myths
    asking the right questions, 240–41
    education role, 245–46
    financial freedom through, 233–34, 247–48
    knowing our interests, 234–37
    Soul Purpose role, 237–40
    universal application test, 243–45
    value proposition, 242–43
destructive liabilities, 200–201
disability insurance, 169, 177–78
Disney, Walt, xiv
division of labor concept, 223
Dodge, Nate, 149
do-it-yourself attitudes, 221–22
dreams, postponing, 35–36, 42–48
Drucker, Peter, 151–52
Durant, Will, 16

E
economics, 78–82
Economics in One Lesson (Hazlitt), 78
"The Economic Value of Certainty" (McGuire), 182
education
    defeating the myths, 245–46
    human life value and, 101, 132
    investing in, 99–100, 106, 118–19, 245–46
    mitigating risk through, 156–61
    paradigm shifts through, 23
    personal finance training needs, viii–ix
    public school systems, 123–25
Eker, T. Harv, 54
elusive obvious, xiii–xvi, 77
Enron, 96–98, 128, 150
entitlement mentality, 87–89
entrepreneurs, 151–52, 183
environmentalism, 98
estate taxes, 44–45
exchange
    currency and, 116–18
    international trade, 17

value determination and, 12–15, 20
velocity through, 50–51
expense reduction, 40–42
exploitation of others, 126–29
external rate of return, 76–77

F
false security
    beliefs about, 87
    consumer views of, 103–6
    from corporations, vii, xiv, 36–37, 88–92, 150
    destructive nature of, 87–92
    financial freedom as replacement for, 92–93
    from government, 36–37, 88–89, 120
fear
    accumulation and, 29, 32–35, 37, 38, 56
    debt and, 190–92
    false security and, 92, 103–4, 106
    money and, 112
    risk and, 143, 148, 167, 180, 184
    scarcity and, 5–7
    of wealth, 83
financial calculations. *See* numbers
financial freedom
    embracing, 93–95
    insurance and, 179–84
    investing in ourselves, 99–101, 118–19, 155–56
    myths about, x, xviii
    producers vs. consumers, 102–8
    productive liabilities and, 199, 206
    quality of life and, 18–19
    replacing false security with, 92–93
    responsibility and self-reliance, 95–98, 128
    stewardship and, 98–102
    utilization and, 38–39
financial institutions. *See Also* numbers
    accumulation theory and, 30–33, 45
    client net worth and cash flow, 54
    myth perpetuation by, viii
    risk mitigation by, 147–48, 158–61
financial security. *See* false security; financial
        freedom
finite pie. *See* abundance; scarcity
formulas for financial freedom. *See* defeating the
        myths
401(k) plans
    accumulation myth and, 44–46
    alternatives to, 46–48
    defeating the myth, 244
    employer matches, 79–80
    Enron, 96–98

"guaranteed" rates of return, 79–80
inheritance of unused assets, 44–45
mitigating risk, 148
Frankl, Viktor, 106
freedom. *See* financial freedom

G
gambling versus investing, 37–38, 141–44, 147–50
Gandhi, Mohandas, 126
Gates, Bill, xiv, 117
goals and visions, 234–36
golden handcuffs, 90
goose that lays golden eggs, 41, 224
government as problem-solver, 36–37, 88–89, 120
Great Depression, vii
greed, 37, 83, 148, 192

H
happiness. *See Also* human life value; Soul Purpose
postponing, 35–36, 42–48
prosperity and, xv, 82–83, 136–37
sources of, 18–19
utilization and, 33–38
Hazlitt, Henry, 59, 78
Hello World, 50
high-risk investing
beliefs about, 141–42
destructive nature of myth, 142–45
gamblers vs. investors, 37–38, 141–44, 147–50
investments vs. investors, 150–53
wise investing as replacement for, 145
HLV (human life value) balance sheet, 207–9
homeowner's insurance, 169, 172, 180
human ingenuity, 15–17
human life value
accumulation theory and, 29, 32–33
character development and, xv, 108, 129, 207–9
definition, xv–xvi, 20, 33
education and, 101, 132
insurance protection for, 176–79
knowing our interests, 234–37
prosperity and, xv–xvi, 129–33
human life value (HLV) balance sheet, 207–9

I
ideas, following through on, 113
income, 40–42
inflation, 72–73
innovation, 16–17
Innovation and Entrepreneurship (Drucker), 151–52

input, 48–49
insurance. *See Also* self-insurance
as asset protection, 184–85
deductibles, 81, 179
disability, 169, 177–78
as freedom and productivity support, 179–84
homeowner's, 169, 172, 180
as human life value protection, 176–79
permanent life, 105, 172–76, 182, 193
reducing expenses, 171–76
replacing self-insurance with, 168–69
risk assessment checklist, 181
term, 105, 172–77
insurance companies, 159–61, 169–70, 173
interest, compound, viii, 45
internal rate of return, 76–77
intrinsic value, 12–14, 114–15, 126, 207
investing. *See Also* 401(k) plans; high-risk investing;
numbers; real estate investments; wise
investing
accumulation theory, 27–32
asset allocation, 27–28
average returns, 70–72
beliefs about, 27–29, 36–38
do-it-yourself attitudes, 221
in education, 99–100, 106, 118–19, 245–46
financial institution roles, 30–33
focus questions, 152
gambling versus, 37–38, 141–44, 147–50
internal rate of return, 76
investments vs. investors, 150–53
loss mindset, 12
market fluctuations, 73–75
in ourselves, 99–101, 118–19, 155–56
risk and reward, 146–47
Soul Purpose and, 37–38
successful people and, 91, 151–52, 156–57
utilizing money versus, 29

J
Jesus and prosperity, 130
jobs, false security from, 89–90
judging wealthy people, 126–29

K
Kennon, Joshua, 28
Kiyosaki, Robert, 129, 151, 156, 216, 219
Kluger, Jeffrey, 5
knowledge. *See* education

L
labor, division of, 223

lawn mowing example, 222
liabilities. *See Also* debt; productive liabilities
    definition, 189–90, 195, 197
    destructive nature of avoiding, 190–94
    increasing productivity with, 202–7
    necessity of, 198
    productive, consumptive, and destructive,
        198–201
life insurance, 105, 172–77, 182, 193

M
macroeconomics, 80–82
Maier, Matthew, 5
Malthus, Thomas, 1, 3
market fluctuations, 73–75
material possessions, xiv–xv, 12–14, 18–19, 128–
    29. *See Also* accumulation; scarcity
McGuire, Les, 104–5, 182, 185
microeconomics, 80–82
Miles, Robert P., 156–57
millionaires, 34, 53–54, 64–66
mindset, 11, 97, 99–100, 107, 202
mitigating risk, 147–49, 153–54, 156–61
money. *See Also* money as power; numbers; price
    characteristics of, 116–18
    financial freedom and, 18–19
    infinite value of, 14
    velocity of, 48–52
money as power
    accumulation theory and, 39–42
    beliefs about, 111–12
    as controlling factor in life, 119–25
    deception and coercion with, 120–21, 127, 129
    destructive nature of, 112–15
    intrinsic value of, 114–15
    "it takes money to make money," 132–37
    judgment and exploitation of others, 126–29
    as prime mover, 122–25
    as root of evil, 115, 121–22, 135–36
    value creation as replacement for, 116
    vulgarity and, 125
money as symbol of value creation
    characteristics of, 114–18
    human life value and prosperity, 129–33
    infinite value of, 14
    utilization and, 39–42
    velocity of, 48–52
mortgage debt, 190, 199, 202–7
mutual funds
    average returns, 70–72
    internal rate of return, 76
    investing vs. gambling, 37–38, 147–48

market fluctuations, 73–75
mitigating risk, 160
myths. *See Also* accumulation; debt; defeating the
    myths; false security; high-risk investing;
    money as power; numbers; price; scarcity;
    self-insurance
    destructive nature of, ix–x
    elusive obvious as replacement for, xiii–xvi, 77
    letting go, x–xii
    origins, vi–ix
    redefining prosperity, xiv–xvi
    as sacred cows, v–vi

N
net worth, 52–56
numbers
    average returns, 70–72
    beliefs about, 59–60
    destructive nature of, 60–63
    financial industry use of, 67–69, 71–72
    inflation rates, 72–73
    macro vs. micro, 80–82
    market fluctuations, 73–75
    prosperity as replacement for, 63
    seen and unseen factors, 76–77, 79–80
    tax brackets, 75–76
    thinking like an economist, 78–80

O
opportunity costs, 157–61, 220–23
output, 48–49
outsourcing, 17
ownership, 98–99, 203

P
Palmer, Stephen, 183
Paul (biblical), 115
Paulson, Tim, 49–50
"a penny saved is a penny earned." *See* price; value
people. *See Also* human life value; successful people
    human ingenuity, 15–17
    intrinsic value of, 12–13, 207
    judgment and exploitation of, 126–29
    money and value creation, 114–15, 121–22
    serving others, 20–21, 55, 82–83, 114–15,
        134–36

permanent life insurance, 105, 172–76, 182, 193
personal finance, viii–ix, 40–42, 59
Piranha Marketing (Polish and Paulson), 49–50
power. *See* money as power
price

beliefs about, 213–14
destructive nature of, 214–18
of insurance, 165–67
terms versus, 227–28
value as replacement for, 218–19
value priority over, 223–26
printing press invention, 16
producers
consumers versus, 102–8
getting out of debt, 204–5
insurance and, 105, 168, 171–72, 176, 178, 180, 185
investments and, 155
price and, 218–19
productivity vs. ownership, 203–4, 207
value proposition and, 153
productive liabilities
definition, 190, 199, 201
human life value balance sheet, 207–9
replacing debt with, 194–95
terms vs. price, 227–28
productivity
accumulation theory and, 36
expense cutting versus, 40–41
focus questions, 219, 223
insurance and, 179–84
liabilities to increase, 202–7
in the present, 42–48
value vs. price, 223–26
prosperity
avoiding, 130–31
happiness and, xv, 82–83, 136–37
human life value and, 129–33
quality vs. quantity, 64–69
redefining, xiv–xvi
replacing numbers with, 63
Soul Purpose and, 82–83, 136–37
through serving others, 134–35

Q
qualified plans, 44–48. *See Also* 401(k) plans
quality versus quantity, 18–19, 64–69
questions, focus, 219, 240–41. *See Also* specific topic

R
Ramsey, Dave, 193–94
Randall, Dee, 21
rate of return, 76–77
real estate investments
as 401(k) alternative, 46–47
debt vs. productive liabilities, 191–92, 199, 205–6
home values, 12–14

investments vs. investors, 151
lease options, 203, 227–28
prosperity and, 131
*See*n and un*See*n factors, 77
terms vs. price, 227–28
trust deeds, 149
as utilized assets, 53–55
velocity and, 51–52
responsibility, 95–98
retirement
accumulation theory and, 32–36
goals and vision for, 234–36
numbers manipulation and, 67–69
scarcity in, 35, 75
Soul Purpose and, 238
retirement planners
accumulation theory and, 31, 45
myths perpetuated by, viii
numbers manipulation by, 60–61, 67–68, 73–76
reward and risk, 146–47
Rich Dad, Poor Dad (Kiyosaki), 129, 216
Riedel, Monica, 118–19
risk. *See Also* high-risk investing; insurance
focus questions, 181
mitigating, 147–49, 153–54, 156–61
reward and, 146–47
self-employment and, 118–19
risk tolerance, 27–28, 141
risk transference. *See* insurance
Roberts, Russell, 17
Rockefeller, John D., Sr., 135
Ruskin, John, 166, 216

S
sacred cows, v–vi. *See Also* myths
savers, 217–18, 220–21
scarcity
abundance as replacement for, 11–12
accumulation theory and, 33–35
beliefs about, 3–4
competition, 9, 12, 19–22
destructive nature of, 4–10
examples, 10
human ingenuity and, 15–17
quality vs. quantity, 18–19
value determinations, 12–14
value exchange, 14–15
school systems, 123–25
security. *See* false security; financial freedom
self-employment, 118–19, 123
self-insurance. *See Also* insurance
beliefs about, 165
destructive nature of, 166–67
risk transference as replacement for, 168–69

stagnant assets with, 169–71
self-sufficiency versus self-reliance, 95–98
serving others, 20–21, 55, 82–83, 114–15, 134–36
7 Steps to 720, 55
Simon, Julian, 16
simultaneous use of money, 51–52
Smith, Adam, 223
social issues
    creating an ideal world, 228–30
    judgment and exploitation, 126–29
    outsourcing and innovation, 17
Socrates, 129
Soul Purpose
    accumulation theory and, 29, 32–33
    definition, xv, 33
    discovering, 239–40
    entitlement mentality versus, 89
    human life value and, 101–2
    investing and, 37–38
    money and, 126, 133, 137
    overcoming the myths, 237–40
    productivity and, 46–48
    prosperity and, 82–83
    stewardship and, 99–101
    value creation and, 42
spenders, 217–18, 220–21
stereotyping wealthy and poor people, 126–29
stewardship
    accumulation and, 36
    consumer vs. producer view of, 102–4
    freedom and, 98–102
    serving others, 20–21, 55, 82–83, 114–15,
        134–36
    utilization and, 45–46
stock market. *See* investing
Stossel, John, 123–24
"Stupid in America" (ABC News program), 123–24
successful people
    characteristics of, xiv, 21–22, 87, 91, 151–52,
        156–57, 183
    myths about, x, xi, 126–29

T
taxes, 44–45, 73, 75–76
Teather, David, 97
term insurance, 105, 172–77
terms versus price, 227–28
Tirone, Phil, 55
Trump, Donald, 156
trust deeds, 149
12 Daily Pro, 154

U
The Ultimate Resource 2 (Simon), 16
uninsured motorists, 167
utilization
    cash flow vs. net worth, 52–56
    definition, 29
    destructive nature of accumulation, 29–38
    productivity in the present, 42–48
    replacing accumulation with, 38–39
    value creation, 39–42
    velocity of money, 48–52
    wealth and happiness through, 33–38

V
Valjean, Jean, 120
value. *See Also* human life value; money as symbol
        of value creation
    creating an ideal world, 228–30
    determining, 12–15, 20
    focus questions, 213, 225, 242
    intrinsic, 12–14, 114–15, 126, 207
    opportunity cost recognition, 220–23
    productivity focus, 219–20, 225–26
    replacing price with, 218–19, 223–26
    terms vs. price, 227–28
value exchange, 14–15
value proposition, 153–54, 242–43
velocity of money, 48–52
victim mentality, 96–97
vulgarity and money, 125

W
Wal-Mart, 5–6
Warren Buffett Wealth (Miles), 156–57
wealth, 14–15, 82–83, 126–29. *See Also*
        accumulation; human life value; Soul
        Purpose
The Wealth of Nations (Smith), 223
White, Garrett, ix, 50
whole life (permanent) insurance, 105, 172–76,
        182, 193
Williamson, Marianne, 56
wise investing
    increasing knowledge to decrease risk, 156–57
    introduction, 145
    investments vs. investors, 150–53
    mitigating risk, 147–49, 153–54, 156–61
    opportunity costs, 157–61
    in ourselves, 99–101, 118–19, 155–56
    replacing high-risk investments with, 145
    risk and reward, 146–47
    value proposition, 153–54